THE
CATHOLIC
EXPERIENCE

THE CATHOLIC EXPERIENCE

Space, Time, Silence, Prayer, Sacraments, Story, Persons, Catholicity, Community, and Expectations

Lawrence S. Cunningham

CROSSROAD·NEW YORK

1985

The Crossroad Publishing Company
370 Lexington Avenue, New York, N.Y. 10017

Printed in the United States of America

Library of Congress Cataloging in Publication Data

Cunningham, Lawrence.
The Catholic experience.

1. Catholic Church—Apologetic works.   2. Cunningham,
Lawrence. I. Title.
EX1752.C835 1985   282   85-19463
ISBN 0-8245-0705-3

CONTENTS

Introduction 1

Chapter One | SPACE 9

Chapter Two | TIME 36

Chapter Three | SILENCE 64

Chapter Four | PRAYER 88

Chapter Five | SACRAMENTS 114

Chapter Six | STORY 139

Chapter Seven | PERSONS 163

Chapter Eight | CATHOLICITY 189

Chapter Nine | COMMUNITY 216

Chapter Ten | EXPECTATIONS 242

Index 266

INTRODUCTION

A few years ago I wrote a book *The Catholic Heritage* (1983) to persuade the willing reader that if Roman Catholicism is anything, it is a community of memory. What it remembers, among other things, are the various ways in which people have lived out their callings as Christians in various ages of the church's life. The late patristic period, to cite one obvious example, was a time of ascetics and pilgrims, but the twentieth century has also produced its pilgrims and ascetics who often look back to that earlier time (i.e., they search the memory of the church) for hints and models for their own peculiar experiences. Thomas Merton was passionately concerned with the life of contemporary literature and contemporary social problems, but he also wrote about, translated, and sought inspiration from the ancient desert fathers and mothers because he was, above all, a monk. He needed to recall his forebearers in faith. *The Catholic Heritage*, then, was about the persistence of tradition and its nourishing value.

This present work is, in a sense, a taking up of that theme of tradition once again but from a somewhat different point of view. That point of view is—isn't it always?—somewhat autobiographical, if not transparently so. With respect to the Catholic tradition I wear two hats. As a professor in a large state university, I have focused my teaching activities on what might be called the "high culture" of Latin Christendom, which, not surprisingly, coincides with my own intellectual instincts. When doing a course on medieval Christianity, for

1

example, I would tend to list as required reading Dante's *Commedia* (as well as Augustine's *Confessions, The Song of Roland*, the *Legenda Major* of Bonaventure) rather than Anselm's *Cur Deus Homo* or the *Summa* of St. Thomas Aquinas, just as my instincts would lead me to Caravaggio or Bernini or the poetry of John of the Cross rather than the canons of the Council of Trent when talking about the Catholic reformation of the sixteenth and seventeenth centuries.

Such a focus on high culture can be a bit misleading as everyone knows. To ignore the gritty reality of the Catholic tradition in favor of its privileged creations would be a bit like trying to explain contemporary New York by concentrating solely on the New York Philharmonic and the Metropolitan Museum. The "classic" exists always in front of a larger reality. A person like St. Francis of Assisi is all the more classic when one understands the violence and squalor (moral and physical) of life in Assisi in the late twelfth century. Raphael and Michelangelo produced masterpieces of human art within the precincts of the Vatican when their papal patrons were characterized by military violence (Julius II), hedonism (Leo X), or simple unworthiness (Clement VII). This is all to say, in short, that the Catholic tradition is a complex and earthy one in which the drab details and failures of daily life, with all their pettiness and rancor, become punctuated with luminous moments of beauty and genuine sanctity. The "classics" are precisely that because they stand in such sharp relief against the everydayness of the tradition itself.

My years of reaching up to the great Catholic classics have passed while I also lived as an ordinary American Catholic attending an ordinary American parish in somewhat extraordinary times. To live in such a manner and in such times makes one acutely aware how extraordinary a "classic" really is. It is impossible not to measure one's life without reference to them. While I have been blessed by knowing extraordinarily holy parish priests, religious, and laypeople, they have been highlights rather than the norm. Most of us (and I emphasize *us*) are ordinary and pedestrian in the exercise of our faith. We are who we are and only fitfully attempt to change. If we think about it, we fear radical conversion since we have some small glimmer of the deep demands involved in such change.

It is that dual role as "professional" and "ordinary" Catholic that prompts this book. What I essentially want to do in it is to bring into focus the knowledge I have gained over the years through teaching and study and my experiences as an ordinary Catholic who attends an ordinary parish. The desire to write does not derive because of some grand insight that I have gained as a result of my studies. The desire comes partly because I want to articulate the gaps, questions, possibilities, trajectories, and hopes that I sense in these particular days of the church's life. I want to enter that lively dialogue which goes on in contemporary church circles about the meaning of Catholicism as we lurch toward a new millennium.

My experiential awareness of Catholicism is circumscribed. I "know" a good deal about Catholicism, but I am not sure that I am better for that knowing. Doctor Rieux, in Camus's *La Peste*, remarks that the learned Father Paneloux was vastly unlearned in comparison to a village priest who sat at the bedsides of dying parishioners. It is that latter kind of "knowing" which, when recognized, reins in, however fitfully, professorial tendencies to arrogance. While I have lived for extended periods in Europe, my Catholic life is, by and large, North American, middle class, and fairly conventional. I have no direct experience of "base communities" and very limited direct knowledge of those creative communitarian and liturgical communities which have sprung up in this country in metropolitan areas or at the fringes of major universities. In fact, living in an area which is largely Protestant (the South) and/or secular (the university), I have often found myself slightly bemused with both the language and the "lifestyle" of those "progressive" Catholics whom I have encountered at professional meetings or other academic/ecclesiastical tribal rites.

Why was this book written? It is an act of homage and confidence in my church by a prickly member who, in his most optimistic moments, calls himself a believer. It is also a statement about what one should "get" out of being a Catholic Christian. It is hardly an exercise in apologetics or foundational theology; it is, rather, a reflection on one person's experience of being a Catholic Christian. It is also a reflection on one person's experience of being a Catholic who still believes that the business of trying to become more Catholic is a worthy thing. In doing this, I did not wish to write a book on Catholic belief since Richard McBrien's *Catholicism* has already done that well, nor write a "What I Believe" confession after the manner of Michael Novak's recent *Confessions of a Catholic.* My aim is a bit more modest: to take a number of common religious categories as starting points for reflections on the experience of being Catholic in these days. I want to ask myself—and the reader—how Catholics experience religious space, time, community, silence, etc.

Behind these chapters are some basic motifs which run through the book like threads. They reflect strong convictions of my own and largely shape my thinking. Let me mention four of them:

1. *The dialectic between past and present:* For all the newness of the post-Vatican II sensibility there is still a strong component of tradition and memory in the Catholic community. The past few decades have been a period of re-searching our roots for models and paradigms of Christian behavior that have deep roots in our collective memory as Catholics. Even when we fail to avert to it, the simple act, say, of the celebration of the liturgy is an exercise so saturated in memory and tradition that we cannot—indeed, should not—try to escape it. To fully articulate that sense of continuity is an urgent part of being Catholic since "being Catholic" means not only participation in a present reality, but insertion into a long tradition extending back into time and space.

2. *Contemplation and action:* I use contemplation here not in its most technical sense but in that widest meaning of the cultivated experiential sense of God in Christ which is central to the attitude of acknowledging the presence of God in the world. It is, in short, awareness of God. By action I mean the very exercise of life—in all its ramifications both private and social—in which the shaping influence of the contemplative attitude impinges on, and gives substance to, our living in the world. I would make my own, then, Thomas Aquinas's dictum that the world was created for the purpose of contemplation. At one level it is the dreariest of clichés to say that one should do on Monday what one professes on Sunday, but at another

angle the banality of the observation gives way to a profound and central Christian truth: being Christian is as much *doing* as saying.

3. *Catholicity:* Catholic, or more precisely, Roman Catholic is the de facto label with which I locate myself on the spectrum of Christian self-description. Used in that sense, the word *Catholic* is a descriptive adjective and will be used as such throughout this book. But Catholic, or, better, "being a Catholic," is also a theological category and I will also treat it as a term worthy of sustained reflection. My conviction is, baldly stated, that the church and its members are never fully Catholic but are in the process of becoming so. The old apologetical arguments about catholicity as one of the characteristic notes of the church do not hold much currency today and I shall not appeal to them. I will attempt to set out some ways (obviously, not all the ways) in which the church struggles to become Catholic.

4. *Christomimesis:* The ultimate issue in Christianity is the making present of Jesus the Christ in time and space. This is so true and obvious as to be overlooked. In the final analysis, the church hands on, not a set of doctrines, but the reality of a person. It demands that we follow not his dictates but his person even when it is his dictates that help us see him as a person. Over and over again we circle this issue: To what degree does the church, both in its remembrance and in its actual practice, help us in the pursuit of Christomimesis? The answer, very briefly, is that from the church in its preaching, teaching, and doing, we find clues, blueprints, exhortations, resources, examples, and models that help us understand how people followed and follow Christ. That some of these strategies are only of antiquarian interest and others useful is clear. Discriminating between the two is not always obvious. Most of us, I think, wonder at times if the church is the place for Christomimesis or an obstacle to it. That is a question we will address directly and often in these pages. This book argues, in fact, that for all its deficiencies, it is the church that has the resources to allow us fully to articulate and cultivate the task of imitating Christ.

This book is not a theological work per se, although it makes generous use of the work of theologians. I am, to borrow a phrase from Andrew Greeley, a consumer, not a producer, of theology. Nor is it strictly speaking a work on spirituality since no one is more conscious than the author of the hollowness of spiritual writing written by those little qualified to write on such a demanding topic; such works should not be attempted by amateurs in the spiritual life. It is surely not a work of apologetics in the classical sense of the term since only the person of rare conviction can write compelling apologetics. It is an *apologia* in that broader and looser sense of being a defense of belief in the church and that in two senses: to make the case (mainly to my fellow Catholics) that the church is not only not irrelevant but a source of Christian hope and to make the case equally (mainly to myself but also to the friendly eavesdropper) that in the church to which we have become so accustomed there are resources and graces to be had if we can only look again with a fresh eye and a certain openness of heart. In the last analysis, this is a book which attempts to look again at the church with a sense of wonder. Wonder, the ancient philosopher reminds us, is the beginning of all wisdom.

Professional theologians will probably not read this book except to see how much I have profited from their work and to check to see if I have misused what I have learned. My intended audience is that relatively well informed Catholic who finds little sustenance in the pieties of the ecclesiastical press and too much bewilderment in the pyrotechnics of the more speculative theologians. I would hope that committed laypeople, members of study groups, college classes, and other audiences of that stripe might find some intellectual nourishment here or, failing that, at least be encouraged that someone is trying to make sense of being Catholic in today's world. The book will most likely offend those who want a church frozen in the amber of Tridentine triumphalism just as it will exasperate those who are called—mainly by themselves—"progressive" Catholics. Perhaps I might get a sympathetic audience from those, who, like myself, try to tread that most treacherous of paths, the *via media*.

In order to focus this work a bit, I have appended a short series of questions at the end of each chapter called, with due

apology to lovers of Ignatian spirituality, "points for meditation." They are designed solely to aid the reader in "rewriting"
the chapters by using some of the questions that the author
first asked himself. It will provide the reader with an opportunity, to borrow Augustine's lovely phrase, to "roam the
spacious halls of memory."

The notes in this book have been kept to a decent minimum.
They reflect my direct sources and some of my reading. I have
also appended to the end of each chapter a very brief bibliography of books which provide some background and context
for my thinking. Zealous readers may wish to consult some or
all of these books to pursue my line of thought or to strike off
on ruminations of their own. There is nothing definitive about
the books I cite. They are suggestions only.

Philip Rieff once remarked, apropos of the conversion of
some of his literary friends (e.g., John Berryman, Allan Tate,
Robert Lowell, etc.) to Catholicism, that the reason for their
move was that they were "looking for new metaphors." I don't
think that Rieff was being totally ironic with that remark.
What he recognized is that Catholicism is a vast storehouse of
memory refracted through a long and complex history of persons
who remember. None of us who claim to be Catholic resonates
with all the metaphors of Catholicism; indeed, some of them
may repel or put off. They are there, however, and amid their
"thereness" we walk. This book attempts to think about some
of them from the perspective of an experience which is North
American, middle class, middle of the road, but still, one hopes,
reaching out toward greater catholicity. It is not everyone's
experience, but one can only trust that others will not find it
that far apart from their own experience. Telling the story,
after all, is the lifeblood of tradition.

This book was written in part while the author enjoyed a
sabbatical provided by the Florida State University; for that
leisure I am grateful to the university. My life as an academic
is made easier by having the help and friendship of two
extremely able colleagues who have served as chairmen of our
department: John Priest and Walter Moore, Jr. Both deserve
my deepest thanks. I am also grateful to Maureen Tobin, Wanda

Franks, and Dianne Weinstein for their invaluable secretarial help. Frank Oveis of Crossroad/Continuum has been a good friend and a wonderful editor; I am happy here to make my thanks public.

As the first draft of this book was being finished, my wife, Cecilia, presented me with our second daughter. This book is for Julia Clare and her mother.

Lawrence S. Cunningham

1

SPACE

Some years ago, while teaching in Italy, I accompanied a group of students on a tour of Sicily. While visiting the great Greek temple complex in Agrigento, one of my students asked me where the worshippers stood in the temple. The question was a fair one, but it assumed that Greek temples were like churches. They are not. The interior of Greek and Roman temples generally housed one large room (called a *cella*) which contained the cult statue of the divinity to whom the temple was consecrated. Visitors to the temple could walk around the exterior of the *cella* on the columned edges of the temple and peer into the dim *cella*, but the acts of worship and sacrifices were conducted outside the temple itself on altars constructed for that purpose. The temple itself was considered to be the house of the divinity, not an assembly hall for its devotees.

I relate this anecdote in order to make some very basic observations which will be pursued in the course of this chapter:

(*a*) To understand architectural space is to understand something about the particularities of religious belief and practice.

(*b*) All religions regularly recognize certain places and spaces as sacred either because a divinity dwells in them (as in the case of the temple) or because sacred power can manifest itself there (at a shrine where healings take place) or because a certain religion marks off (i.e., consecrates) a certain place as appropriate for worship as in the case of a church or a mosque.

(*c*) The Catholic tradition recognizes churches as "houses of God" (and, in that sense, they are rather like temples), but

9

Catholic churches also house worshippers. Within these churches spaces are further marked off for other sacred functions such as baptism or the hearing of confessions or have chapels dedicated to Mary and the saints or repositories for the Blessed Sacrament, and so on.

I make these general observations because a close look at how we organize sacred space (i.e., architecture) or how we acknowledge it (e.g., at shrines or sanctuaries) can tell us a good deal about how we express and experience our own faith. This is especially helpful in the case of the Catholic tradition since that tradition had its origins in the "sacred" world of the ancients and because Catholicism has had such a long history of organizing, in the most complex ways imaginable, spaces into architectural places. Is it not true, for example, that the great basilica of St. Peter's in the Vatican is almost synonymous with Roman Catholicism—a sort of shorthand symbol of all that Catholicism stands for? In the popular mind, St. Peter's is the center of Catholicism's world and an organizing metaphor of its complex historical reality.

The Church Building as Sacred Space

Everyone has had the experience of walking into a cool quiet church from the bustling life of the streets. There is a recognizable sensation about making a transition from the street into the church. A church interior has its own peculiar aura; it is an almost indefinable composite of stillness, the lingering odor of wax, incense, and human smells, the flickering of votive lights, the quiet presence of the solitary worshipper fingering beads, the statues, the stained glass. It is a presence which is quite clearly not like the world "out there." That sensate aura enhances our feeling of having passed from profane to sacred space. In fact, the English word *profane* comes from two Latin words *pro* (before or in front of) and *fanum* (temple); *profanum* means literally the place—say, a marketplace or a square—which was outside the precincts of the temple itself. It was the area not of the gods. Likewise, the word *templum* (Latin for temple) has a strong spatial connotation. The word is used in Latin to mean a sanctuary for the gods, but it can also mean a space marked off where a vision might occur as, for instance, an area of the sky which the ancient augurs would watch to see if there were signs that would predict future events.

The point to be understood here is that the going into a space like church space, especially when we are distressed or in need of quiet or desirous of time for reflection, is one way in which we symbolize our relationship to God. Simply being in that space is an act of religion.

On more formal occasions—most typically when we go to Mass on Sunday—we surround our entrance into church with a complex form of etiquette to symbolize our presence in church. We are usually dressed better; we keep quiet; men doff their hats; holy water is taken as a sign of our desire for purity; before taking our seats, we may make a ritual bow to the cross or genuflect; we spend a moment or two on our knees in silent prayer before sitting to await the beginning of services. All of these gestures, so practiced as to be nearly automatic, have behind them the freight of long tradition. They are learned experiences which pass from one generation to another. The gestures of the individual worshipper are paralleled by any number of similar gestures in the liturgy (the sprinkling of holy water; the use of incense, etc.) which officially reinforce the sense of being in the house of God.

That the space of the church is experienced as sacred by the believer seems obvious. But there is a further point to be made. The architectural organization of sacred space admits of many variations. A careful observer soon perceives that the ways in which the architectural space is organized reflects different perceptions of how the sacred is experienced. To say it another way: different architectural styles reflect quite different understandings of how one enters into the world of the sacred. To illustrate that point, I would like to describe some church interiors from the past history of Christianity in order to reinforce this point. I have chosen four different architectural styles from rather widely differing eras of church history: the Roman basilica of the fourth and fifth century; the romanesque church of the late eleventh century; the Gothic cathedral; and the Roman baroque church of the post-Reformation period.

With the Edict of Milan (312 A.D.), which provided toleration for Christians in the Roman Empire after nearly three centuries of intermittent persecution, the church began to build public houses of worship in Rome, usually with state aid and under the patronage of the emperor. The first great churches in Rome like old St. Peter's and St. John Lateran were built in the basilica style. Although there were some variations, the Christian basilica, based on pagan models which had served many functions, was a great hall (with side aisles to help support the roofing of the entire building) with an altar at one end and behind that altar a curved area for the assembly of the clergy and the bishop's throne. The roof, most typically of wood, was high and had a series of lateral windows (called the "clerestory") between the central roof and those which covered the side aisles.

The primary design of the basilica was to accommodate a large assembly of people who would face the altar and the assembled clergy with its bishop. It was a building, then, for public worship. There was nothing about the basilica which fostered either private devotion or movement once the assembly was in place. Richard Krautheimer has underscored the sociopolitical significance of the basilica: "Laid out lengthwise, it was focused on the apse where the bishop was enthroned, Christ's magistrate, as it were, and on the altar where in the sacrifice of the Mass Christ revealed Himself to His people. . . . To fourth century men, then, the Lateran basilica and Constantine's other churches would evoke most closely within the genus basilica the emperor's audience halls, and, beyond that, imperial palaces in general."[1]

In another place Krautheimer describes the social impact of those churches:

> . . . The new basilicas loudly proclaimed the standing of the Established Church. They claimed the status of monumental public architecture, of government building and of palatial reception halls. They were large, they were conspicuous, and they rose high above their surroundings. By the fifth century the skyline of Rome must have been thoroughly altered by new Christian structures: structures that were meant to compete with palaces and public buildings and the temples of the gods, from the greenbelt into the very heart of the city.[2]

The Christian basilica, then functioned both as a place for solemn and sacred assemblies and as a social statement which now proclaimed the status of a religion which once met quietly in house churches and whose legal position was ambiguous at best and illegal at worst.

When one compares the rather chaste design of the basilica (however lavish its interior decoration may have been) with the great romanesque churches which were built on the pilgrimage routes of Europe (like St. Sernin at Toulose or St. Madeline at Vezelay or Santiago of Campostella), one sees a strikingly different kind of architectural floorplan.

The most conspicuous difference between the basilica and the romanesque church can be seen in the apse (altar end) of the church. The apse of the romanesque church has a series of semicircular bulges fronted by an aisle space which runs around the back of the altar. The bulges are recessed areas for a series of small chapels since, by this time, the practice of priests saying individual masses each day had become firmly established. The aisle (called the "ambulatory") provided access to these chapels and as a way for pilgrims to walk around the entire apse area to get greater access to the reliquaries housed in the church.

Two things, then, happened over the centuries which affected the shape of the romanesque church. One was the shift in the understanding of the eucharistic liturgy. While the Mass was still considered a communal celebration, there was an increasing tendency—noticeable since the sixth century—of celebrating votive Masses offered for the needs of the faithful as services at which the faithful need not necessarily be present. This led to a multiplication of Masses celebrated by individual priests without the presence of a conspicuous congregation. Hence the need for more chapels, especially in places (like monastic or cathedral churches) where large groups of priests lived.

The other development was the increasing medieval passion for pilgrimage. The ambulatory helped with the traffic of pilgrims which became particularly acute during festive times. Many romanesque churches were designed for mobile congregations of occasional visitors and for the stable group of priests who required particular chapels for their own liturgical offices. The basic point to keep in mind is this: the romanesque church was taking its shape from the gradual complexification of liturgical and devotional practices which were developing in Western Christendom. One witness to that process was the changing character of church architecture.

The Gothic churches which began to be built in France in the twelfth century had much in common with many of the romanesque churches. They also felt the intense pressure of pilgrimages (Chartres, for example, was a major pilgrimage site). For that reason they needed the radiating chapels and the ambulatories which were a feature of romanesque churches. The complexity of Gothic design derives both inside and outside the church (with the "flying buttresses" characteristic of the style) from the need to support the ever increasing height of the walls. There was also a desire to thin the walls and pierce them so that they could afford more space for windows. By the late Gothic period the churches were taking on the appearance of masonry skeletons erected as frames for the ever more number of stained glass windows; hence the name *rayonnant* (French for "radiating") style was chosen to describe the gigantic radiating compositions of the rose windows, which at that time became both larger and more complex in their divisions.[3]

While we tend to think of Gothic in terms of its height, it was, as Otto von Simson has argued in a classic study, light (luminosity) which is the real characteristic of the Gothic.[4] That luminosity was made possible by the Gothic technical achievement of attaining greater verticality. Height had a theological as well as a functional importance in the Gothic period. Anyone who gets the opportunity to visit a true Gothic church can perform a simple test to see this. Enter the church, turn your back to the altar, and watch those who come in after you. Almost inevitably entering visitors will tilt back their heads and look up. The reason for this reflex is not hard to divine. Every line in a Gothic church seems to be a vertical one. The elongated clusters of columns, the pointed arches, the pinnacles decorating the frames of windows, pictures, and altars, all have an upward thrust. In the Gothic sense there is an overwhelming feeling of being lifted from this world to the transcendental world of God. To enter a Gothic church is to have one's mind (and eye) freed from the ponderousness of gravity for a glimpse of the world beyond. In that sense the Gothic church reinforced the medieval idea that life is an ascension from the weight of this world into the pure lightness (in two senses) of God. That sense of moving up was so much a commonplace of medieval thought that it was a major theme of Dante's *Commedia*: the pilgrim poet actually felt the shedding of weight as he climbed up the mount of purgatory readying himself for the journey to the presence of God who was understood to be a pure light at the very heart of the universe.

Verticality, then, had a close connection with light in the Gothic church. The sun pours through the windows bathing the church interior with its blues and reds. That suffused light also illuminates the sacred themes depicted in the windows themselves. Medieval theoreticians, borrowing ultimately from platonic sources, saw the analogy immediately: the sun is like God who illumines the story of creation and redemption depicted in the windows. The light of the sun is not seen directly, but nothing is seen without its illuminating power. The profound significance of Gothic light has been vividly described by Georges Duby in comparing the Gothic abbey church of St. Denis in Paris (the first Gothic church) with earlier monastic pilgrimage churches:

> At Saint Denis the relic chamber emerged from the penumbra of sacred grottoes, the dim half world of magic where a groveling religion had confined it, and merged into the radiant openness of the church itself, its reliquaries visible in broad daylight. The remains of Saint Denis himself, swathed in gems, triumphantly occupied the center of the church and shone with uninterrupted light. It was the light of his [Abbot Suger of Saint Denis] own theology—a reflection of God, a mirror of divinity, helping the faithful to find enlightenment.[5]

In many ways the Gothic cathedral was so unique a symbol of medieval culture that some scholars have seen the cathedral as a physical analogue for the entire structure of medieval philosophy and theology. St. Peter's in the Vatican is a post-medieval church which was begun in the late fifteenth century (the original was a fourth-century basilica-style church) when the Renaissance was at its apex and finished nearly one hundred and fifty years later at the noonday of the baroque. Its early architects included such figures as Bramante and Raphael, but its true architect was the Renaissance genius Michelangelo who designed a central, planned, Greek cross church with an imposing dome over it. That dome was not finished when Michelangelo died in 1564. In subsequent years it was decided to add a long nave and an imposing façade to the church (thus effectively obscuring Michelangelo's dome; it is best seen from the Vatican gardens behind the building) with the great baroque artist Gianlorenzo Bernini designing the main piazza and colonnades in front of the basilica as well as the canopy over the papal altar and the so-called altar of the Chair in the apse.

Anyone who has ever walked into St. Peter's knows immediately that it was not designed for intimacy or quiet meditation. Its scale is not for the individual; it is for the crowd. Its overwhelming size, its high tunnel vaulted ceilings, its rich, bronze, decorated canopy (baldachino) over the papal altar draw the eyes, not to the heavens, but straight ahead to the papal altar and beyond to the altar of the Chair. One can fully appreciate the impact of St. Peter's only when it is ablaze with lights, festooned by damask hangings, resonant with the voices or the polyphonic Vatican choir, thronged with a polyglot congregation watching a papal ceremony. I was in St. Peter's for the coronation of Pope John XXIII in 1958 when a companion turned to me and said, "To hell with Ringling Brothers. This is the greatest show on earth!" His remark, wittily irreverent, was on target. There is only one adequate word for the Roman baroque: theatrical.

It is in the very nature of the baroque to emphasize outside proportions, emotions, vividness, and a certain visual clamor. St. Peter's was built to make an overwhelming statement about the nature, power, and prestige of the papacy. It was an apologetic statement, created in the clamorous decades after the Reformation (which was triggered, as we know, by the promulgation of indulgences to raise funds for its building) to give witness to papal claims. That is why the style of St. Peter's (and much of the Roman architecture of the seventeenth century) has often been called "militant baroque." St. Peter's is a celebration of the glory of the militant church triumphant in *this* world. It shares none of the ethereal spirituality of the Gothic nor the fortresslike otherworldliness of the romanesque. It is a church, like every church, of its time. It reflects the hopes and concerns of that time and tells us much about the faith of its age.

How does all this relate to the typical parish church? Can we even say "typical" since there seems to be no paradigmatic parish church from which we can generalize?

North American parish churches built in the modern period either echo the architectural style of the past (e.g., ersatz Gothic or New World baroque), as can be seen in any older section of a major American city, or they have tried, timidly for the most part, to create a modern idiom out of the general modernism of post-Frank Lloyd Wright America. The styles, however, are not relevant to what we want to discuss here. Our concern is with the organization of interior space. How do these churches reflect, in their layout, a sense of communion with God?

Those churches which were built before the impact of the liturgical reforms of the Second Vatican Council had at least two things in common, both of which demanded some later form of renovation. First, the tabernacle was a prominent, if not central, focus of the building and, second, the altar and its space was designed in such a way as to be cut off from the rest of the church. There was a clear demarcation between altar and congregation, usually signified by an altar railing which also served as the place where one normally received communion. In fact, one can see in such churches a two-story area of the sacred: the first was the church space itself and the other was the area circumscribed by the altar rail. Behind that line the laity went only on rare occasions. It might be noted, in passing, that women did not enter that space at all except to be married or to clean!

The obvious significance of this kind of architectural organization was to underscore the sacramental presence of Christ in the tabernacle (an emphasis strongly insisted on after the Council of Trent in opposition to Reformed teaching) and the hieratic status of priests who attended that presence. Ceremonies like Benediction of the Blessed Sacrament involved a highly ritualized "presentation" of the eucharistic Christ as the tabernacle was solemnly opened, the Eucharist displayed, and finally, reposed. Private "visits" to the church—a devotional exercise much praised in the church—were likened to a person coming into the presence of a monarch. The pious would silently and humbly enter, make their petitions, and quietly retire. This sacred presence was surrounded by a complex rule of etiquette: genuflections each time one passed in front of the tabernacle; laypeople not touching the sacred vessels; etc.

Churches then exuded a sense of the continuing presence of the eucharistic Christ in an aura of sacrality and mystery. It is difficult to convey in words the feeling that such an understanding could engender in believers. Thomas Merton, writing about his first communion as an adult convert, gives some sense of it:

> . . . The bright sanctuary was all mine. I could hear the murmur of the priest's voice, and the responses of the server, and it did not matter that I had no one to look at, so that I could tell when to stand up and kneel down, for I was still not very sure of these ordinary ceremonies. But when the little bells were rung I knew what was happening. And I saw the raised Host— the silence and simplicity with which Christ once again triumphed, raised up, drawing all things to Himself—drawing me to Himself.[6]

One of the more conspicuous impacts of the Second Vatican Council was to shift liturgical consciousness in such a way as to cause a diminishment of that sense of the sacral presence of Christ in the Eucharist. A shorthand proof of that diminuition has been the decline of devotions like Benediction of the Blessed Sacrament.

A personal anecdote might help to underscore this shift in sentiment. While doing research for this book, I was a member of a Catholic community (too small to be called a parish; it is a mission) in a rural North Florida County which dedicated its first permanent church after some years of using a Methodist church (itself a significant fact!). It is the first Catholic church in the area. The monies were raised by the parishoners who also took an active role in clearing the land, designing the building with the aid of the diocesan architect, and decorating the interior. Parishioners built the altar, refurnished second-hand pews, sewed the altar cloths, and a local potter (my wife) made bowls for the holy water, and so on. The church, a modest affair but typical of today's churches, has no altar rail, no side altars; the tabernacle is attached to the left wall of the santuary; and the altar faces the people. The organization of that church space is such that the emphasis is on the weekly celebration of the liturgy, not on the housing of the eucharistic presence. The space does little to emphasize the permanence of the sacred; it does much to emphasize its occasional nature. Indeed, the community uses the building for "nonsacred" purposes, such as meetings, and at least a few members have suggested that, with a few decorous shiftings to block off the altar area, the building could be utilized for that most Catholic of secular rituals: Bingo on Wednesday nights.

Am I suggesting that our church is a desacralized building? Not at all. What I am suggesting is that the theological and liturgical focus of much of contemporary Catholicism has shifted from a static to a dynamic one. If one were to press me about the sacred character of our little church, my honest response would be that the sacred (read: the presence of Christ) is best experienced not by being in that building but *when* something happens there. In other words, it seems to me that in the post-Vatican II church there has been a significant shift away from the sacrality of space toward an emphasis on the sacredness of *time*; a shift from *where* to *when*.

This distinction should not be understood in any absolutely dichotomous fashion; it is not an either/or proposition. The Second Vatican Council's *Constitution on the Sacred Liturgy* insisted that when new churches were built, "great care be taken that they be suitable for the celebration of liturgical services and for the active participation of the faithful."[7] It was inevitable, given that mandate, that there would be a greater focus on the communitarian aspects of the liturgy, the need for scriptural proclamation, and the emphasis on the pedagogical function of the liturgy. Church space would accommodate itself to those foci to the detriment of those values which emphasized the passive presence of Christ the "Divine Prisoner of the Tabernacle" as one of the more extreme formulations would have it.

There is no doubt that the Catholic community still regards

the church as "God's House." After all, it is set off and consecrated for that purpose. Within its precincts the holiest rites of celebration—baptisms, weddings, funerals—are solemnized. Still the sacredness of the building is increasingly seen as flowing from those celebrations rather than as a characteristic of the building itself. This shift from the sacredness of space to the sacredness of time has been one of the hallmarks of the contemporary Catholic experience, but it has received little formal notice. In a recent essay Thomas O'Meara has written that the church building is not the object of faith but its medium.[8] It is through the building that something is communicated. So we must insist that to understand the medium is, at another level, to understand the message.

The shifting meaning of the church building as sacred space can be appreciated by another common phenomenon in the post-Vatican II church: the increasingly common practice of celebrating important rites of the church outside the confines of the church building itself. Examples abound: Masses celebrated outdoors, in college dormitories, in private homes, and so on; nor is it uncommon for a priest to baptize a baby in the privacy of a home in familiar domestic surroundings. Such celebrations underscore a move away from the "sacred space" of the church with celebrations taking place in "profane" space by the recreation of sacred moments through ritual.

What is one to make of this shift? Two observations seem to be in order.

First, one might be tempted to say that the decline in the sense of the sacredness of space is a dramatic symptom of the force of secularization sweeping the church, i.e., the erosion of the sense of the sacred and the concomitant exaltation of the human and the secular. One such critic has seen the contemporary liturgy as moving away from the goals of objective worship as worship of God to a fulfillment of the needs of the worshipper. Instead of talking to God the congregation now talks to each other. Such a liturgy becomes, in this critic's words, a *therapeutic* liturgy and "no longer the objective source of unity and continuity throughout the church but a means of celebrating the unity, friendship, and camaraderie of groups within it."[9]

That argument has been made loudly both by conservative critics within the church as well as by those non-Catholics who have a nostalgic respect or aesthetic hankering after the old usages of Catholicism. My own feeling is that it has been too easy to invoke the term "secularization" as a club with which to beat change. I am inclined toward Andrew Greeley's argument that what we are seeing is a shift in consciousness, rather than the forces of secularization.[10] Given the priorities and orientations of the Second Vatican Council, such a shift was both inevitable and of gigantic significance. It was not unanticipated. As the critic and liturgical scholar Louis Bouyer pointed out before the council, the price the church paid for its Tridentine liturgical laws and its sacramental usages was a congregation who ended up watching—rather than sharing in—a sacred drama enacted at a distance.[11] Church became sacred theater (the baroque culture was decisive here) with sharply defined roles for actors and audience. The fruitful participation (*actuosa participatio*) which was a key concept in the council meant inevitably a move away from a hieratic view of the liturgy to a more incarnational and communal one. That the times contributed to that shift seems obvious. For all the tacky tawdriness of post-Vatican II experimentation with guitars, banners, and "relevant" liturgical formulations (and how quickly we forget the saccharine tackiness of the older liturgical formulations) the new liturgy has provided, at its best, a vivid sense of worship for the modern Catholic. All theology begins in anthropology, Karl Rahner insists, and nowhere is that more true than in the sacred times we spend in worship. If we do not always have the actuality, we certainly have the potentiality of sensing that Christ who guaranteed his presence when "two or three are gathered in my name."

This brings us to a final point. It is helpful to remember that in the earliest days of Christianity the common place of worship was in the private household. Contemporary scholars have rightly insisted that the early worshipping community inserted itself in the family structures of its community. The obvious merit of such a situation was that it fostered a sense of intimate community with those gathered in his name. The obvious disadvantage was that the practice could lead to social stratification if one family happened to have the wealth to afford a house commodious enough to shelter a community of worship. In any event, it is useful to recall that St. Paul uses the expression the "household of the faith" as an expression of the church as a whole, an obvious metaphor derived from the early communities gathered in private homes.

While it would be anachronistic to suggest that the contemporary church could go back to such an arrangement, it is helpful both to recall the earliest places that Christians worshipped and under what circumstances. To have large formal structures for worship is fine but not normative for the church. The earliest experience of the faith was to localize its worshipping community in far more intimate and less sacralized surroundings. It should be also noted that a consideration of the "house church" may also shed light on the concept of the local church and how it is structured and governed. A reflection on localization in space leads almost inevitably to large considerations about the community itself.[12]

Another View of Sacred Space

The Christian basilicas of Rome were built in a city which had had an indigenous religious culture for over a millennium. Roman religion, like its Greek forebearer and like most religions of the ancient world, accepted as axiomatic that there was another world beyond ours—the world of the sacred—which could, and often did, break through into our world. This "breaking through" could occur to an individual through a dream or sign or it could be provoked by various religious rites or the sacred, in the person of divinities or spirits, could appear in certain places like a grove or a cave or a mountain, and show forth their power. When such hierophanies happened, it was not at all uncommon for a shrine or sanctuary to be erected over the place as a continuing hope that such prodigies would continue to occur.

Christianity grew in a culture which had so nurtured this religious *worldview* that it was impossible to avoid experiencing it in the very texture of everyday life; even the days of the week were named in honor of the pagan deities. How did

Christianity cope with this massive and long-standing tradition of alien religious ideas as it gained ascendency in the West? The relationship of Christianity to Rome is a notoriously complex question which must be addressed both at the level of intellectual cross-fertilization and at the more mundane level of primary contact, i.e., what does one do about pagan customs, shrines, language, and so on? On that second question we can say that the Christian church adopted one of three strategies (or any number of combinations of them): (1) they attempted to destroy and root out the vestiges of paganism; (2) they attempted to change such usages to a manner consonant with Christian practice; or (3) by a process of cultural osmosis, pagan elements were simply absorbed into the Christian world-view. An example might help to frame the Christian strategy. About a block from the Roman Pantheon (itself now a Catholic church and burial place of notables including Raphael the painter) there is a Dominican church called Santa Maria sopra Minerva—St. Mary over Minerva. The title is instructive since it manages to say two things at once: the Dominican church is built over the remains of a temple to Minerva and St. Mary has triumphed over that feminine pagan deity.

That religious exchange has been put into action often in Christianity. In 1519 the Spanish explorer Cortes landed on the island of Cozumel off the Yucatan Peninsula. One of his first acts there was to replace the Mayan goddess of the moon with an image of the Blessed Virgin Mary who had a half moon under her feet (cf. Rev. 12:1: "A woman clothed with the sun and the moon under her feet") as a visible sign that the Virgin had supplanted the native religion of the New World. There was a conscious pastoral strategy behind such substitutions and it was articulated early in the church's history. Writing to the missionary monk Mellitus who was departing for Britain in 601, Pope Gregory the Great instructed him in this manner:

> The idols are to be destroyed, but the temples themselves are to be aspersed with holy water, altars set up in them, and relics deposited there. For if these temples are well built, they must be purified from the worship of demons and dedicated to the service of the true God. In this way, we hope that the people, seeing that their temples were not destroyed, may abandon their

error and, flocking more readily to their accustomed resorts, may come to know and adore the true God. And since they have the custom of sacrificing many oxen to demons, let some other solemnity be substituted in its place, such as a day of Dedication or the festivals of the Holy Martyrs whose relics are enshrined there. . . . They are no longer to sacrifice beasts to the devils, but they may offer them for food to the praise of God, and give thanks to the giver of all gifts for the plenty they enjoy. . . . For it is certainly impossible to eradicate all errors from obstinate minds at one stroke, and whoever wishes to climb a mountaintop climbs gradually step by step, and not in one leap.[13]

This process of adaptation has been called "missionary adaptation" or "missionary accommodation" and its history is long and checkered in church history. Resistance to such accommodations were fierce in certain periods of church history because of the cultural imperialism of the church. The futile struggles of the great Jesuit missionaries in China in the sixteenth and seventeenth centuries to harmonize Catholic teachings with the Chinese reverence of ancestors, Confucian ethics, and the Mandarin language are only the most conspicuous example of such tensions. The current hesitations of the papacy over the "Africanization" of Catholicism on that continent is a sign that this issue, replete with so many philosophical and theological issues, has not yet been resolved. While the Second Vatican Council affirmed that the church could be enriched by "the customs and traditions of their people, from their wisdom and learning, from their arts and sciences,"[14] it is still difficult to put that spirit into practice.

Obviously not all Christian shrines and sanctuaries grew from the practice of replacing pagan holy places. Using a schema proposed by Victor and Edith Turner,[15] we can classify the "holy places" of Catholicism according to a number of separate categories. All these sites are objects of pilgrimage.

1. *Prototypical Sites:* Places closely identified by history or inference with the founder of the religion and/or his closest disciples. The great shrines of the Holy Land and the apostolic shrines of Rome would be prime examples of these kinds of holy places.

2. *Syncretistic* or *Archaic Sites:* Places which are now devoted

to Christian use, but which once had older non-Christian religious value. Our Lady of Guadalupe, built over a Mayan shrine in Mexico, would be one example; the famous shrine of Glastonbury in England, once a Celtic site, would be another.

3. *Medieval Sites:* Places which emerged concomitantly with the growth of medieval piety and the cult of the saints or relics. The most conspicuous of these were also famous pilgrimage destinations: Canterbury in England; Loreto in Italy; Chartres in France; Campostella in Spain; etc.

4. *Modern Sites:* Many of these shrines, mostly Marian in character, came into prominence in the nineteenth and twentieth centuries almost, it seems, as a conscious reaction to the prevailing skeptical mood of the times. They would include such shrines as Lourdes and La Salette in France; Knock in Ireland; Fatima in Portugal; Beauraing in Belgium, etc. Such shrines, while prominent in the modern period, are "in tone . . . actually anti-modern, since they usually begin with an apparition or vision and they assert miracles do happen."[16]

If anyone wishes to experience a sense of continuity with the archaic religious sensibility, a visit to one of these shrines, especially the more successful of them, would provide an ample sense of such a spirit. The Marian shrine at Lourdes is an excellent example. Between February and July in 1858 a young ill-educated girl, Bernadette Soubirous, experienced a series of apparitions of the Blessed Virgin Mary. Among the many instructions Bernadette received was one which told her to wash and drink from a spring that came forth when Bernadette dug in the sandy soil near the grotto of Massabielle outside of the town of Lourdes. That spring, in time, gained a reputation for its healing powers. Pilgrimage to Lourdes became so intense over the years that in the centenary year of 1958 over six million people visited the area. Even today Lourdes attracts between one and two million visitors a year.

The entire Lourdes phenomenon—its apparitions, the grotto, the springs, the visits of the sick, the bathings, the healings— puts us in touch with the earliest strata of human religious experience. Thousands of the sick and infirm, carried by their more able fellow pilgrims, wait daily to be blessed by the priests of the shrine or to bathe in the healing waters of the spring. Each night there are serpentine processions of candle-carrying pilgrims singing the "Lourdes hymn" with almost hypnotic repetition. It is easy to see the parallels between this behavior and that of the ancient healing sanctuaries of Greek or Roman religion (after all the nursing brothers of Saint John of God run a hospital on an island in the Tiber in Rome on which once existed a temple to Asclepius), but it would be useful to underscore the conviction that stands behind these sanctuaries: In *this* place—and the place is well defined; the sanctuary has its precincts so as to demarcate sacred from profane space—the power of God can break through and act. That is a conviction, no matter how contested it might be in modern culture, which is witnessed to in the Catholic accept-ance of holy places and holy shrines.

We should also notice that many shrines serve deep socio-political needs for people. Scholars have pointed out that the apparitions at Lourdes coincided with the period when the papacy's secular prestige was on the wane and anti-Catholic rationalism on the rise.[17] Other Marian apparition sites—most notably La Salette and Fatima—had strong apocalyptic over-tones to them with cries for penance, warnings about the impending cataclysm of war, and secret "messages" about the future of the world. Some great shrines have a strongly tradi-tional tie to the nationalistic or social aspirations of a people. Our Lady of Guadalupe, for example, has been the traditional protectress of the Indians of Mexico (in contrast to Our Lady of the Remedies who is the patroness of the "Spanish" segment of the populations) who are the traditional poor and downtrod-den of the country. It is no accident that it was her image which stood at the head of the armies of Mexican revolution and as the rallying point for the *braceros* who attempted to organize themselves in the agricultural fields of California in the 1970s. An even more striking example of this connection between Marian piety and nationalism can be seen in the symbolic place the shrine of Our Lady of Czestochowa plays in contemporary Polish life. The Black Madonna has been a symbol of Polish cohesion since 1656 when King John Kasimir proclaimed the Virgin as the "Queen of Poland" after a Polish victory over the Swedes. In the past few years world television has seen her image prominently displayed with the banners of the Solidarity movement. The great pilgrimages to honor the icon of the Virgin of Czestochowa at Jasna Gora ("Shining Mountain") has been a potent sign to the communist government of Poland of the power of the church over the hearts and minds of the people. Pope John Paul II has openly said that his call to the papacy was connected to his devotion to that great shrine and, as many scholars of the papal mind have argued, that admission had bound up in it a complex brew of Marian devotionalism, Polish nationalism, and a vivid sense of social messianism.

The connection between a "sacred" place and the spirit of national pride and sense of social purpose is not peculiar to Catholicism. A visitor to the tomb of the Unknown Soldier in Arlington National Cemetery recognizes immediately the quasi-religious nature of that place. The solemn guards, the measured cadences of their march, the chaste marble, and the respectful silence of the visitors all enhance that sense of solemnity which celebrates sacrifice for the commonweal. The difference between that site in Arlington and a shrine is that the latter is a focus of power; shrines do not only solemnize, but exude power. Things outside the ordinary happen there. Forces "break through" to heal or warn or reveal. There is an eruption of the sacred possible at any time.

That sense of the sacred is as old as Christianity itself and, as we have already noted, continues a tradition in religious experience which goes back behind Christianity. It is curious but not surprising, however, that such places, while common enough both in Latin America and, to a lesser degree, in Canada, are relatively rare in the United States. While thousands of American pilgrims visit the great shrines of Christendom around the world, there are very few such locales in this country. The few shrines that do exist are either linked to historical events in American Catholicism (e.g., the Shrine of Nombre de Dios in Saint Augustine, Florida, or the Shrine of the North American Martyrs in Auriesville, New York) or are erected, like the National Shrine of the Immaculate Conception in Washington, D.C., for some devotional reason. There are no significant "healing" shrines in this country.

The reason for this paucity is not hard to find: the Catholic church in the United States did not begin to enjoy a shaping growth until the last century. The church grew in this country at a time when the sacral aspects of Catholicism were already in some kind of decline in Europe except for modern shrines. The "sacred world" of Europe was already eclipsed by the rise of science and urban rationalization. There was no large-scale indigenous culture (like the Mayan or Aztec) upon which the older Catholic culture could be grafted. The American Catholic experience of sacred space was largely confined to the experience of the church building itself. The church, in the cities of the United States, represented a safe and familiar haven, a bulwark, against whatever was alien in American culture. It was largely an urban church without ties to the archaic religious spirit which was deeply rooted in the countryside. For those who craved the sacral in space there was but one thing to do: go on pilgrimage to foreign lands like the Celtic monks of old.

The Ambiguity of Sacred Space

Mircea Eliade and others have argued that archaic cultures not only marked off sacred places like temples as places of worship, but also consecrated their own habitations in a sacral manner. The idea was that the place in which one settled (either singly as in a home or communally as in a village) was like a "second creation" after the manner of the creation of the world. In the beginning such consecrations provided a sense of security against the feeling of homelessness and anarchy. My home is not just a home; it was a place which reflected what the gods had done. It was order against chaos. One consequence of this belief that one settled a place after the pattern of divine example was the tendency to think of a god as bound to one place or one people exercising divine power against the gods of other places and other peoples: divinity as protector of turf.

This sense of particularity was not completely absent from ancient Israel. Yahweh had chosen a people, dwelt among them, entered into a covenant with them, and made his presence felt in spatial ways—in the Ark of the Covenant and in the Temple of Solomon. Yet there was also a counterweight in ancient Israel—best articulated by the great prophets of the eighth century—that the God of Israel transcended spatial and national boundaries that claimed power over all the earth. There was, in short, a nudging sense of Yahwistic universality. That corresponded to an increasing resistance to spatial particularity. Herbert Schneidau has underscored that resistance nicely with reference to this notion as it appears in the New Testament: "In his 'eschatological discourse' (cf. Mk. 13; Mt. 24; Lk. 21), Jesus had warned that not a stone of the Temple would be left standing: this prophecy knits together the biblical symbolism that appears in the stories of Babel's towers and Jericho's walls. The only thing stones can do, in the Bible, is fall."[18]

It is instructive, in this regard, to reflect on the Gospel portrait of Jesus. While he was born in a particular place and lived in a very circumscribed area during his life, there was in the life of Jesus a certain rootlessness. He was born while his parents were on a journey; he was carried as an infant into short exile; and, after spending his youth in the town of Nazareth, he had an adult life of itinerant ministry, travelling "round the whole of Galilee teaching in their synagogues, proclaiming the Good News of the kingdom, and curing all kinds of diseases and sickness among the people" (Mt. 4:23). He once described this life of itinerancy in stark terms: "Foxes have their holes and the birds of air have nests, but the Son of Man has nowhere to lay his head" (Lk. 9:58).

In his own life one sees a dialectical relationship with sacred places. He goes out into the desert to pray (the desert being a "natural but sacred" place par excellence in biblical religion); goes up to mountains for solitude; frequents the temple in Jerusalem; reacts violently against those who would profane it; and so on. At the same time Jesus feels no constraint being placed on him by the sacredness of place. When Jesus encountered the Samaritan woman by the well, the discussion turned on the sacredness of place. The woman contrasts her sacred place, Mount Gerizim, with his—the temple in Jerusalem. Jesus relativizes both places in unmistakable terms:

> Believe me, woman, the hour is coming
> when you will worship the Father
> neither on this mountain nor in Jerusalem. . . .

But the hour will come—in fact it is here already—
when true worshippers will worship the Father in spirit and
truth:
that is the kind of worshipper
the Father wants.
God is spirit,
and those who worship
must worship in spirit and truth. (Jn. 4:21–24)

The concept of space was often internalized in the New Testament. Places became sacred in remembering the works of Jesus ("When two or three are gathered in my name") or allegorized to stand for interior piety ("Know ye not that you are temples of the Holy Spirit?"). Early Christians were known as people of "the Way" and it was on pilgrimage, not in place, that they sought to make sense of the message of Jesus who was the Christ.

Behind these relativizing tendencies was the felt conviction that the old places and spaces could render true faith static at best or deformed at worst. Christianity did not reject places holy to God to be sure, but they did think out a whole series of images to keep that faith from becoming space-bound. These images of pilgrimage and movement waxed and waned in the history of the church, but it was one of the great advances of the Second Vatican Council's *Dogmatic Constitution on the Church (Lumen Gentium)* to reassert them forcefully. The church is to be thought of not only as extended in space and time but also as a mystery in time, a gathering of the people of God in place, and as a pilgrimage through human history.

It is difficult, to be sure, to hold in mind simultaneously the idea of our faith being concretized in a specific place (e.g., "my" parish) and transcending that place. But that enlarged sense of transcending my place is one of the deepest meanings of what it means to be Catholic.

Nobody escapes the limitations of time and place nor would we be better off trying to do so. We need "go aside" into different places and at different times to make real the presence of the sacred in our lives. We need to locate ourselves in those spaces where traditionally the sacred speaks to us. We do that both by crossing the threshold of the church Sunday after Sunday and at those informal times when we feel the need for the quiet of a retreat or a monastic pause in our lives. The Catholic tradition provides ample scope for the fulfillment of this need but with the understanding that we turn again to the burdens of the day. The paradigm for this going aside to places is rooted in the example of Jesus who made use of the desert, the mountain, the garden of olives, the temple, and the synagogue to give structure to his life amid the whirl of life.

At its very worst the sacralization (or better: pseudosacralization) of space has demonic implications. It was, at the very best, a mixed blessing to give a piece of geography the title "Holy Roman Empire" just as it was a deformity to so absolutize the *holy places* that they became an energizing metaphor for violence and aggrandizement. The Constantinian heritage of identifying place—Empire, State, City—with the special presence of God can be a pernicious thing as the sad history of the church has so clearly shown.

The way we sacralize space can undergo profound shifts over the centuries. Latin America is dotted with huge baroque churches, many of them lavishly decorated, which date back to the period of Hispanic colonial domination. It is a commonplace today to hear people complain about the waste of monies on these exuberant structures. The complaint is all the louder from those who have even a glancing experience with the poverty and squalor of the region. This has always struck me as an anachronistic criticism. Apart from reminding such critics that Jesus had some words to say to Judas who complained about the wasting of money when the feet of Jesus were anointed with precious perfumes, there is another, less polemical, point to be made. In earlier times the sense of the sacredness of space was more intense because of the strong emphasis on the sacramental presence of Jesus in the Eucharist and a stronger sense of the transience of this life. To sacrifice wealth for the glory of God was a fitting thing; if the sacrifice of wealth was painful, there was an added merit to be gained. It was expected that God should get the very best and the most precious of our gifts. The quality of art and the lavishness of decoration were visible signs of the devotion of the donors and the dedication of the populace. To erect beautiful buildings had an almost sacramental meaning.

That attitude strikes me as a plausible, and, in many ways,

an admirable, way of relating to God. But, by and large, it is not our way. Our sense of material abnegation is directed in other directions as a result of a growing sense of human solidarity; at its best, our sense of sacrifice is more incarnational. The martyred bishop of San Salvador City in El Salvador, Oscar Romero, refused to finish the cathedral of his see city as a visible sign of his commitment to the poor of the country. The raw concrete building, ugly in its unfinished concrete, is a spatial statement about a different set of religious priorities.

To recall an earlier observation: For the past generation there has been a noticeable shift away from a hieratic and vertical view of the Eucharist in the church to one that emphasizes the communal sharing of a meal; the recognition of the Lord in "the breaking of bread." That shift—and it has been a profound one—has brought with it an inchoate sense that Christ is not encountered in *place* but in relationship. With such a shift it would seem to be desirous to extend that sense of relationship beyond the immediate community of worshippers. To spend modestly on a decorous church and use the surplus monies would appear to be something beyond merely being "good-hearted"; it would be, in fact, a deepening of the faith we have in the celebration of the Eucharist in the Christian community. The words of St. Paul seem germane in this regard: "As it is, the parts are many but the body is one. The eye cannot say to the hand 'I do not need you' nor can the head say to the feet 'I do not need you' " (1 Cor. 12:20–21). One practical way to express this concern, as I suggested in an earlier work,[19] would be for every parish in the industrialized world to pair with a parish in the third or fourth world and tithe for the maintenance of that parish. Such a scheme would be of material help to the church of the poor while giving the churches of advanced societies a better sense of Catholicity. It would also help nurture the sense of the church as being "metaspatial"—crossing and connecting spatial boundaries.

This shift which has occurred in the contemporary church has triggered both bitterness and alienation among some Catholics, especially older ones. Anyone, like myself, who is concerned "professionally" with things Catholic is told repeatedly that "the church isn't the same" or "we are becoming just like Protestants" or—as someone told me casually at a cocktail party—"When they dropped Latin, I dropped them." Those complaints are symptomatic of a deeper feeling that the "sacredness" has gone out of the church and that the circle has been shattered which bound us (religion: from the Latin *religare*, to bind) to the mysteries of the transcendent order. There is a deep nostalgia and a profound longing in those sentiments. It is not enough to insist, as we have insisted, that the long view of history provides both explanation and, following on that, comfort. But things do change and horizons shift and broaden. Neither is it a consolation to be reminded that we may well be living "between the times" as new understandings are aborning (as they surely are) and old ones passing away. If, as I say, such observations give us scant comfort, they still need to be said. The very dynamic character of the church cannot permit us to luxuriate in the past. We need to remind ourselves that nostalgia can be a peculiarly deadening temptation. The great theologian Henri de Lubac wrote some salutary words on this issue more than a generation ago. He spoke of certain temptations concerning the church to which some people easily succumb:

> For them the church is a certain order of things which is familiar to them and by which they live; a certain state of civilization, a certain number of principles, a certain complex of values which the church's influence has more or less christianized but which nonetheless remains largely human. And anything which disturbs this order or threatens this equilibrium, anything which upsets them or merely startles them, seems to them a crime against a divine institution.[20]

Such is the temptation to absolutize the concrete. While it is true, to use Rosemary Haughton's lovely phrase, that Catholic faith must have a "local habitation and a name,"[21] it would be very wrong to absolutize either the place or the naming. It was against that temptation that the prophets and Jesus spoke so urgently.

Points for Meditation

1. If Mass were to be celebrated in your home for some special occasion, what would you do to "prepare" for that event by way of cleaning and decorating? How

much of that activity would be ritualistic? What would the preparations mean to you, not as the householder, but as the participant/host of the liturgy?

2. Have you ever been in a church building that you found completely repellent to your spiritual sensibilities? If so, why?

3. Have you ever looked really closely at the shape and makeup of your own home parish church? What, beyond the familiarity brought by time, do you find comforting and/or disconcerting about it? Do you link that building to certain important memories in your life?

4. If you were called upon to design a church interior that would express your sense of faith, what would you absolutely insist on being included and excluded?

5. Are there any nonecclesiastical places which have a sacred significance for you? If so, how did that take on the character of sacredness and how did these places function in your life?

6. In what places do you think Jesus would be most comfortable today? Is that question even askable?

Notes

1. Richard Krautheimer, Three Christian Capitals: Topography and Politics (Berkeley: University of California Press, 1983), p. 20.
2. Richard Krautheimer, Rome: Profile of a City, 312–1308 (Princeton: Princeton University Press, 1980), p. 35.
3. Jean Bony treats the rayonnant style in French Gothic Architecture of the Twelfth and Thirteenth Century (Berkeley: University of California Press, 1983), p. 357ff.
4. Otto von Simson, The Gothic Cathedral (New York: Harper Torchbook, 1964).
5. Georges Duby, The Age of the Cathedrals: Art and Society, 980–1320 (Chicago: University of Chicago Press, 1981), pp. 102–3. For a complete text of Suger's writings on the theology of light, see Erwin Panofsky, Abbot Suger (Princeton: Princeton University Press, 1946).
6. Thomas Merton, The Seven Storey Mountain (Garden City: Doubleday Image Book, 1970), p. 273.
7. The Documents of Vatican II, ed. Walter Abbott (New York: Association Press, 1966), p. 175.
8. Thomas Franklin O'Meara, "The Aesthetic Dimension in Theology," in Art, Creativity, and the Sacred, ed. Diane Apostolos-Cappadona (New York: Crossroad, 1983), p. 214.
9. William McSweeney, Roman Catholicism: The Search for Relevance (New York, St. Martin's, 1980), pp. 238–39.
10. Andrew Greeley's The New Agenda (Garden City: Doubleday Image Book, 1975) is a representative example of this position.
11. Louis Bouyer, Liturgical Piety (Notre Dame: Notre Dame University Press, 1955).
12. Wayne A. Meeks, The First Urban Christians (New Haven: Yale University Press, 1983), pp. 75ff.; Elizabeth Schüssler Fiorenza, In Memory of Her (New York: Crossroad, 1983), pp. 175–84.
13. This letter is preserved in the Venerable Bede's A History of the English Church, trans. Leo Shirley Price (Baltimore: Penguin, 1955), pp. 86–87.

14. From the *Decree on the Church's Missionary Activity* in *Documents of Vatican II*, p. 612.

15. Victor and Edith Turner, *Image and Pilgrimage in Christian Culture* (New York: Columbia University Press, 1978), pp. 17–19.

16. Ibid., p. 19. For a fuller treatment of this theme, see Alan Neames, *The Happening at Lourdes: The Sociology of the Grotto* (New York: Simon and Schuster, 1967).

17. The many accounts of Marian apparitions reported from around the Catholic world, especially those like the Bayside, New York, apparitions which are linked to traditionalist Catholic themes, can be seen as reactions to the cognitive dissonance triggered by ecclesial and cultural turmoil.

18. Herbert Schneidau, *Sacred Discontent: The Bible and Western Tradition* (Baton Rouge: Louisiana State University Press, 1976), p. 119. I would not like to push that point to the extreme of saying that the biblical tradition secularizes all space.

19. Lawrence S. Cunningham, *The Catholic Heritage* (New York: Crossroad, 1983), pp. 222–23.

20. Henri de Lubac, *The Splendour of the Church* (New York and London: Sheed and Ward, 1956), p. 208.

21. Rosemary Haughton, *The Catholic Thing* (Springfield, Ill.: Templegate, 1979), p. 147.

Selected Readings

Apostolos-Cappadona, Diane, ed. *Art, Creativity, and the Sacred.* New York: Crossroad, 1984. A useful bibliography enhances this anthology of essays on sacred art.

Eliade, Mircea. *The Sacred and the Profane.* New York: Harper Torchbook, 1961. A classic study of sacred space and time.

Giedion, Sigfried. *Space, Time, and Architecture: The Growth of a New Tradition.* Cambridge: Harvard University Press, 1963. The Norton Lectures of 1938–39 are a model of how to think about architectural space.

Martin, David F. *Art and the Religious Experience.* Lewisburg: Bucknell University Press, 1972. A philosophical analysis with some useful remarks on architecture.

Scully, Vincent. *The Earth, the Temple, and the Gods.* New Haven: Yale University Press, 1982. A brilliant exercise in thinking about space and the sense of the sacred by one of American's master teacher-lecturers.

Wolterstorff, Nicholas. *Art in Action: Toward a Christian Aesthetic.* Grand Rapids: Eerdmans, 1982. A study by a non-Roman Catholic scholar.

2

TIME

The noted scholar Mircea Eliade asserts that for a religious person (*homo religiosus*, to use his term) time is not an inexorable march from past to future unrepeatable and unrecoverable. Sacred time, Eliade writes, "is reversible in the sense that, properly speaking, it is a primordial mythical time made present. Every religious event, any liturgical time, represents the reactualization of a sacred event that took place in a mythical past, 'in the beginning.' "[1]

With only a moment's reflection on the central act of Christian liturgical worship, the Eucharist, we can see that what Eliade says is true. The New Testament clearly teaches that on the night before Jesus died, he shared with his disciples a meal of bread and wine which was in some manner a sharing in his body and blood. The New Testament is careful to record that this event, which happened in a specific setting at a specific moment in history, was to be repeated, as St. Paul says, "until the Lord comes" (1 Cor. 11:26). The sanction for this repetition is the express command of the Lord. Paul emphatically says that "This is what I received from the Lord, and, in turn, passed on to you . . ." (1 Cor. 11:23).

From these early apostolic memories recorded in St. Paul's First Letter to the Corinthians and in the synoptic gospels (Mt. 26:26–29; Mk. 14:22–25; Lk. 22:15–20) the liturgy, as we know it today, slowly and tortuously grew over the centuries. We not only re-create, re-present, and re-enact that once-in-a-moment event in time, but we explicitly recall the words

36

which have been passed on to us from the New Testament church. We recall the memory of those words not simply by reading or proclaiming them—although we surely do that also— but by acting them out in formal ritual action. To use Eliade's terminology: The New Testament account of the Eucharist is the *mythos* (story) and the liturgy is the *ritual* by which the *mythos* is made vivid and actual.

The many meanings of that ritualized *mythos* need not concern us here; we shall speak about those meanings in various contexts in this book. What is our concern is the element of *time* involved in that activity which we call the "eucharistic liturgy." At a certain determined time and place— say, a dreary Sunday morning in January, 1985—I go to Mass. When, by faith, I participate in that celebration, I have stepped out of the ordinary course of time (just as, by entering that space of the church, I have stepped out of regular space) in order to live ritually in an event which happened two millennia ago. That contemporary event, rooted in a historical moment, takes on a new meaning and an immediate actuality. By my participation in the re-creation of that event it happens again. In that act Christ becomes vivid to me in my time. On the road to Emmaus the disciples recognized the Risen Lord after he broke bread and shared it with them: "Their eyes were open and they recognized . . ." (Lk. 24:31).[1] Most commentators think that the Emmaus incident has been shaped by reading back the eucharistic experiences of the early Christian experience into that incident. At our participation in the liturgy we stand in that succession of moments which link us by liturgical moments with that early believing group at Emmaus. The very ordinary act of going to Mass, when properly perceived, is the dearest and strongest act of tradition and continuity we possess. Our time becomes part of the time which extends back to the first eucharistic community and extends forth into that future which will not end until "he comes again."

On this occasion when we most vividly experience that sense of the liturgy as community not only with our fellow celebrants but with the historical continuum of believers we gain a profound sense of the suspension of ordinary clock time. There is nothing all that mystical about the experience of stepping out of clock time. We simply do not often reflect on the experience or relate it to our religious experience. It is a common enough human desire to escape from the oppressive sense of ordinary clock time. In an airport, waiting for a delayed plane, we will buy a magazine or a paperback novel in order, as we say, to "kill time," i.e., to enter into the fantasy life of fiction so that we are not so aware of the slow passing of the minutes and our increasing sense of frustration at that slowness. Another example: We go to an early afternoon movie which places us in the grip of a well-paced story. When the movie is over (it might tell a story which imaginatively encompasses three generations of a life), we emerge, blinking into the sunlight, to discover that only two hours have passed by. We again begin to sense the weighty passage of ordinary time. Eliade believes that those immersions into the time of fictional or filmic mythos give us a taste, however attenuated, of the experience of sacred time: "When modern man 'kills' time with a detective story or enters such a foreign temporal universe as is represented by a novel, reading projects him out of his personal duration and incorporates him into other rhythms, makes him live in another 'history' ".[2]

I insist on the specific character of time in the Eucharist in order to make a general observation which may serve as an entry point for some specific considerations of the element of time in the Catholic experience. The general observation is that to be a Catholic is to live at least in two kinds of time: the time of ordinary existence and that time, by means of ritual activity, when we step into the mode of liturgical time to re-present to ourselves the presence of Christ who lived in history but whose presence is metahistorical.

I would say further that we live "at least" in those two modes of time since, as closer examination shows us, the Catholic experience has a complex view of time not merely reducible to the category of liturgical and profane time. Catholicism, to put it another way, has many eyes: It looks back in time to assess its fidelity to the things which have been handed to it, i.e., its tradition; it looks beyond time to the eternal present which is God; it looks to the future from its own present for the promised Kingdom. It is that complex character of observed time which the poet T. S. Eliot described in the opening lines of *Four Quartets*: "Time present and time past/Are both perhaps present in time future,/And time future contained in time past."

The Liturgical Year

The liturgy of the church is, at its most basic, an act of worship, but "it likewise contains abundant instruction for the faithful. For in the liturgy God speaks to His people and Christ is still proclaiming His Gospel."[3] That statement by the Fathers of the Second Vatican Council solemnly enunciates what we almost instinctively know from experience or observation: What most Catholics know about Christ and his teachings is learned principally through a continuing contact with the formal proclamation of the Gospel in the celebration of the liturgy. From the time of early childhood Catholics hear the readings of the scriptures and listen to homilies on those readings and repeat prayers which are drenched in the images of the Bible. While it is true that many people have attended Catholic schools and some have come from homes rich with prayer and observance, most Catholics have, as their primary point of contact, that hour a week in which the liturgy is celebrated.

With the restoration of the vernacular liturgy and the renewed emphasis on preaching, the church has recognized more than ever the teaching role of the liturgy even though we all recognize from bitter experience that the quality of instruction in the liturgy is more often an expressed ideal than an actual reality. We have all suffered through routinized Sunday celebrations, banal sermons, and garbled readings. We also suffer from an overfamiliarity with the liturgy itself. We settle into our pew on Sunday prepared (or resigned) to hear something which we have heard all of our lives. The Gospel refrains are a familiar buzz; a kind of pious "white noise." Indeed, the familiarity of the liturgy, set as it often is in a familiar and comfortable parish church which we have known all of our lives, can be a positive impediment to genuine *hearing*. "The old words of grace," Walker Percy writes in sadness, "are worn smooth as poker chips and a certain devaluation has occurred, like a poker chip after it has been cashed in."[4] At best, we are comforted by the regularity of the words and the familiar actions; the liturgical proclamation does not pierce as a double-edged sword. It envelopes like a well used robe. The comfort of religious language is part of the larger issue of religious language itself; we shall return to that theme again. At this point I want to focus on the designated times when, by tradition, we have listened to those words. Those designated times are usually treated under the rubric of the liturgical year.

Chapter five of the *Constitution on the Sacred Liturgy* devotes itself entirely to the cycle of liturgical time.[5] It is a chapter which breaks no new ground, contenting itself with a summary of the accumulated tradition of the Western church. That tradition, however, is somewhat complex. First, the council emphasizes that the "Lord's day is the original feast day" (art. 106) because it honors the core mystery of Christianity itself: the paschal mystery of Christ's death, burial, and resurrection. The feast of Easter recapitulates what is celebrated each Sunday which is the Lord's resurrection (art. 102). Sunday, then, is the microcosm of liturgical time and the liturgical year is the larger framework which structures the passage of individual Sundays during the year. In that annual cycle the church "unfolds the whole mystery of Christ, not only from His incarnation and birth until his ascension, but also as reflected in the day of Pentecost, and the expectation of a blessed, hoped for return of the Lord" (art. 102).

Within this larger orbit of the church year there are three other subservient cycles which celebrate the principal feasts of the Blessed Virgin Mary, the saints of the universal calendar, as well as those "various seasons of the year [in which] according to her traditional discipline, the Church completes the formation of the faithful by means of pious practices for soul and body, by instruction, prayer, and works of penance and of mercy" (art. 105). To those outlined in the official liturgical year we should also mention those days in which the national churches also hold religious observance to celebrate holidays peculiar to its own experience. In the United States Thanksgiving would be an example of such a day in which the civil religion of the nation has the cooperation of the church itself.

We focus here on the great cycle of the church's year because it is that cycle which presents the mystery of Christ to us.[6] In that cycle which begins in Advent as the church "waits" for Christmas, we follow the annual unfolding story of Christ's birth, ministry, passion and death, resurrection, ascension, and Pentecost gift of the Spirit. After Pentecost we meditate on the Gospel on the "ordinary Sundays" until Advent comes again. That great cycle is, of course, the product of a finished development since the various parts of the year (the Lenten season, Holy Week, the Easter and Christmas cycles) developed at their own pace during the long history of the church.

The appropriation of Christ, according to the temporal order of the church year, is twofold: the weekly liturgical encounter and the annual unfolding of the mysteries of Christ in the course of the liturgical year. In this twofold observance of day and year we are given a framework of time for the formal celebration of faith. We come aside to re-create and re-fresh ourselves in order to live a more fully Christian life. The Sunday liturgy is the repeated act of communion with Christ in the context of a faithful community while the annual cycle of the liturgy is the basis for our hearing and absorbing the story of Christ which is at the center of our faith.

That is the ideal. How does this ideal work out in practice?

Not very well for most of us. The reason is simple. The manner in which we organize our time does little to encourage our sense of following the cycle of the seasons (upon which the liturgy is based) or the shifting back and forth from mundane to contemplative time.

A consideration of our work week should make that clear. The contemporary work week now falls into a five-day period of labor (or study or whatever) and a two-day "weekend." This is the pattern of all industrialized and postindustrialized societies as the six-day and five-and-a-half day work week became less common. We should realize that the very notion of a "weekend" is quite recent in society. There is no corresponding word for it in many European languages; in languages like French and Italian the English word is just carried over as a loan word. According to the *Oxford English Dictionary* "weekend" first appears in English in 1879 and, significantly enough, it referred to leisurely trips for the middle class from urban centers. Soon, "weekend" referred to the upper-class custom of spending those days at a country estate. The traditional six-day work week and Sabbath day of rest were being replaced by a five-day work week and a two-day period of recreation and leisure. Sunday store openings and other such activities are a direct result of the slow absorption of the Sabbath observance into the larger time frame of the weekend of rest. Sunday religious observances have become one more activity in a time period of two days rather than the time period itself. Sunday morning, as Wallace Stevens said in a celebrated poem, has lost its meaning as "the green freedom of the cockatoo/Upon a rug mingle to dissipate/The holy hush of ancient sacrifice."[7]

The fuller cycle of the liturgical year has fared little better than the sacred time of Sunday. The annual cycle of the following of Christ no longer functions in our culture as a series of benchmarks to mark the passing of the year. We may still speak of "Christmas break" or the "Easter season," but they are conventional designations not closely tied to our actual perceptions of the year in any religious sense. Furthermore, while it is a commonplace that our major religious feasts like Christmas and Easter coincide with the observance of seasonal changes (Christmas at the winter solstice; Easter at the spring equinox), our culture, except in agricultural settings, is not much concerned with the changes of nature. We do not live close to nature; we go out to seek it as a conscious decision. My university office, for example, is windowless and climate-controlled. The only way I know if it is cool or warm outside or raining or bright or early or late is by inquiry or inference. It does not really matter. My time follows other signs—the clock or the bell.

Shifts like this in our pattern of life have distanced us from the rhythms upon which much of liturgical time is based. We simply do not mark our day by the sound of the Angelus bell or the seasons by the great feasts of the parish. It does little to lament this passing or yearn for its return (as if it ever fully existed outside the structures of the monasteries). It is an irreducible fact of the way we are and, as such, it raises a question: How does a person in the late twentieth century living in a postindustrial culture maintain some sense of the sacred times of the liturgy?

The difficulty in coordinating the value of liturgical time with the ordinary course of our life does mean that we have lost the need for celebrative moments in our life. Ordinary reflection on our own lives would show the contrary. What is at issue here is the blurring of our sense of Sunday as a special day of worship and celebration and the general trend away from a sacralized sense of the year (the ongoing reduction in "holy days of obligation" is a mark of that trend). Such an erosion is a cultural fact of life. The need to go aside and the need to ritualize certain moments of time are constants in our existence. We now have a plethora of choices when we do want to "go aside" and some of those choices, seemingly secular in character, have taken on a semisacred character as anyone who has ever had to endure a lecture from a dedicated runner about the "highs" of his daily discipline can attest. Contemporary society is not as culturally homogeneous as it has been in the past and the heterogeneity of culture does mean that our choices are dictated neither by tradition nor by our elders. The fact that not as many people go to Mass today as did a generation ago has often been blamed on the liturgical turmoil following the Second Vatican Council. But the dropping off of Sunday observance might also be interpreted as a result of our culture providing more options for the "rest and recreation" of Sunday.

Andrew Greeley has argued persuasively that religious stories are no longer self-evident in our society; these stories need interpretation and mediation.[8] If that is the case, and it surely is, a rather simple, almost self-evident, yet crucially important conclusion can be drawn from that fact: The observance of liturgical time—that hour of formal worship at the liturgy— had better be freighted with some kind of intelligibility or people, free from the older constraints of tradition and culture, will find alternatives to that hour.

There was a time when people went to Mass on Sunday because it was an absolute duty. It was not a question of whether one "got something" from Mass; it was a simple irreducible fact that one went because that was part of being a Catholic. It was attendance and not participation that was expected; if one participated, that was all to the good, but the crucial issue was: Were you there before the Gospel and did you remain at least through communion?

The first Sunday the priest looked out at his congregation and declared "The Lord be with you!" instead of *Dominus vobiscum*, a radical transformation took place in the Catholic church. There was, for the first time in centuries, a direct intelligible link between priest and congregation without the mediation or the mystification of liturgical Latin. People heard and understood or, more likely, heard and did not understand. Congregations were now forced to assess the liturgy not on an aesthetic plane, but on a conceptual one: Is this saying something to me? The various tinkerings with the Roman liturgy, both formal and informal, were attempts—often well-meaning and often inept—to translate the distant mystery—the "blessed mutter" of the Mass—into something which could be grasped directly in a spiritually nourishing way. That this did not always happen was simply a result of a massive change taking place when few had thought out what might follow from it. There is an interesting volume to be written on the sociology of change using the liturgical reforms of the 1960s as the starting point of discussion. It was one thing to have a desire for certain results; it was quite another to anticipate what could happen.

Change is a fact and, except for the dreaming nostalgic, it is a fact without much chance of reversal. The great challenge to the contemporary church is to learn how to translate the accumulated riches of the liturgical tradition into something which is significant in its manifestation and in its content; a translation, in short, which understands both medium and message. By and large the liturgical medium today is woefully undernourished precisely because the modern church has an impoverished aesthetic sense.[9] There simply has not been much emphasis on the categories of the beautiful and the fitting. Liturgical reformers in this country have not engaged our poets ("our" not necessarily meaning Catholic) to provide us with worthy liturgical texts. This may seem at first blush a small matter, but if it does seem small, it is because we have no regard for poetry. Poets are irrelevancies in our age despite Karl Rahner's wise reflections on their quasi-priestly role as the evokers of those primordial words (*Urwortes*) which touch on the very mystery of existence itself.[10] Poets, as that Catholic haunted genius of words, James Joyce, asserted, transubstantiate base reality into something glorious through language.

The chaste use of art, language, and music is not a peripheral issue in liturgical matters. It takes little knowledge of the Catholic tradition to know that the marriage of art to liturgy has been one of the hallmarks of that tradition. If one hopes to provide any sense of the deep mystery expressed in the liturgy, some sense of the numinous must be part of that exercise. Some would insist that the liturgy should reflect everyday life. I think that a misguided position. If that Sunday hour is to be marked off as significant, it must be bracketed off from the banality of the quotidian. That does not mean that the liturgy must be lavish; it means only that it should have high sense of the serious and the beautiful. The late Dorothy Day loved to quote Dostoevsky's dictum that "the world will be saved by beauty." The same dictum, I would submit, has applicability to the liturgy.

What I am suggesting is that everything should so conspire as to provide a palpable countertime to the ordinary time of life. When a person goes to church on a Sunday morning, there ought to be a perceived feeling that what is happening is new, profound, and strikingly different from what one sees and experiences during the ordinary unfolding of the week. This is not a plea for lavishness; it is a plea for seriousness. While there was a tendency to slough off ceremonial—some of it well worth sloughing off—in the period of the 1960s, we should realize that the use of ceremonial carries with it a genuine insight into religious need. It is easier to say that this should be so and another to carry it through to practice. Nobody would want a consciously ugly or slovenly liturgy. But the unwillingness to do something concrete is not a trivial matter. The eruptions of emotionalism in contemporary Catholicism, reflected in everything from Marriage Encounter and Cursillo to the Charismatic movement, is symptomatic of a deep hunger for high-intensity religious experience currently not being found in formal worship in the church.

Beside the medium of the liturgy, there is its message—words and actions which are meant to convey something. It is a commonplace among educated Catholics to observe that we have a crisis in religious language. The entire burden of David Tracy's revisionist project in theology, the most ambitious on the Catholic horizon, is to retrieve a meaningful theological language which will correlate what Tracy calls "common human experience and language" and the "authentic interpretation of Christian texts."[11] Such a discussion is far beyond the scope of this book, but Tracy's project underscores what we wish to signal here: There is a critical need for the contemporary liturgy to provide its words and actions some existential currency. In the Byzantine liturgy of St. John Chrysostom the deacon cries out to the congregation just before the reading of the Gospel: "Wisdom! Attend!" Here is the issue: How do we *attend* to that wisdom?

The revisioning of theological language is not simply the task of the systematic theologian; it also springs from the use of formal religious language as that language is mediated in those sacred times when we gather in worship. I would make my own the manifesto of Amos Niven Wilder:

> It is in the area of liturgics—the idioms and metaphors of prayer and witness—that the main impasse lies today for the Christian. . . . Before the message there must be the vision, before the sermon the hymn, before the prose the poem. . . . Before any theologies however secular and radical there must be a contemporary theopoetic. The structures of faith and confession have always rested on hierophanies and images. But in each age and climate the theopoetic of the church is reshaped in inseparable relation to the general imagination of the time.[12]

The liturgy is, by instinct, conservative (and rightly so) since it hands down what is received. But it must also take account of the dynamic nature of religious understanding. To say that worship is conservative is not the same as saying that the preservation of texts, rituals, and what-have-you should be done in the manner of a museum. We cannot enshrine words which do not resonate with human experience. Pheme Perkins has written that "such a demand fails to recognize the internal dynamic of the biblical heritage on which those institutions are built. Faith never provided a hold on an 'unchanging' reality. It demanded faithfulness, trust in God's word, and a promise for the future that was often obscured by the turmoil in which God's people lived."[13]

I take Professor Perkins's words to mean that the values of the Gospel do not come easily; one must listen in openness and be ready for response. For those who try to live moments in the aura of liturgical time there must be, in that deep manner which Simone Weil invested the expression, an openness to *wait in patience.* For those who have the responsibility to celebrate the liturgy there must be a concomitant willingness to give.

It has been widely said that the multiplication of ministries in the contemporary church has reduced the priest to the role of a "liturgy machine"—someone whose sole function has become those of celebration and absolution. Some say this in denigration, but, even if it were fully true (which it is manifestly not), it could still be seen as an unparalleled opportunity; a role of grace. I can think of no other comparable social role in contemporary society which permits a person the chance to speak to a large voluntary community week after week who wait hungrily for something which will touch the very fundaments of their existence. The abstract nature of that opportunity has yet to be impressed freely into the consciousness of those who celebrate the liturgy. Nor is there strong evidence— indeed, some counterevidence—that the younger clergy have learned how to provide bread instead of stones.

For all the problems and puzzles connected with worship people still come aside at *times* and express their hope-filled desire to meet Christ in the liturgy. The times are not always satisfactory and their sacred character blurred, but people still wait in patience for those moments which do count the most.

Time and Personal Growth

We can know time either as a detached reality like dates on a calendar which marks the passing of time or as a deeply felt experience of our own evolving personhood. In the former sense we know that "It is already March; how time flies!" while in the personal instance we say with the poet "I grow old. I grow old." It is in that latter sense that we experience both our mortality and our human growth.

All religious traditions give mythical and ritual significance to those stages on life's way. It is hard to think of life in a human community without those ritual moments of observing a birthday, an anniversary, the passing into adulthood, or the passing away from this life.

In archaic societies these moments in the life cycle are invested with a profound religious significance. The ceremonies by which a person passes from childhood to the ranks of the hunter or warrior (in the case of the male) to become eligible for marriage and childbearing (in the case of females) are called "rites of passage." These rites, thoroughly studied by Arnold von Gennep and others,[14] often include the mythic pattern of ritual death and rebirth. One dies to the old state and is reborn into the new. That ancient paradigm of death and rebirth is so rooted in our human consciousness that when we see it referred to in the most banal of circumstances, we do not recognize it for what it is. Each year, for example, we see the "old year" as an ancient man go off to die as the newborn year, date emblazoned on its diapered bottom, arrives on the scene. The symbolism there is as old as humanity.

The Catholic church places great weight on life-cycle rituals. Rites such as the observance of anniversaries, the reception into religious orders, and other quasi-sacramental or sacramental rituals can be analyzed as the marking off of both time and "life stages." The official sacraments are obvious examples. The theological underpinnings of baptism reverberate with scriptural motifs of dying to the old in order to enjoy a new life in Christ. There is an ancient tradition of seeing an analogy of the baptism of the adult, with the going down into the waters and a return from them, as similar to the death, burial, and resurrection of Christ. Just as Christ went into the tomb only to emerge in new life, so, the fathers insisted, the new Christian is buried in the waters of baptism in order to emerge as a new creature.

The entire sacramental system, as it is elaborated in the traditional seven sacraments, can be seen as a series of moments which parallel moments of human growth. Baptism and its complement, confirmation, initiate one into the life of the church; the Eucharist sustains that life on pilgrimage; penance is a form of reconciliation on that pilgrimage while the anointing of the sick is a "crisis" intervention, with both Holy Orders and matrimony pertaining to the maintenance of social community in the church.

We shall speak of the sacraments at some length later in this volume. At this juncture I simply want to insist on the "timeliness" of the sacraments with respect to the growth of human life. Contemporary discussions, both pastoral and theological, have shifted our attention away from the sacraments as signs of the church in the abstract and forced us to think more closely about the sacraments as they intersect with our own growth as maturing persons. The issue of the appropriate link between first communion and the sacrament of penance (should these two sacraments be linked or separated; is penance a natural first step toward the reception of holy communion, etc.) is actually a discussion about the timeliness of the sacrament of penance itself. Does a child have the mental and spiritual maturity to fathom the concept of sin, reconciliation, and so on? The relation of penance to communion is a historico-theological issue while the advisability of penance for young children is an issue of timeliness which has a developmental as well as theological dimension. The same thing is true of infant baptism. Should all infants be baptized upon request or should there be some sign that the parents have a commitment to the Catholic faith and some willingness to exercise their parental responsibilities of religious nurture? What is the proper time for baptism? To engage that issue is to remove the sacrament of baptism from the arena of custom (and abstract theology) to focus on the sacrament as being intimately linked to the church as a believing community.

The issue of timeliness becomes more sharply centered when we think about the sacrament of matrimony in the light of current social realities. A recent book by Theodore Mackin argues that Christian marriage is a covenant founded on love.

If the covenant of love disintegrates, there is no marriage because the sign value of the marriage has been irretrievably lost.[15] Mackin then deduces from that fact that remarriage in the church becomes a possibility. In a review of this provocative book Thomas Weinandy rejects Mackin's thesis, arguing that "Christian marriage mirror's Christ's covenant with his church and thus it is indissoluble as the new covenant in Christ is indissoluble."[16] Weinandy goes on to say that marriages fail because many people enter marriage without the Christian maturity to live out a life of covenanted love. What Weinandy could not consider in his brief review is the issue of the relationship of social maturity and Christian maturity. They are not necessarily the same thing.

If matrimony as a sacrament is a sign of the bond between Christ and the church (as the theology deduced from Ephesians 5 would have it), does one have to demonstrate some commitment to that notion in order to be married in a sacramental fashion? To put it another way: Should the church celebrate a marriage between two Catholics who are canonically eligible simply because they request such a marriage? Is that a *timely* thing to do? Our hypothetical couple, after all, quite possibly live in two spheres of time, the one being social and the other religious. In social terms they may be of the age of consent, sexually prepared, financially ready, and socially pressured to marry. They may also live simultaneously in a certain religious cycle which has not reached that same point of maturity. Their desire for a church wedding may derive from parental desires, their own sense of tradition, or their love for the parish church or their friendship with a certain priest. All this is well and good. It reflects a sense of tradition, filial sensitivity, rootedness, and family solidarity, but it does not suggest, per se, a sense of Christian commitment to a life of covenanted love as that is understood by the church.

At this point let me offer a different model—totally hypothetical—to illustrate my point.[17] Could we envision marriage in the church as a series of incremental steps (akin to the process by which one takes vows in a religious community) which would eventually (but not necessarily) lead to a solemn and permanent public profession of life-long commitment after the model of the relationship of Christ and the church? Could we envision, to be more specific, a church rite to solemnize the desire to live together in a bond of matrimony to be followed by renewed commitments at other occasions? I have in mind something like solemn reaffirmation of marriage vows to be celebrated in tandem with the baptism of the first child of the marriage or after a certain number of years of joint sharing in the sacramental life of the community. Could we not distinguish, in short, the right to marry from the right to the sacrament of matrimony, the latter reserved to those who make a conscious choice to partake in that sacrament at the time when they feel their spiritual life and social life are at a certain level of maturity? Such a dynamic model of matrimony, patterned on the incremental steps of the catechumenate, the religious life, and the various orders of sacerdotal ministry would be an effective way to highlight the appropriation of the Christian life as something which happens in tandem with life growth.

Such a rethinking of the sacrament of matrimony in dynamic terms would be an effective way to link matrimony to the maturation process both of human growth and of spiritual maturity. The church would not have to be overly prescriptive in this matter. Some people would be mature enough to enter into a sacramental marriage right away while others would want to grow toward such a plateau. For younger marriages it might be one way of underscoring the family orientation of marriage to cluster the sacrament of matrimony with the baptism of a child as one way to reaffirm both the marriage and the Christian duty of child nurturing. By celebrating these two events together (in the context of a solemn eucharistic liturgy), one would signify the relationship of sacrament to human maturation and responsibility in a powerful manner.

Closer linkage of sacramental action to the cycle of human growth would be one way of giving emphasis and significance to the sign value of the sacraments. Recent sacramental theology has gone a long way in shifting our attention away from the causality of the sacraments (i.e., sacraments work *ex opere operato*) to a consideration of their value as signifiers of our faith, our sense of worship, our communion with the church, and our conviction of the presence of Christ "among us." Living in faith, despite the claim of the fundamentalists, is not a once-in-a-moment conversion experience but a gradual deepening—a series of conversions if you will—to faith as that faith is experienced and tested in life. We may have been confirmed at the age of twelve, but it may take years of interior struggle in faith before we begin to grasp the commitment to faithful obedience in our Christian vocation. If, as the consensus of sacramental theologians would have it, confirmation is meaningless apart from baptism, it may well be advantageous to repeat those "confirming" anointings/impositions of hands just as we repeat our baptismal vows (e.g., at the Easter Vigil) not to "multiply sacraments" but as a timely and processive way of reminding ourselves that strengthening is required throughout our lives.

Signs of the Times

To this point we have considered time in relationship to the liturgy and the sacramental life of the church. Our most common experience of sacred time occurs either in the context of the official worship of the church (going to Mass on Sunday; receiving the sacraments in due season) or in those myriad quasi-liturgical experiences which we use to mark off sacred moments in an unofficial way (daily prayers in the family or before meals). When those moments are completed, we then pass naturally back into the daily round of life. Nobody lives exclusively in the world of the sacred; we live in the midst of ordinary activities and to the degree that we are mindful in our faith relate those moments back to the experiences of our moments of faithful worship. It is obvious that we are called upon to connect our worship with the ordinary life that we lead.

The awareness by which our commitment in faith suggests courses of action in the concrete circumstances of life occurs at those moments when our faith and the action of life intersect. By and large these moments come to us almost reflexively and most often as a moral imperative: I need to be more loving toward my family; I should not be so indifferent to a neighbor; I ought be more helpful to this or that poor person; and so on.

Such reflexive applications can also have a more narrowly Catholic ring to them: I should be more faithful to the life of prayer; I should do nothing that implicates me in abortions, and so forth. Such reflections arise naturally enough in our lives and they are certainly not to be underestimated as shapers of our religious character. Such reflections can cause conflict or create tensions in that they demand of us that we reflect on our choices, our priorities, and our commitments to a range of values. Generally speaking, the tensions which arise are clear-cut in that they polarize around should/should not or act/don't act. It is out of these simple tensions and polarities that Christian maturity arises and strengthens.

Because of the peculiar character of contemporary cultural experience we have been called upon to widen our sense of how to apply the faith which we possess to the problems that confront us. We are asked, to use a current phrase taken from the Second Vatican Council, to scrutinize the "signs of the times."[18] The active involvement of the American bishops in matters like the control of nuclear arms and economic policy is a direct result of the conciliar insistence that the teaching church must be concerned with issues which are wider than the more traditional "Catholic" issues. The church, the council says, cannot be satisfied with using its moral suasion only when the issues involve parochial school funding or family planning issues.

In the modern world a lot of things happened to convince concerned Catholics that the church could not operate as an entity sealed off from the cares and concerns of the world. From the time of the last century sensitive Catholics recognized that the vast working classes of Europe were not only not active in the church, but saw it as an alien institution allied to power, money, and the forces of social oppression. After the Second World War Christians in general and Catholics in particular had to face the ugly truth that not only did a large number of individual Catholics sit idly by while Hitler committed genocide against the Jews, but institutions of the church were equally silent. How could the church be so distant from the realities of what was going on around them that they could not see the world crumbling and going mad?

There has always been an impulse, deep in the consciousness

of the church, to reach out to the poor and the neglected. From childhood we were taught not only to contribute to, but to *sacrifice* for, the poor of the world. Giving up allowance money for the missions is a vivid memory of my youthful observances of Lent. In this day and age, however, something new has been added: a vividly visual awareness of suffering, poverty, and injustice. It was one thing to hear about the "poor starving babies of Africa" from the pulpit or the classroom. It is quite another thing to see such starvation, in vivid color, in one's living room on the evening news. It is hard to overstate the effect of the dramatic visualization of the world on our consciousness today. What we have not begun to think about in a sustained manner is the impact that such strong visual information is having on our religious sensibility.

In his book *The Shock of the New* Robert Hughes argues that Picasso's *Guernica* is the last great monumental war painting of a kind that goes back to Uccello in the fifteenth century, runs through Goya in the nineteenth, and finishes with Picasso's great protest against the mechanized bombing of the Basque village of Guernica in the Spanish Civil War.[19] Hughes, upon reflection, is quite right. When we remember subsequent wars in an *iconic* fashion, our images are not of pictures, but of photographs (the raising of the flag at Iwo Jima or the little Vietnamese girl fleeing napalm) or we think of television color footage on the evening network news.

That strongly visual turn in our perception of the world developed during the same time when Catholic theology, ever so slowly, began to shift its focus from the "high christology" of Jesus as the Son of God to a "low christology" of Jesus as the compassion of God and faithful companion (from *cum pane*—to share bread with) of humanity. "The message of Jesus had to do first of all with the prayerful and compassionate fidelity of God," writes Monika Hellwig. "Living among people who were harshly oppressed, bewildered, and discouraged, Jesus became for many of them the joyful discovery that God never abandons his creatures, that God is infinitely compassionate, and powerful to implement his compassion in ways beyond human ingenuity and understanding."[20] It is from that basic view of Jesus, Hellwig argues in a standard introduction to

Catholic theology, that all subsequent reflection on the meaning and power of Jesus must spring. It is the basic view of Jesus which should form all further speculation, devotion, and example.

This orientation "from below" was already at work when the Second Vatican Council convened. It was partially a result of that more horizontal view of theology in general and christology in particular that the council saw fit to look at the larger world. In a striking departure from tradition one of the major documents of the council (*Pastoral Constitution on the Church in the Modern World*)[21] was addressed, not to the church, but to the human family: all people of good will. In that pastoral letter to the world the church affirmed its desire to scrutinize the "signs of the times." This phrase, first used by Pope John XXIII in his encyclical letters, was a capsule notion which lent the church's presitge to the task of building up the human community. That document is now part of history, but its impact cannot be overstated. By pledging to watch the "signs of the times," the council committed itself to look at the world with genuine interest and with prophetic concern. It was a profoundly humanistic (in the very best sense of that word) move away from the more aloof theology of the past. It came as a pledge in the precise period when people, in vast numbers, first began to really *see* the world in an immediate and vivid manner. When the council used the phrase "signs of the times," it meant that the church had a duty to scrutinize the "main facts which characterize an age."[22] It is the task of discernment and, hence, is part of the prophetic office of being a Christian in community.

Everything from the notion of liberation theology to the entrance of vowed religious men and women into the public arena of politics has been justified by an appeal to the conciliar insistence on the church's involvement in the "facts which characterize an age." The church, this argument would run, has been called upon to be concerned with *this* world; to incarnate the compassion of God in Jesus for this time and place. How well all of these applications of theory to practice have worked out is a judgment for historians. What is perfectly clear is that this official attitude, expressed in the conciliar documents, has slowly filtered down to the church at large, with varying degrees of sophistication and commitment. It is reflected in everything from Latin American *comunidades de base* to parish-run soup kitchens for the inner city homeless in the United States.

We have, then, a conjunction in the church of a demand to scrutinize the facts of our culture and a concomitant visual assault on our eyes depicting those facts. The "typical" parishioner sees vivid images of starving children in refugee camps, displaced Haitians coming to his or her shores, and so on, every night on the news. The abstract concept of poverty becomes concretized in visual images. Some few respond to those images by a form of activism, but I would not like to suggest that most do. What I would argue is that images which are so direct and compelling have lessened the psychic distance between our own relative well-being and the miseries of the world. We no longer need the reports of returning missionaries to tell us about the sufferings in other parts of the world. We have the "stuff" for the fertilization of the religious imagination; world hunger is no longer an abstraction.

The office of the church is to remind us, no matter how we want to resist the reminder, that the making concrete of the Christian vision cannot be located only within the space of our own limited vision. We cannot avoid the larger dimensions of the facts of culture. Peter Maurin, one of the founders of the Catholic Worker movement, used to say that people need only step outside the door and begin doing good. That was the key to the active life of Christ. The point I would insist on is that the door now opens to a larger vista. Being attentive to the "signs of the times" carries with it an openness to the larger world; a *catholic* vision of solidarity with the larger realities. We are called on, in short, to see both locally and globally or, in the phrase of René Dubos, to live locally but to think globally.

It is one thing to assent to that notion in the abstract and quite another to make it concrete by action; the latter task always carries with it some degree of discomfort to either our material well-being or our cherished convictions. Perhaps an example will help. In the part of the country where I live

(Florida) there is a raging debate over the ethics of capital punishment as more and more Florida death warrants are signed and executions proceed apace. The entire Catholic hierarchy of the state has taken a stand against executions. Their common rejection of the death penalty is in direct conflict with the sentiments of the majority of their parishioners who, like the rest of the state, favor executions by about 70 percent to 30 percent of opponents. Historically the church has tolerated the death penalty. The great Catholic theologian St. Thomas Aquinas makes a reasoned argument for its legitimate use by the state.[23] Well into the 1960s it was not even considered a "Catholic" issue. How then do we explain this rather dramatic change in official Catholic thinking over such a short period of time? It seems to me that three things happened to create the current anti-death penalty consensus and all of them bear on our topic.

First, those who scrutinize the "signs of the times" note the general decline in the use of the death penalty in Western society. In the West today it is used only in the United States, South Africa, and behind the Iron Curtain. Its gradual decrease has been one of the several signs of the humanization of law in our time.

Secondly, there has been a conscious effort (looked at with some suspicion by some conservatives) on the part of the bishops to link their anti-death penalty stance to the larger issue of respect for human life, a respect which, in their estimation, should embrace the innocent, the guilty, and the life of nations. Respect for life, the bishops say, should be a seamless issue which embraces every effort to attenuate the move to violence and bloodshed.

Finally, there is the desire—and I grope for a word here—to apply the "Jesus ethic." The state may have the abstract right in law to execute (and I, for one, cede them that right), but it would be more in line with the Gospel to encourage the state to resist that right in the name of mercy and forgiveness. It may be that the state should protect itself from the violent by removing them from society, but a relinquishing of the ultimate penalty says, in effect, that even for this or that terrible and heinous crime there is room for mercy and compassion. In such situations where we resist the tendency to strike out in retribution we are exercising a form of compassion when we are at least inclined to be compassionate. Such a holding back of the arm of retributive justice is a small step toward the application of the hard and paradoxical value of forgiveness and love. When we can forgive this or that heinous criminal, we have made a quantum leap in the application of the Jesus ethic. We have moved from bare justice to justice tempered by love.

The long debate over the death penalty also helps to remind us how slow the acquisition of a Christian conscience about disputed matters may be. A Gospel sensitivity about disputed issues like the death penalty is a slow incremental process as we learn to look at the issues which are part of the world and begin to see how they mesh with the values which we profess as Gospel values. Being alert to the signs of the times helps us to resist the simple acceptance of things as they are. There are many instances in our own history when we as a church simply tolerated the status quo, only losing those passive attitudes through a painful process of learning. Being alert to the signs of the times does not mean trimming the demands of the Gospel to the fashions of the day; it is not a Gallup Poll morality. We should remember that a generation ago a high percentage of American Catholics in the South thought segregation compatible with Gospel values. That percentage of the population was wrong, but the drive to implement racial justice, however, came, not in a rush, but as a burdened enlightenment of the conscience. Its most generous implementation is still not fully realized.

At this point, we should enter a cautionary note. It is one thing to say that we are alert to the signs of the times while it is quite another to read those signs with exactitude. Many conservatives, not always unreasonably, are suspicious of the contemporary conjunction of theology and activism. They insist that a good deal of "relevant" theological praxis is, in reality, a reduction of faith to a pious celebration of the zeitgeist; an uncritical acceptance of fashionable ideology. Without passing on the fairness of this critique with respect to particular instances, it does seem that some socially active Catholics seem to equate the Kingdom of God with the left wing of the Democratic party. To scrutinize the "signs of the times" is not to fall prey to the enthusiasms of the hour. Walker Percy's novel *Love in the Ruins* (1971) is a devastating satire of the Catholic church in the United States turning into a schismatic triad of three churches ranged from right to left, each blending political ideology and Catholic culture. Whether Percy is a prophet or merely a scold is still not clear despite the deep divides that separate Catholics on social and political issues. It may be that in the last analysis a healthy tension over social issues is salutary for the church.

To be aware of the signs of the times requires that sense of spiritual maturity which is capable of disentangling ends from strategies. At their most fundamental level certain ethical issues in culture are either conformable to the demands of the Gospel or they are not. Some may tolerate torture as an imperative of realpolitik, but nobody, in the name of Christ, can tolerate it in the name of Christian realism. It may be a fact of life that children starve or are abused or misused, but Christian Catholics cannot accept that as tolerable in the name of a greater good. It is not a matter of indifference that people starve, lack shelter, or suffer human degradation. Honest people may disagree about strategies for the alleviation of such conditions, but the conditions themselves are not morally neutral. Strategic disagreements can never be paramount. When we look at the "signs of the times," we must begin with certain categorical "shoulds" and "should nots" which form the core of our scrutiny.

That each Christian must live in a specific time and take that time's temperature seems patent. Alertness to the times should produce more than moral indignation. Alertness to the signs of the times is inextricably entwined with Christian vocation. By vocation, as is clear, we do not mean a vocation to the religious life, but that is clearly a facet of it. By appealing to vocation I refer to that conviction, that calling, if you will, to see the incompleteness of the salvific work of the Gospel in actual circumstances and the concomitant conviction about our role in making that salvific work more actual. It is that enlarged sense of existing in community—a community not only in the ecclesial and sacrament sense but the community which is the human family.

That enlarged sense of community provides the most authentic tie between our celebration of liturgical time and our life "in these times." By recreating the mysteries of Christ as real experiences we are better equipped to replicate them in our ordinary lives. Ideally, our perception of the liturgical mysteries should help us enlarge our vision as it ripples out from the community with whom we worship to the neighborhood in which we live to the world in which we dwell. The life of liturgical time, in short, ought to provide a concomitant growth in our experience of human community.

Not everyone develops this sense of enlargement to the fullest. It is something that grows as the spiritual life grows. It is the great saints of our tradition who provide us with markers to check our progress. One luminous figure of our era, the late Teilhard de Chardin, had a genuinely mystical sense of this unity of all things. Teilhard was a scientist and a traveller who often found himself in remote parts of the world. Without a congregation he would offer a sort of spiritualized liturgy which he called the "Mass on the world." Teilhard thought of the great expanse of the world itself and his own role as a priest as he offered the world back to God in prayer. From his written version of that exercise we get a glimpse of one of the most compelling visions of human community ever written.

> This restless multitude, confused or orderly, the immensity of which terrifies us; this ocean of humanity whose slow, monotonous wave-flows trouble the hearts even of those whose faith is most firm: it is to this deep that I thus desire all the fibres of my being should respond. All the things in the world to which this day will bring increase; all those which will diminish; all those too which will die: all of them, Lord, I try to gather into my arms, so as to hold them out to you in offering. This is the material of my sacrifice; the only material you desire.[24]

That compassion for the world—one finds it in Therésè of Lisieux, Mother Teresa of Calcutta, Pope John XXIII, Thomas Merton, Dorothy Day—grows out of the deep experience of remembering, recreating, reliving Christ as worshipped and encountered. Those acts then extend out to the world. That sense of the world has always been the most authentic meaning of the word *Catholic;* a meaning which is difficult to arrive at with clarity and conviction.

Time: A Recapitulation

Our concern has been the experience of time as recreated in the liturgy, experienced in personal growth, and as a necessary condition of our being in the world. There was a period in the Catholic experience when time was endured for the sake of eternity (eternity: no time): What significance does this world have from the perspective of the eternal? The mysticism reflected in the Gothic cathedral was a mysticism which forced our eyes beyond time *up* to the world of God, which is the world of the timeless. Our experience today, both secular and religious, underscores our responsibility for the present time; we are asked to redeem the time. We see the gift of God not as something given to endure time (it is not an opiate) but as an experience of God who opens time for us into a future which we accept in a radical act of faith. We, as finite beings, living in an actual historical moment, look to both our individual and common future with the conviction that there is, in that future, someone beyond our present comprehension. Richard McBrien catches the idea well:

> We are constitutionally restless in our quest for truth and in our search for love. Only God, who is the fulness of truth and love itself, can finally satisfy that radical human longing. To say there is no God is to say that there is no possibility of ultimate human fulfillment, for the fulness of truth and love obviously transcends our unaided human capacities.[25]

To cultivate that hope-filled existence is very close to what the total contemporary experience of faith is all about. Such a sensibility is holistic in the fullest sense of the term. It roots our daily life in the life of God; it overcomes any tendentious split between the life of nature and supernature; it values what is human and immediate in our life; it insists on the worth of the present time while encouraging us to redeem that time and look for the future. In that sensibility we already live in God; we taste that presence in the times we mark off as sacred and in our increasing awareness of the holiness of life itself.

Points for Meditation

1. Do you have regular times in your life which are important for the nurture of faith or for the deepening of your sense of the presence of God in Christ in your life? What are those times? Why are they important?

2. To what degree is your participation in the liturgical life of the church a routine? Under what circumstances has that sense of routine been shattered?

3. We ritualize certain moments in our life and invest them with sacred significance. Which of these times have been most meaningful for your life? Have other times, not formally religious, been more significant? Can you suggest the shape of a particular liturgical ritual to religiously solemnize a moment like an official engagement or a parent's anniversary?

4. Does the passage of time in your own life ever preoccupy you? To what degree do you think of the passage of *your* time as being shaped by God?

5. Under what circumstances have you best experienced a re-creation of the presence of Jesus in your life? In the liturgy? In prayer? At odd, unexpected, moments?

Notes

1. Mircea Eliade, *The Sacred and the Profane* (New York: Harper Torchbook, 1966), pp. 68–69. Eliade distinguishes sacred and liturgical time; the former recreates mythic beginnings and the latter, historical events. I use the terms here interchangeably.

2. Ibid, p. 205.

3. *Constitution on the Sacred Liturgy*, art. 33, in *The Documents of Vatican II*, ed. Walter Abbott (New York: Association Press, 1966), p. 149.

4. Walker Percy, *The Message in the Bottle* (New York: Farrar, Straus and Giroux, 1975), p. 116.

5. *Constitution on the Sacred Liturgy*, art. 102, in *Documents*, p. 167.

6. The classic study of this cycle and the mystery of Christ is Odo Casel, *The Mystery of Christian Worship* (Westminster, Md.: Newman, 1962). For a recent survey of scholarship on the liturgical year with some pastoral reflections see Robert Taft, "The Liturgical Year: Studies, Prospects, and Reflections," *Worship* 32 (1981) 3–23.

7. Wallace Stevens, "Sunday Morning," in *The Collected Poems* (New York: Knopf, 1969), p. 66.

8. Andrew Greeley, *Unsecular Man* (New York: Delta Books, 1974), pp. 240ff.; and *The Religious Imagination* (New York: Sadlier, 1981), pp. 1–21.

9. Is it a hopeful, or retrograde sign that Hans Urs von Balthasar's *The Glory of the Lord: A Theological Aesthetics* is now appearing in a multivolume translation a generation after its original publication? *Volume I: Seeing the Form*, trans. Erasmo Leiva-Merikakis, ed. John Riches (San Francisco: Ignatius Press/New York: Crossroad,

1982); *Volume II: Studies in Theological Style: Clerical Styles*, trans. Andrew Louth, Francis McDonagh, and Brian McNeil, ed. John Riches (San Francisco: Ignatius Press/ New York: Crossroad, 1984.

10. Karl Rahner, "Priest and Poet," *Theological Investigations*, vol. 3 (Baltimore: Helicon, 1967), pp. 294–320; and "Poetry and the Christian," *Theological Investigations*, vol. 4 (Baltimore: Helicon, 1966), pp. 257–67.

11. David Tracy, *Blessed Rage for Order* (New York: Seabury, 1975).

12. Amos Niven Wilder, *Theopoetic: Theology and the Religious Imagination* (Philadelphia: Fortress, 1976), p. 1. See also David Power, "Cult to Culture: The Liturgical Foundations of Theology," *Worship* 31 (1980), 482–95.

13. Pheme Perkins, *Who Is This Christ?* (Philadelphia: Fortress, 1983), p. 136.

14. Arnold Von Gennep, *Rites of Passage* (Chicago: University of Chicago Press, 1960).

15. Theodore Mackin, *What Is Marriage?* (Ramsey, N.J.: Paulist, 1982).

16. In *Theological Studies* 43 (1983) 710.

17. As a background for this model I found the following useful: Edward Kilmartin, "When Is Marriage a Sacrament?" *Theological Studies* 33 (1973) 275–86; Bernard Lee, "Marriage as a Process Sacramentology, in *Theology Confronts a Modern World*, ed. Thomas McFadden (West Mystic, Conn.: Twenty-Third Pubns., 1977), pp. 203–28; Joseph Martos, *Doors to the Sacred* (Garden City: Doubleday, 1981), pp. 399–452; James Schmeiser, "Marriage: New Alternatives," *Worship* 32 (1981) 23–24; Ladislas Orsy, "Faith, Sacrament, Contract, and Christian Marriage: Disputed Questions," *Theological Studies* 42 (1982) 379–98.

18. For a theological understanding of this concept, see G. Gennari, "Segni dei tempi," *Nuovo dizionario di spiritualità*, ed. DeFiores and Goffi (Rome: Edizione Paoline, 1982) pp. 14–22.

19. Robert Hughes, *The Shock of the New* (New York, Knopf, 1981).

20. Monika Hellwig, *Understanding Catholicism* (Ramsey, N.J.: Paulist, 1981), p. 61.

21. *Pastoral Constitution on the Church in the Modern World*, in *Documents*, pp. 199ff.

22. This is the meaning the council assigned to the term; see *Commentary on the Documents of Vatican II*, ed. Herbert Vorgrimler, vol. 5 (New York: Herder and Herder, 1969), p. 99

Selected Readings

Adam, Adolf. *The Liturgical Year.* New York: Pueblo, 1982. A study of postconciliar developments.

Capps, Walter. *Time Invades the Cathedral.* Philadelphia: Fortress, 1972. Reflections on the appropriation of time from the perspective of the theology of hope.

Eliade, Mircea. *Cosmos and History: The Myth of the Eternal Return.* New York: Harper Torchbooks, 1959. A profound meditation on the uses of time in religion.

Power, David and Mary Collins, eds. *The Times of Celebration.* Concilium 142. New York: Seabury, 1981. A series of essays on worship and the calendar of the church.

Searle, Mark. *Liturgy and Social Justice.* Collegeville: Liturgical Press, 1981. A study of prayer and activism.

3

SILENCE

It seems almost perverse to write an entire chapter on the subject of silence. One is tempted to do something after the manner of a Zen koan (or a Dada trick) and leave twenty or so pages empty under the title of silence. Alas, that will not do in a book of this sort. Besides, upon reflection, we know that silence plays its part in the Catholic experience. We recall stories of the old Trappists using sign language in an attempt to maintain silence in their monasteries. We know that the mystical tradition has described the experience of God as a gradual growth in silence. St. Bonaventure, at the end of his *The Soul's Journey to God*, cries out: "Let us die then and enter into the darkness; let us impose silence upon our cares. . . ."[1] We also know that there are times when we reproach God for his silence. Silence, in fact, is a key category for understanding a number of issues crucial for contemporary culture. Silence, after all, is a word often used when talking about the absence of God in a secularized culture.

Silence has many meanings in the Catholic experience. It can come in the form of a discipline by which we enter into a spirit of re-collection. It is in that spirit of silence that the traditional life of prayer has been pursued. Most religious foundations observed the "Great Silence"—the quiet which was to be observed from the end of night prayers until the end of the liturgy the next day. Monks, St. Benedict warns, "should try to speak as little as possible, but especially at night."[2] Religious houses, traditional havens of silence, are not only

64

important for the life of their inhabitants but as centers of quiet and silence for those who wish to "retreat" from the world for a time. Those who live the regular life of the contemplative find silence as an integral part of their spiritual formation. Physical silence is the context for the search for interior silence. Thomas Merton caught that idea perfectly in his luminous "Fire Sermon" in *The Sign of Jonas*:

> Between the silence of God and the silence of my soul, stands the silence of the souls entrusted to me. Immersed in these three silences, I realize that the questions I ask myself about them are perhaps no more than a surmise. And perhaps the most urgent and practical renunciation is the renunciation of all questions.[3]

Silence is also a way of speaking about God. In that sense silence is not instrumental as we described it above but an actual (if metaphorical) category for understanding God. It has both a positive and a negative history as a concept. Negatively, silence indicates the absence of God; God's inability or unwillingness to communicate with creation: God as absence. The silence of God has been a leitmotif in a culture which has felt bereft of the possibility of belief. In Ingmar Bergman's classic film *The Seventh Seal* the allegorical figure of death speaks to the searching knight:

KNIGHT: I want knowledge, not faith, not suppositions, but knowledge. I want God to stretch out his hand to me, reveal himself, and speak to me.
DEATH: But he remains silent.
KNIGHT: I call out to him in the dark but no one seems to be there.
KNIGHT: Then life is an outrageous horror. No one can live in the face of death, knowing that all is nothingness.[4]

The silence of God, understood in this fashion, is a terrible burden for the authentic searcher. This silence is most conspicuously felt at moments of crisis. The implications of God's silence do not reassure: There is no meaning, no framework, no meaning for our lives. Silence, in that sense, means no-other; it means a world of solitude.

The silence of God, then, can signify the absence of God.

But silence is not only to be construed as negation. It is one of the paradoxes of silence that it can "speak" with fierce directness. Silence, the hoary cliché tells us, speaks volumes. There is no more poignant moment in the gospels than that brief incident recounted in Luke 22:61–62 after Peter denies knowledge of Jesus: "At that instant, while he was speaking, the cock crowed and the Lord turned and looked straight at Peter, and Peter remembered what the Lord had said to him: 'Before the cock crows today you will have denied me three times.' And Peter went outside and wept bitterly." Jesus spoke only with his silence.

I would like to pursue that positive concept of silence— silence as communication—a bit further. By thinking of silence, not as absence, but as a kind of presence, we might get a fresh angle on an ancient idea in the Catholic experience: the awareness of God in the natural world around us.

God as Silence

The First Vatican Council (1869–70) taught as Catholic truth that the human mind, unaided by supernatural revelation, can arrive with some certainty (*certo cognosci posse*) at a knowledge of God. That affirmation canonizes a commonplace in the Catholic tradition which went back well into the early Middle Ages, i.e., that the human mind can know of God by the instrumentality of disciplined philosophical reason. That belief systematized what St. Paul had said to the Romans: "For what can be known about God is perfectly plain since God himself has made it plain. Ever since God created the world his everlasting power and deity—however invisible—have been there for the mind to see in the things that he has made" (Rom. 1:19–20).

It is important to underscore that the First Vatican Council did not teach that every person did, in fact, come to a knowledge of God through reason; the council taught only that humans had that capacity. In actual practice many people may not come to such a knowledge either because of lack of interest or obtuseness or because of a simple unwillingness to consider the issue. Furthermore, at least at the popular level, a knowledge

of God deduced from life could (and often does) yield a deficient
and indefensible image of God: God as "The Man Upstairs"
or the "First Person" of the universe. God is not another being
among beings even if he is affirmed as the "greatest being."
To think of God in that fashion is to think of God as a discrete
object of knowledge among many other objects of knowledge.
But God is prior to and behind all that is and all that can be
thought: the being beyond being; the Ground of all being. For
that reason we need to draw a sharp distinction between our
creatureliness and that deep reality behind creation which is
God. Karl Rahner, with characteristic majesty, writes:

> This absolute incomprehensible reality, which is always the
> ontologically silent horizon of every intellectual and spiritual
> encounter with realities, is therefore always infinitely different
> from the knowing subject. It is also different from the individual,
> finite things known. It is present as such in every assertion, in
> all knowledge, and in every action.[5]

This reality which has been called variously Mystery, Ground,
Thou, and Absolute Horizon expresses, however haltingly, the
most authentic notion of God. Such a reality is elusive and, in
the deepest sense of the term, mysterious. Again, Rahner
writes:

> . . . Our basic starting point seems to say that God is everywhere
> insofar as he grounds everything and he is nowhere insofar as
> everything that is grounded is created, and everything which
> appears in this way within the world of our experience is
> different from God, separated by an absolute chasm between
> God and what is not God.[6]

The attempt to truly encounter that deep reality which is
God has been the traditional goal of the deep person of prayer—
the mystic. All of the forms of traditional spiritual discipline—
quiet, meditation, etc.—are preparatory to that expected meeting with something other than our own creatureliness and
limitation. That experience is so radically different that when
experienced it is difficult to describe. The mystic finds that
language fails and, as a consequence, he or she reaches for the
paradox or the oxymoron: *todo y nada* (all and nothing); brilliant
darkness; and so on.

Deep contemplative prayer is not the province of a spiritual elite; it is available to everyone in the church. In fact, many people may well have experienced moments of deep mystical prayer—what Sigmund Freud has called an "oceanic feeling"— but have not been able to name it. The very fact that people pray—as opposed to merely saying prayers—is testimony to their desire to somehow "reach out" to some deep experience of God. But, if God is not another object among objects, what is being reached for? How is the elusive presence of God to be known:

It is at this point, and in response to those questions, that the analogy of silence, understood in its positive sense, may prove helpful. More specifically, let us consider the role of silence in music.

We go to a concert hall to hear a majestic work like Beethoven's Ninth Symphony. The performance of that demanding concert piece is framed by silence. We quiet down after the conductor's entrance is greeted with applause; that quieting down takes on an air of expectancy. We wait in silence for the first notes, in all their softness, to come to us. At the conclusion of the symphony we are irritated (at least, I am irritated) by premature applause. We want the notes to die out in silence. Musical compositions are quintessentially temporal pieces of art. It takes x number of minutes to perform a composition and those minutes are bracketed off by silences. Furthermore: The music of the composition would be unintelligible were it not organized against the background of silence. The "rests" in music are punctuations of silence which permit the unfolding of the internal logic of the music. Silence is the canvas on which the musician paints.

In music, then, one hears the music only because of the silence. Without silence music would be garble if it were anything at all. In a very specific sense we must "hear" the silence if we are to hear the music. Silence is the sine qua non of music; there is more than showmanship or eccentricity in the experiments of the avant-gardist John Cage with his "silent" compositions; they explore an absolutely crucial part of music.

Consider the observations of the aesthetician Gisèle Brelet writing on silence and music[7]; I have chosen to paraphrase just a few of her observations to make the point:

★ One might say that silence is the very substance of music, since in it the individual sounds dissolve into the possibility of all sounds.

★ Becoming and movement, too, arise from silence. Absolute continuity would be confusion—and it would be immobility.

★ Thus silence [in music] exists only to change vacuity into plentiude.

★ When music lapses momentarily or definitively into silence, that silence is not nothingness or privation, but possession and fulfillment.

The analogy is not hard to see. The world comes into being, exists in time, and goes back to God as a musical composition is brought into being, perdures, and ends in silence. Furthermore, as we have noted, the intelligibility of the musical composition depends on the interaction of sound and silence. In a similar fashion we must not think of the world as having been created by God and left "out there" as a discrete entity. God, the Catholic tradition teaches, creates and sustains the world. God is *Pantocrater*—the One who holds all things in his hand. The world, Catholic belief affirms, is intelligible because it is undergirded by the creative power of the creator. God is silence and the world notation. Without that silence there would be garble and chaos.

Dietrich Bonhoeffer, writing from a Nazi prison in 1944, uses a somewhat similar musical analogy to describe the human relationship to God:

> . . . God requires that we should love him eternally with our whole hearts, yet not so as to diminish our earthly affections, but as a kind of *cantus firmus* to which the other melodies of life provide a counterpoint. . . . Where the ground bass is firm and clear, there is nothing to stop the counter point from being developed to the utmost its limits. . . . Only a polyphony of this kind can give life a wholeness, and at the same time assure us that nothing can go wrong so long as the *cantus firmus* is kept going.[8]

To pursue our analogy by way of reflection: To truly know the mystery of existence as we live it out is to somehow reach that deeper mystery from which it ultimately springs, and which sustains it in being. To know and love the world we must learn to "listen" for the silence which is both beyond and beneath it. Such listening is impossible without some commitment to a life which expects "something more" than merely going through the paces. The sense of God in our life is as elusive (and allusive) as silence is to music. That presence is there as an absolute presupposition for life, but it requires a spirit of genuine humility in order to be heard. Rahner writes that the transcendent God "presents itself to use in the mode of withdrawal, of silence, of distance, of being always inexpressible, so that speaking of it, if it is to make sense, always requires *listening to its silence*"[9] (my emphasis).

Two questions arise from a consideration of this analogy: (1) Why is it useful to think of God and the world in terms of this analogy; and (2) What pertinence does Jesus have in this schema, i.e., what is Christian about this attitude?

To live in the world with a developing sense of its mystery is to acquire a sense of basic wonder at the universe (and those who inhabit it) which leads, in turn, to what I consider to be the basic religious sentiment of the genuinely spiritual person: existential gratitude. As with many things G. K. Chesterton said it best; he is discussing, of all things, attitudes toward dandelions:

> And all such captious comparisons are ultimately based on the strange and staggering heresy that a human being has a right to dandelions; that in some extraordinary fashion we can demand the very pick of all the dandelions in the garden of paradise; that we owe no thanks for them at all and need feel no wonder at them at all; above all no wonder at being thought worthy of them. . . . Now I not only dislike this attitude as much as the Swinburnian pessimistic attitude but I think it comes very much to the same thing; to the actual loss of appetite for the chop or the dandelion. And the name of it is Presumption and the name of its twin brother is despair.[10]

This basic sense of existential gratitude is not a vague sort of Wordsworthian nature mysticism. It is a basic orientation which understands both giver and gift; it is able to distinguish them. The goal of this basic orientation is an acquisition of that feel for life which senses its preciousness, its manifold possibilities, and, most of all, its final integrity and meaning.

To "hear" the silence which is God is to know that ultimately it "all adds up"—that the world is grace-ful.

The person who understood this better than anyone else in Christianity was St. Francis of Assisi (1181–1224). Francis, Chesterton argued, was not a "nature mystic"; he was "a mortal enemy of all those mystics who melt away the edges of things and dissolve an entity into its environment. He was a mystic of the daylight and the darkness, but not a mystic of the twilight. He was the very contrary of that sort of oriental visionary who is only a mystic because he is too much of a skeptic to be a materialist."[11] It was the simple fact of God's creative generosity which led St. Francis to his vast love for the world. St. Bonaventure makes it quite clear that it was not sentimentality but deep faith in God as creator and giver that undergirded the Franciscan love of nature: "When he (i.e., Francis) considered the primordial source of all things, he was filled with even more abundant piety, calling creatures, no matter how small, by the name of brother and sister, because he knew they had the same source as himself."[12] Francis, in short, did not love nature (he never used the word) but creation in all of its particularities, but behind those particularities he heard silence which is God.

The link between God and the world understood in the full theological sense of God's sustaining creativity over the world provides the basis for an actively prayerful attitude toward the world and life in it. From that prayerful attitude flows not only gratitude but compassion for one's fellows. It is an attitude which is activist in the sense that, even at a human level, one takes responsibility for the gift when it is received with the same seriousness that parents take responsibility for their children. If there is ever to be a "spirituality of ecology" at the physical and human levels, it must derive, not from sentimentality, but from that profound feeling for the interrelatedness of life itself. That feeling, in turn, springs from an even deeper sense of the world as gift.

Cultivation of the presence of God as silence, in the last analysis, gives us a way of linking the two poles—contemplative and active—of the spiritual life. By listening to the silence of the world, our sensitivity to mystery is sharpened while our taste for gratitude and responsibility is heightened. In that dynamic interchange we live the full and rich lives promised to the children of God.

Silence as Discipline

In order to "hear" the silence which is God we must also learn the value of personal silence as a spiritual discipline. The entire Catholic tradition of spirituality testifies to the desirability of such discipline. The traditional endorsement of recollection, of periodic retreat, of silent pauses in the liturgy, the institutionalization of silence in religious houses, and the praise of withdrawal all have their part in the ascetical tradition of the church. The spiritual commentators from antiquity have noted that Christians should imitate the example of Christ whose active ministry was punctuated by moments of withdrawal into the prayerful silence of the desert, the mountain, or the garden. Silence is the guarantee that human activity does not become obsessively frenetic but mindful and reflective.

The role of silence is complex in the Catholic tradition. For purposes of our discussion we can utilize the distinctions proposed by John Teahan[13]:

1. *Public* or *ritual* silence: silence as an antithesis to the acclamations of song or word to enhance the dynamic of the liturgy or paraliturgy, e.g., a moment of silence at some public memorial service.

2. *Ascetical* silence: a practice or discipline used to factor out external activity in order to be better prepared for prayer or meditation.

3. *Meditative* silence: Silence in tandem with the exercise of prayer. Such silence "directs our attention away from everyday ratiocinative and emotional turbulence, fosters inner calm, and thus makes the meditator more aware of his innermost self."[14]

Although there is some overlap in these categories, we can distinguish in all of them (or in any combination of them) two levels of silence: exterior silence which is oriented toward the cessation of noise and clamor and that deeper interior silence which is a fuller, more directed, possession of the self.

About exterior silence we need say little about its desirability since it is self-evident that people in every walk of life—apart from deep spiritual concerns—seek some "peace and quiet" in life, some break from the frantic pace of that which ordinarily fills up the hours. We insist that children spend some "quiet time" as avidly as we seek it for ourselves. The desire to escape the city, the television, or the crowd is re-creation in the original sense of that word. The religious experiences we have already mentioned in this study—the entering of sacred space or the marking off of sacred time—are all exercises which can be understood as searches for exterior silence.

External or exterior silence is an instrumental means for cultivating that deeper interior silence which can be described as possession of the self as free as possible from distraction and illusion. Interior silence is crucial for the development of a genuine spiritual life. It is the context out of which genuine prayer develops. It is that silence which is characteristic of the contemplative personality. Thomas Merton writes:

> Contemplation is essentially a listening in silence, an expectancy. And yet in a certain sense, we most truly begin to hear God's word when we have ceased to listen. What is the explanation of this paradox? Perhaps only that there is a higher kind of listening, which is not attentiveness to a particular wave length, a receptivity to a certain kind of message, but a general emptiness that wants to realize the message of God within his own apparent void. . . . He waits on the word of God in silence, and when he is "answered" it is not so much by a word that bursts into his silence. It is by his silence itself suddenly, inexplicably, revealing itself to him as a word of great power, full of the voice of God.[15]

Interior silence, then, is that expectant waiting for the presence of God to become more explicit in what is the normal clutter of our daily life. Exterior silence "clears the air," but internal silence is more. It is not merely absence of noise; it is that expectant readiness to enter into dialogue; to be open, in Martin Buber's words, to the Eternal Thou. In a real sense the cultivation of interior silence already is prayer.

Interior silence understood as openness to God should not be construed in a purely vertical manner. Interior silence does not mean a spirituality whose goal in life is the extinction of human relationships or the erasure of human contacts in order to be *solus cum Solo* (alone with the One). Contemplative monasticism, in its silence and isolation, does not conceive of itself as linked only with God; monasticism has always had an ecclesial, which is to say a communitarian, dimension. Inner silence is necessary both for an awareness of God and an awareness of others. Even St. Anthony of the Desert, the most assiduous seeker of solitude in the ascetical tradition, shut himself into the solitude of an abandoned fortress for decades only to throw open the gates in order to act as an exemplar of sanctity and a doctor of souls. The interiority of his life was both for his own spiritual growth and for that of others.

The person who has learned the secret of interior silence has also learned, if his or her silence is authentic, the secret of communicating with others. When St. Benedict, in the *Rule*, speaks of silence, he generally uses the word *taciturnitas*, not the word *silentium*. The monk, Benedict says, is a taciturn person. "Taciturn" has a rather frosty ring to it; we generally use it to describe someone who will not speak beyond conventional grunts; the person of few words. But even in the use of taciturn in that sense there is the added idea that the taciturn person is one who knows what to communicate and when. The archetypal cowboy in the movies is taciturn, but his actions speak as loudly as his words. He knows what to do. So with the monk. Ambrose Walthen has noted that Benedict's monk, as a taciturn person, is one who has first listened and so is able to speak what is needed to be said:

> To receive the word of another, to listen, to be obedient, demands that we stop for a moment speaking our own words and accept the word spoken by the "other." To listen, however, is only possible when we are silent for a moment, when all the noises, both external and internal, quiet down so that the word of reality can be heard. By hearing that word that gives being, man receives the word that can be returned to the speaker, to the "other." Man is by nature dialogical, one who is bound to the "other," by word heard, received, spoken, and returned. Man cannot remain forever silent; his very being demands that he speak to the one who speaks to him.[16]

The cultivation of genuine silence, paradoxically, is a form of communication which moves in quite different directions. It allows a person to hear God and others in a way that invites response. It is a holistic way of being in the world which values alertness to the silence which is God and the reality of others who enter into dialogue with us. The person of interior silence actually listens to people: no one is simply an object out there making sounds. Such silence is partially a gift (which is to say, a grace) and partially a discipline. We all have the capacity for silence, but it is only a willingness to cultivate it which makes it present to our consciousness in this life of noise and activity.

Silence and the Word of God

The silence we spoke of above is the disciplined silence of individual prayer. Indeed, we could say that genuine prayer is listening rather than speaking. But what of silence and the reception of the word of God? We "hear" God's word both in our study of the scriptures on an individual or collective basis and by listening to its proclamation in the liturgy. In the former case we need only say that when we read the scriptures in a prayerful manner it would seem obvious that the disciplined silence of readiness would be a necsessary condition for that reading. To meditate on the scriptures fruitfully requires a prior disposition to listen to what the word says to us. In the parlance of modern criticism: The text should read us in our very act of reading the text. In the monastic tradition of *lectio divina* (divine reading) the reading of the scriptures (with reading understood in a very broad sense) was crucial for the spiritual development of the monk. *Lectio* was not merely the perusal of the text nor its scholarly study. In the technical sense *lectio* was that life-long process by which the word of God was internalized as it was heard in the liturgy, remembered from reading, visualized in art, absorbed through instruction, and acquired in study and instruction. The operative word here is *internalization* (and not mere memorization), which is to say, hearing by making space for God's word within oneself.

The entire Christian tradition of meditation—in all of its variegated forms, schools, and methodologies—is nothing more than a development of that silent readiness to have the word of God shape and change us. The suggested circumstances for meditation (quiet, solitude, and so on) set the person ready for reception. Such circumstances aren't an end in themselves (the Catholic tradition has had a great distrust of quietism) but a seedground for receptivity. Such silence is not prompted merely to "have a look" inside oneself but to acquire that spirit of "letting go" in order to be a receiver. Such a discipline is an attempt to actualize that nascent faith, hope, and charity which we have received as gifts (i.e., as grace) by the very fact of being a follower of Christ "because the love of God has been poured into our hearts by the Holy Spirit which has been given to us" (Rom. 5:5).

The contemporary spiritual writer William Johnston has some very trenchant observations on the relationship of meditation and silence. He notes that all meditation begins in words (the words of scripture, of a teacher, of a text of spiritual writing) which in time begin to simplify as fewer words are required. It can happen that the persistent person of prayer no longer needs words; saying has been replaced by being. Even in that state there will be an awareness of presence (what the theologians call an "awareness through love"). When that awareness has been lost, we are at that mystical apex which St. John of the Cross has called *todo y nada*—all and nothing. Yet—and this is a crucial point—out of that silence of meditation come those stirrings or impulses (to love, to action, to further conversion) which demand formulation. Speech comes again. Johnston writes:

> And so we find in meditation a cyclic process. One begins with words, which give way to silence, and the silence, in turn, gives birth to words, and the words to silence once more. . . . When words become abundant and reach their fulness or saturation point, silences ensue. And out of the deep silence emerge words. . . . One should never make efforts to abandon words and enter the void. Neither should one disturb the void in order to form words. Do not awaken love before its time. Let the contemplative process unfold smoothly and quietly at its own pace and in its own time.[17]

The ordinary person may find this a bit, well, mystical. It seems so solemn and time-consuming. In the harried life most of us live there is precious little time for periods of prayer, withdrawal, and meditation even if there were a taste for such a thing. Taking care of children or working for a living makes the simple act of sitting down to scan the morning paper with a cup of coffee seem a luxury. Unfortunately, a good deal of contemporary spiritual writing barely takes into account the sheer burden of getting on with ordinary life. Many of our most popular spiritual writers today are either celibate academics (Nouwen, Dunne, et al.) or religious (Pennington, Johnston, Merton, etc.) whose style of life differs greatly from those who have neither the institutional structures nor the support system to follow the life of sustained prayer. I do not say this in denigration of their labors since, clearly, they have had an immense impact for good on people. I am constantly amazed (and edified) by the range of persons, both in and outside the Catholic church, who have been touched by the writings of the late Thomas Merton. Nonetheless, there is far too little focus on the spiritual life of prayer as it relates to the ordinary experience of people.

The Catholic tradition does provide many resources for those who would like to deepen their ordinary lives by a more intense life of contemplative prayer. There is, for example, a great book yet to be written to explore the "Little Way" of Therésè of Lisieux for the needs and conditions of contemporary people. There is another method which I would like to mention, a method once much preached in the church: the practice of the presence of God. That devotional practice, rooted in a very ancient tradition of the church, was formalized by the Carmelite laybrother Lawrence of the Resurrection (1611–91) who served for thirty years as a simple laborer and cook in a Paris friary of his order. Brother Lawrence, in some extraordinary documents found after his death,[18] bids the striving Christian to simply reflect on particular moments during the day and raise those moments as moments of prayer: we see a child and thank God for the creative beauty of the universe; we pass a hospital and utter a silent word of solidarity with those who suffer; we speak to a friend or a chance acquaintance and recall the words of Jesus on love of neighbor. The practice of the presence of God is, to borrow a Buddhist phrase, mindfulness.

I have described this mindfulness as a method simply to underscore that it is not an occasional thing or a moment of intuition; it can be a deliberately cultivated discipline. It is not dissimilar to the Ignatian practice of recalling the points of the morning meditation at various times throughout the day to see how they are being applied in actual life. A generation ago most Catholics were taught, as part of their daily prayers, the "Morning Offering." That prayer (older Catholics may recall a copy of it pasted to their bathroom mirror as a reminder) was a formal offering of every "thought, word, deed, and action" of that day to God. The practice of the presence of God is nothing more than a reinforcement of that morning prayer at disparate moments during the day. Such moments of recollection tie us to a sense of both the otherness of God and the worth of our neighbors. It is a practice which deepens our prayer life and our sense of human solidarity.

With the disciplined practice of the presence of God we acquire a better grasp of the intersection of time and silence as religious categories. By those conscious moments of recall we separate ourselves, however momentarily, from the flow of events to quiet down into reflection. Those moments help us gain once again that primordial wonder and gratitude which is at the heart of prayer. From those moments grow a richer sense of the gracefulness of the world we inhabit.

What of silence and the liturgy? To be sure, the very observance of a sacred time and the entering of a sacred place is a form of silence: It is a going aside into stillness. Furthermore, the eucharistic liturgy allows for ritual moments of silence: the silent pause before the absolution at the beginning of the liturgy; the silence before the collect prayer; the moment of silence for private petitions at the offertory; the silent interlude after communion. They are all pauses which punctuate the doing and saying of the celebration.

Most liturgical celebrants, alas, have a perfunctory attitude toward these moments; they are rarely more than mechanical pauses. As a consequence there is little felt sense of an interchange between utterance and silence. More's the pity since so much of the liturgy is an interchange of hearing and receiving along with proclaiming and doing.

But we must be realistic and deal with what is. As a consequence, the silence of the liturgy must be generated consciously both as an external discipline and as a cultivation of that internal discipline which we have already treated. We must consciously recall that the liturgy is both a place and a time to "quieten down" in order to receive as well as to give. That much is a truism. Beyond that we should learn to re-call the liturgy in terms of how we live outside its structure; that, after all, is the charge we are given at the dismissal. We need learn to bridge the formal act/language of the liturgy and our ordinary world. We need to hear with enough intensity so that what we hear resonates beyond the liturgical hour and liturgical place.

Some years ago in London on a Good Friday I decided to attend services at the church of St. Martin in the Fields. For some undefined reason (was it the Oxfordian tone of the curate who read the lessons as if he himself had written them and found pleasure in the result?) I was dissatisfied. I left the services in progress and wandered up to Piccadilly Circus. On a sidewalk, surrounded by curious onlookers, I saw a disheveled man of indeterminate age, unconscious and breathing with gasping shallowness. A bored but efficient ambulance attendant said to nobody in particular that the man had probably over-dosed on drugs. One of the onlookers muttered "Small loss." I do not want to sentimentalize that moment, but it struck me—as it never had before—that the vignette was the most graphic example of abandonment and desolation I have ever experienced.

Since that day I have never been able to hear the Good Friday liturgy without thinking of that dying junkie. *Ego sum vermis et non homo*—"I am a worm and no man"—always reminds me of matted hair, dirty fingernails, soiled clothes, labored breathing, and "small loss." It is not an outrageous correlation to link the dying junkie and the passion of Christ. Mother Teresa would approve of it. It is—at least for me—one luminous example of how to "desanitize" liturgical language. It forces me to be silent before the awful majesty of the words of liturgical piety and to think about them in a new and weirdly different manner. The words of the liturgy take on depth, thickness, and a freight they never had before.

That incident in central London was not something I consciously engineered. It happened and the happening was, fortuitously, on a Good Friday. What has exercised me since then is to think of ways in which I can make conscious bridges from the formality of the liturgy to the texture of life. What I have been looking for is something akin to Eliot's famous "objective correlative"[19]—those words, actions, signs, or what-have-you which can evoke the precise character of the word I hear in the liturgy. That is a hard currency to earn; the best I can offer the reader is the advice which runs as a leitmotif through this chapter: We need be silent in order to hear. It is that silence which shall provoke us finally to action.

To hear the word of God in the liturgy (or, for that matter, in any encounter with that word)—to truly *attend* to the language in a pregnant manner—requires a silence, like the silence we foster before music begins, which is expectant and receptive. When we begin to hear in that manner, whether in the liturgy or in meditation, we are doing something that is not only profoundly prayerful but profoundly ecclesial. It has often struck me of a Sunday while listening to the readings that my hearing is shared, in a welter of tongues and modulations, all over the world. I am part of that community of listening and recalling which waits for the Gospel now as it has waited for millennia. We never fully possess the meaning of the word of God. Year after year, generation after generation, we, as a community, reach up to it without ever having it fully in our grasp. We listen, absorb, apply, integrate (and, truth must say, resist, deny, turn deaf), and still come back for what is not yet learned. It is in that silent readiness to come back for more that we find the true contemplative dimension of the liturgy. It is that silent readiness for more which keeps our worship from being only an act of doing or acting. The contemplative participation in the worship of the church, at both formal and informal levels, springs from exterior and interior silence. That ritual celebration is prayer-ful. It is the great sign (*magnum sacramentum*) of the presence of God in our individual and social lives.

The Dark Side of Silence

In her wonderfully evocative book *Silences* the American poet Tillie Olsen distinguishes natural silences (lying fallow, the period of gestation, the retreat for renewal) from unnatural ones. Unnatural silences in literature are those in which literary work becomes aborted, deferred, denied (as in Kafka or Hopkins); in which work suffers from any one of the various forms of censorship; in which work has silence as a foreground to it (the poet Wallace Stevens kept silent until he was middle-aged). Most of all—and here Olsen is thinking like Virginia Woolf before her—of those silences of women, oppressed as a class, who have "no room of their own." Here is the result of that condition:

> When the claims of creation cannot be primary, the results are atrophy; unfinished work; minor efforts and accomplishment; silence. (Desperation which accounts for the mountains of applications to the foundations for grants—undivided time—in the strange bread line system we have worked out for our artists.)"[20]

The silences which Tillie Olsen describes are those which are painful, destructive, wounding, unwarranted. They are the absences which deserve to be filled; the gaps which cry out for words of support. They are the dark silences. Unlike the silence of God, which we may experience with sorrow or nostalgia or, even, relief, the dark silence of humans is ungodly, painful, and, in the end, sinful.

This dark silence is the obverse of prophetic speech and that boldness (*parrēsia*) characteristic of those who feel an urgency to utter truth in a timely fashion. The great prophetic calls of the Old Testament are filled with images which indicate a person's life being changed from silence to speech; from muteness to utterance: Isaiah has his lips cleansed with a coal by an angel (Is. 5:6–7) in order to become the Lord's messenger; Yahweh puts his hand on the mouth of Jeremiah (Jer. 1:9);

Ezekiel is fed a scroll of "lamentations, wailings, moanings" (Ex 1:10); Amos had visions (Am. 1:1); and Jonah, as we know, vainly flees God in order to maintain his safe silence.

Prophetic speech is not only denunciatory; it is also that bold, affirming proclamation by which the vacuum of silence is filled with the substance of truth. When the early martyrs (martyrs-witnesses) made their public witness of faith, they not only proclaimed their Lord but, simultaneously, rendered judgment on the evil of the persecutor and the vacillations of those who would not make professions of faith. They show a compulsion to speak; the early proconsular acts record the urgency of their boldness:

> Cittinus said: "We fear no other except the Lord who is in heaven."
> Donata said: "Honor to Caesar as Caesar; fear God alone."
> Vestra said: "I am a Christian."
> Speratus said: "I am a Christian."
> And they all agreed.
> Saturninus the proconsul read from a tablet: "They confess to following the Christian religion and obstinately persevere so they are to be put to the sword according to Roman law."
> They said in unison: "Thanks be to God."[21]

The great antithesis to dark silence in the church has been enshrined in those who utter truth as martyrs, preachers, missionaries, or theologians as the moment demanded. It is that spirit of bold speech whose paradigm is Jesus: "Some pharisees in the crowd said, 'Master, check your disciples!' but he said, 'I tell you, if these keep silence the very stones will cry out!'" (Lk. 19:41).

The most notorious discussion on the dark side of silence in the recent past was the furor raised by the play *The Deputy* written by the German Protestant Rolf Hochhuth.[22] The thesis of his drama triggered an impassioned discussion which produced a mountain of pamphlets, charges, countercharges, and resulted in the premature publication of the secret wartime archives of the Vatican. *The Deputy* charges that the late Pope Pius XII knew in fine detail about the systematic annihilation of the Jews by the Nazis, yet never spoke out because of his own Germanophile tendencies, his concern for church goods, and his obsessive fear of communist Russia. The play's surface plausibility derives from the incontestable fact that the pope never publicly condemned the death camps by name during the war period.

It is hardly possible to rehearse this complicated story even in generalities. Those who chastise the papal silence point to the pope's reticence in the face of horrors about which he surely knew. Defenders of Pius's course of action argue that the papal silence, however wrongheaded the decision was, came as a tactical decision to ward off worse atrocities (as happened when the Dutch hierarchy made a denunciation). Defenders underscore the efforts the papacy did make in behalf of Jews during the Nazi period.

The issues surrounding the "silence of Pius XII" are so complex and emotional that even today they cause pain and dissension when they are discussed. Our task is neither to absolve nor to condemn the silence of the papacy. We do need to pose a very simple question: When faced with pure evil, must one break silence, whatever the consequence, and speak? Whether it would have resulted in more persecution for the church in Nazi countries or accelerated the operations of the death camp are very real, but ancillary issues. The main issue is, again: Must silence be broken in the face of evil?

My suspicion is that most people, from the safe vantage point of historical hindsight, would answer in the affirmative. Even if it means persecution of the church, the pope should have loudly, unambiguously, and totally condemned the Nazis. Pius XII should have spoken the words in public with which he threatened an Axis ambassador in private: words of fire.[23]

When we speak against the darkness of silence, we must be prepared at worst for persecution; at the least, ridiculed indifference. It again comes down to the judgment about the signs of the times: When is it time to speak? The recent pastoral letter of the American bishops on nuclear war is a case in point. That 1982 pastoral letter was a bold word against the horrors of nuclear war. We know that the letter was a product of debated consensus. It tried to take account of the horizon of episcopal opinion while maintaining something like a united front of moral purpose. It ran a course somewhere between the most hawkish views of deterrence and the loud but minority option for pacifism. What is most interesting is that it triggered in American life an immense debate that went well beyond the confines of the American Catholic community. The American bishops—perhaps haunted by episcopal silences on burning moral issues in the past—felt compelled to speak out on what they saw as one of the clearest moral issues of our time—an issue which involves all of the human race. By refusing to yield to those who feel that the "bishops ought to stay out of politics," they added to the great (and generally productive) debate about war in the nuclear era. The bishops spoke out decisively about the first strike use of weapons and clearly defined how far they could accept the notion of nuclear deterrence. What is important about their pastoral is that they set out clearly and unambiguously the moral parameters for nuclear war. If that cost the American bishops some prestige in certain quarters (it is an open secret how strongly the White House tried to influence their deliberations), it was prestige well worth giving up. They were alert to the signs of the time and they said what had to be said. "They didn't swerve from their apostolic responsibility as pastors and teachers," wrote the Canadian scholar J. M. Cameron, who added, "American Catholics have reason to be proud of their bishops and the whole Christian world owes them a debt."[24] What the practical effects of that letter will be is difficult to gauge. What is very clear is that the bishops spoke clearly on an issue that demanded comment. Many of their flock are passionate patriots and may have wondered if this was a patriotic thing to do. That, clearly, was not the issue for the bishops who saw a larger moral responsibility.

The bishop's pastoral on nuclear arms is hardly as dramatic a public response as an appeal of Pius XII would have been in wartime Germany; I did not intend to parallel them from the point of view of history. There were many in this country who gave moral and psychic comfort to the bishops in their deliberations. My point, simply, is that when evil is regnant in actuality (the persecution of a people) or is a real threat (nuclear war), there is a need to break silence, to become a "nay" sayer, even if that is discomforting or likely to provoke hostility. To do otherwise is to acquiesce to the silence and that will not do. Against the silence we must speak; otherwise the "very stones will cry out."

Modern high culture has been obsessed with the problem of silence. Silence has been an essential part of the aesthetics of avant-garde musicians like John Cage (who titled his assembled writings *Silences*) and the Irish dramatist Samuel Beckett. Silence stands as a thread behind Wittgenstein's desire to bridge language and the world while Heidegger brooded on silence and being throughout his life as a thinker. Silence has become, as Susan Sontag observed in an influential essay, an aesthetic akin to a spirituality for an age that not only does not believe in God but also has severe doubts about the truth of language and communication itself.[25] Silence, for others, seems the only decent course in an age of indecencies: "No poetry after Auschwitz!" proclaimed Theodor Adorno. That fearful silence is the silence of nothingness. It is the silence of the mute universe which terrified Pascal; it was the silent, uncaring skies of Algeria which, in its indifference, outraged Camus.

It is the peculiar task of the contemporary church to preach the Gospel against the background of the dark side of the silence of nothingness and moral complicity. The mystic testifies to the beauty and complexity of that silence while the prophet argues against its nihilism and threat. That is the deepest meaning of the bedrock affirmation of the Christian tradition. As Christians we accept the fact that the creative word of God broke into the silence of primordial chaos and, in the fullness of time and in symmetry with that first utterance, Word became enfleshed so that the silence would never engulf us:

> At various times in the past and in various ways, God spoke to our ancestors through the prophets; but, in our own time, the last days, he has spoken to us through his Son, the Son that he has appointed to inherit everything and through whom he made everything there is. (Heb. 1:1–3)

Points for Meditation

1. Under what conditions (when? where?) do you find that positive silence which gives you rest or peace or times of reflection? Do you consider silence as part of your religious life?

2. As you look back on the development of your life, do you remember times of silence on your part which still haunt you? What do you say (or can you say)—if only in your imagination—that would fill up those silences?

3. How would you suggest silence be integrated into formal worship?

4. Have you ever experienced silent (i.e., nonverbal) states of prayer? Under what circumstances? What were the consequences of such moments?

5. Have you ever considered reading the scriptures as part of the disciplined inner silence of your spiritual life? Would you be able to undertake such a practice? Under what circumstances? How would you proceed?

6. Have you ever felt the strong need for the silence of a retreat or a day of recollection? If you have gone on such retreats, have they been satisfactory experiences? Why?

Notes

1. In *Bonaventure: The Soul's Journey into God, the Tree of Life, the Life of Francis*, trans. Ewert Cousins (Ramsey, N.J.: Paulist, 1978), p. 116.

2. *Rule of Saint Benedict*, chapter 42.

3. Thomas Merton, *The Sign of Jonas* (Garden City: Doubleday Image Book, 1956), p. 344.

4. *Four Screenplays of Ingmar Bergman* (New York: Simon and Schuster, 1966), p. 111. For a development of this theme, see Arthur Gibson, *The Silence of God* (New York: Harper and Row, 1969).

5. Karl Rahner, *Foundations of Christian Faith* (New York: Seabury, 1978), p. 77.

6. Ibid, p. 82.

7. Gisèle Brelet, "Music and Silence," in *Reflections on Art*, ed. Suzanne Langer (New York: Oxford Galaxy Book, 1961), pp. 105–21; specific page references are in the text. I have pursued this same analogy in a somewhat different form in Lawrence S. Cunningham, "On the Silence of God," *Spiritual Life* 26, no. 3 (Fall 1980) 137–42.

8. Dietrich Bonhoeffer, *Letters and Papers from Prison* (New York: Macmillan, 1962), p. 175.

9. Rahner, *Foundations*, p. 64. On the crucial role of creation and the development of a specifically Christian mysticism, see Andrew Louth, *The Origins of the Christian Mystical Tradition* (Oxford: Clarendon Press, 1981), p. 76 and passim.

10. G. K. Chesterton, *Autobiography* (London: Hutchinson, 1965), p. 332.

11. G. K. Chesterton, *Saint Francis of Assisi* (Garden City: Doubleday Image Book, 1957), p. 87.

12. "The Life of Francis," in *Bonaventure*, pp. 254–55.

13. John Teahan, "The Place of Silence in Thomas Merton's Life and Thought," *Journal of Religion* 61, no. 4 (October 1981) 364–83.

14. Ibid., p. 365.

15. Thomas Merton, *Contemplative Prayer* (Garden City: Doubleday Image Book, 1971), p. 90.

16. Ambrose Walthen, "The Word of Silence: On Silence and Speech in the *RB*," *Cistercian Studies* 17 (1982) 208. The pertinent chapter in Benedict's *Rule* for silence is number 6.

17. William Johnston, *The Mirror Mind* (San Francisco: Harper and Row, 1981), pp. 76–77.

18. Brother Lawrence, *Practice of the Presence of God*, trans. Donald Attwater (Springfield, N.Y.: Templegate, 1962).

19. See T. S. Eliot, "Hamlet," in *Selected Prose of T. S. Eliot*, ed. Frank Kermode (New York: Harvest Books, 1975), p. 48. Kermode's introduction has some cautionary words about Eliot's understanding of the "objective correlative."

20. Tillie Olsen, *Silences* (New York: Delta Books, 1982), p. 13.

21. I have translated and edited these lines from the *Passio Sanctorum Scillitanorum* in the *Enchiridium Fontium Historiae Ecclesiasticae Antiquae*, ed. C. Kirch (Rome: Herder, 1960), pp. 53–54.

22. Rolf Hochhuth, *The Deputy*, trans. Richard and Clara Winston (New York: Grove, 1964).

23. Herbert Jedin and John Dolan, eds., *History of the Church*, vol. 10 (New York: Crossroad, 1981), p. 94.

24. In *Commonweal*, February 24, 1984, p. 121. The pastoral of the bishops is *The Challenge of Peace: God's Promise and Our Response* (Washington: United States Catholic Conference, 1983).

25. Susan Sontag, "The Aesthetics of Silence," in *The Susan Sontag Reader* (New York: Farrar, Straus, and Giroux, 1982), pp. 181–203.

Selected Readings

Dauenhauer, Bernard. *Silence: The Phenomenon and Its Ontological Significance.* Bloomington: Indiana University Press, 1980. An important philosophical study.

Picard, Max. *The World of Silence.* South Bend: Gateway, 1977. The reissue of a classic work by the Swiss philosopher who had a great influence on Thomas Merton.

Philosophy Today 27, no. 2/4 (Summer 1983). This issue is devoted to the subject of silence; it has extended discussions of Dauenhauer's work.

Rahner, Karl. *Encounters with Silence.* Westminster, Md.: Newman, 1960. A classic of Rahner's spiritual writing.

Steiner, George. *Language and Silence.* New York: Atheneum, 1967. A brilliant literary study of the place of silence in modern letters.

4

PRAYER

In the last of the *Four Quartets* the poet nudges the reader to visit Little Gidding, which in the seventeenth century had been the home of a quasi-monastic circle of devout Anglicans under the direction of the saintly Nicholas Ferrar. If you visited that place, Eliot writes, it should not be out of curiosity or information, but:

> You are here to kneel
> where prayer has been valid. . . .

Eliot had a powerful sense of the continuity of the Christian tradition and its sign value in culture. He could not help but savor the historic spirit represented by as holy a place as Little Gidding. It was there that the ancient faith of English Catholicism had manifested itself and where it had been under attack (the experiment had been shut down by the Cromwellian parliament of 1647 as incorrigibly papist) by the iconoclastic forces of antitradition.

The notion of a place being the locus of valid prayer is another way of speaking about the sacred nature of place. It is an old and honored part of the Catholic tradition. Besides those places where sacred power erupts in hierophany (e.g., in shrines), there are those other places where the spirit of prayer and contemplation is nurtured as a primary focus of life. It is a fact of contemporary experience that Catholics are drawn to those monastic contemplative centers where the seasons and times are devoted to worship. Part of the reality of prayer is the gestural act of locating oneself for prayer.

Setting aside places for prayer and finding places to pray is, upon reflection, a commonplace in Catholic spirituality just as it is a commonplace in religion generally. While Jesus encouraged his disciples to pray always, we do not fail to note that he himself went to specific places to pray: to the temple, to the garden of Gethsemane, to the desert, to the mountaintop. He likewise encouraged his disciples to go away from the admiration of the crowds and pray in the privacy of a shut-off room. In the long evolution of Christianity those places—rooms, deserts, mountains, house churches, retreats, convents, monasteries—become the loci of prayer both liturgical and private.

The localization of prayer has also been accompanied by its temporalization. Again, the New Testament instructs us to pray always, but very soon we note that times were set aside for prayer whether that time was construed as "the first day of the week" or at specific times in the unfolding of a single day. The structure of daily prayer in the early church is a subject of some scholarly dispute, but we know that in the course of time the temporal structure of prayer would exert a powerful influence on the structure of culture. Indeed, as David Landes has argued in a charmingly learned book, the very invention of clock time in the West derived from the monastic desire for precision in the execution of the daily offices of the monastic liturgy.[1]

The development of prayer as an activity organized in time and space is a rather staggering phenomenon when one thinks about it. One almost sees why the church appropriates to itself the line from Malachi the prophet: "From the rising of the sun to its setting my name is great among the nations and in every place incense is offered to my name and a pure offering; for my name is great says the Lord of Hosts" (Mal. 1:11). Stepping back from the particularities of our own circle to see the church as a whole, we see it ahum with the life of prayer. At certain venerable places (e.g., the monastery at St. Catherine's in the Sinai) the liturgy has been celebrated and the offices sung without interruption for well over a millennium. At any time during the day or night somewhere there is prayer which is valid. I have often remarked to my students—a bit melodramatically to be sure—that as they drift home from the weekly beer bust or sorority party the Trappist monks up at Conyers, Georgia (Georgia is "up" from where I live), are rising for Vigils. My students usually receive this news without comment, but I find it strangely consoling.

In 1851 the poet and critic Matthew Arnold, on his honeymoon, visited the Grand Chartreuse in France. He was a man of failing religious faith, but he sensed in that ancient bastion of prayer and asceticism a force which he could only express in poetry; it was a statement of his own doubt and the power of that place of prayer:

> Wandering between two worlds, one dead,
> The other powerless to be born,
> With nowhere yet to rest my head,
> Like these, on earth I wait forlorn.
> Their faith, my tears, the world deride—
> I come to shed them at their side.
> *(Stanzas from the Grand Chartreuse)*

I have often felt that sense of prayer in place when visiting one of those older parishes in the settled cities of the Northeast or in the villages of a European country. It is impossible to wander down the aisles of those churches, often identified with the ethnic character of the neighborhood, and not sense some spiritual residue in them. It is not just the impregnated odor of beeswax, incense, and human smells but the rather haunting aura of past events: the joyful baptisms, the festive First Communions, the lavish weddings, the tragic funerals—not to mention the endless round of Masses, Benedictions, and other devotions. In those buildings there is a spirit of rootedness and continuity; it is tradition and prayer made tactile.

Matthew Arnold stood on the grounds of the Grand Chartreuse as an outsider simultaneously recognizing the tradition of monastic prayer as an ancient datum in culture and his own receding faith as a datum of his age. We may—or may not—also experience doubt about the possibility of prayer (am I talking or listening to myself when I pray?), but, aside from the deeply existential question, there is the issue of that long hum of the church at prayer. What is one to make of it?

A rather simplistic explanation would be to see the totality of prayer as a vast hymn of praise arising from the earth as a positive counterpoint to the cacophany of despair, hatred, and destructiveness that marks so much of human discourse. In that understanding of prayer we tend to see analogies with power houses and dynamos. The argument has often been advanced that our contemplative monasteries supply the spiritual power which advances the good of the church and, as it were, keeps the cosmic lights on. Now, it is true, that there is a close connection between contemplative activity and active missions,* but to see contemplative centers solely as spiritual dynamos is a misleading notion; it is an idea against which Thomas Merton wrote a good deal especially in his posthumously published volume of monastic essays entitled *Contemplation in a World of Action*.

Such a view of prayer betrays a number of unexamined and rather shaky assumptions not the least of which is the too sharp distinction between the life of prayer and human life generally or, to use the traditional language, nature and supernature. Furthermore, it focuses too exclusively on the formal structures of prayer in an abstract manner, not taking account of those small gestural prayers (at meals, before trips, etc.) which arise as extensions of purely human needs for expression and assurance. In short, we need to understand prayer within the fabric of human creativity, not as a counterpart to it.

To understand prayer in its most capacious sense we must affirm that prayer is an intensely human activity. We will affirm that it is a distinctly human characteristic; just as human beings are builders (*homo faber*) and players (*homo ludens*), so they also pray: *homo orans*. We have already touched on this fact in many parenthetical ways as we insisted on the deeply human need to locate sacrality in space and time and to search for the transcendent both in solitude and in community. In these discussions we have referred to analogues with other, less formally sacralized activities as referrents for

* Many activist orders (e.g., the Maryknoll Sisters) have a contemplative branch within the order to preserve the spirit of prayer in the order.

such impulses. It is useful to see prayer, understood at its most fundamental level, as linked to the development of what it means to be a full human person. Prayer, in this paradigm, is not a flight from reality but a thirst for it.

We can say further that prayer, understood in such a human framework, is not alienation but healing and reconciliation. That has been the clear conviction of every spiritual writer of this generation from Karl Rahner and Hans Urs von Balthasar to the late Thomas Merton. To pray is to affirm, however indistinctly, the potentialities of human life. Merton insisted on that aspect of prayer throughout his mature writings. His position is clearly enunciated in a conference he once gave to his fellow monks at Gethsemani:

> Prayer is freedom and affirmation growing out of nothingness into love. Prayer is the flowing of our innermost freedom, in response to the word of God. Prayer is not only dialogue with God: it is the communion of our freedom with his ultimate freedom, His infinite Spirit. . . . Prayer then is not an abject procedure although sometimes it may spring from our abjection.[2]

Merton, of course, is speaking of prayer and not the saying of prayers. Often, when we speak of prayer, we are not referring to that simple act of attentive awareness but to the articulation of formulas, the "saying" of the rosary, or the formal liturgical acclamations to which we add an "Amen." Too often in contemporary writing that kind of prayer does not receive the attention due it, but, in fact, we must make account of it in any discussion of prayer in the Catholic Christian tradition.

Prayer is difficult for many moderns because of our collective inability to "imagine" the other to whom prayer is addressed. We all know the quip attributed to one of those funky, quasi-theological comedians (was it George Carlin? Mark Russell?) that speaking to God is called prayer but God speaking to us is called schizophrenia. It is hard for us to think of Someone up there who listens to all those petitions or to visualize a Lady who sits above us as "Ave" resonates through the ether. Prayer, when "seen" at that visual level, seems to be a primitive, naïve, and alien exercise.

Nonetheless we pray or we seek to pray almost impulsively

and/or out of deep need. It is not always necessary to reflect on that need; most of the time we don't. Those who do often reduce the impulse to pray to some atavistic dependency gesture or some symbol of our own finite and precarious hold on life. It may be that, but it is, upon examination, more. One of the domestic chores I have is to put my daughter to bed each evening. As I lay her down in her crib with her blanket and current favorite doll, I almost impulsively touch her head and wish for her a happy, untroubled night. It is not a sentiment addressed to her alone but an expression of (and an inchoate faith in) the benignity of the world to keep an innocent child unharmed. Peter Berger has pointed to such primordial gestures as examples of what he calls "signals of transcendence," i.e., gestures by which a person affirms his or her faith in the essential gracefulness of the cosmos; a sign signifying one's faith in the essential trustworthiness of the universe. Those "signals" as explicitly recognized are also forms of prayer in the largest sense of the term. Berger writes:

> Every parent (or at least every parent who loves a child) takes upon himself the representation of a universe that is ultimately in order and ultimately trustworthy. This representation can be justified only within a religious (strictly speaking, a supernatural) frame of reference. In this frame of reference the natural world within which we live and die is not the only world, but only the foreground of another world in which love is not annihilated in death, and in which, therefore, the trust in the power of love to banish chaos is justified. . . . The parental role is not based on a loving lie.[3]

It is in these primordial gestures and from our perceptions of them that we should seek the fundament of prayer. It may be that we project a loving God onto the universe (as Feuerbach and Freud insist), but one could make the case that such a projection is rooted in the experience we have in the exercise of our daily lives. We do not always fully appreciate or articulate that experience, but it is part of our being human. If there is an underlying thesis to this chapter on prayer, it is that prayer is a deep existential attitude before it is a conscious and explicit act. Neither attitude, nor act exists, however, in a pure, undifferentiated state. It is always made explicit in the forms of culture. If we take that as a given, then we should proceed, as we will do, by speaking of prayer as deeply human but denominated in its express forms as Christian and Catholic.

Prayer and Horizon

We are extremely indebted to theologians like Karl Rahner and Bernard Lonergan for converting the philosophical notion of horizon into a manageable theological category which aids our understanding both of the human condition and of its transcendental character. It is a rich resource for understanding the very foundations of spirituality.

What is horizon?

Let us begin with common human experience. We may be on a road driving toward a definite destination. Our energy and attention are focused on a point (down the road, the next hill, the approaching signs of a town, etc.) while only vaguely aware that there is a vast arc of space—the horizon—which gives our point of view direction and specificity. We are moving to a certain point relative to the arc of that horizon. As we move closer to our destination, the horizon shifts, changes, enlarges, and takes on a new character. We are only aware of it as a peripheral context for the point toward which we are driving.

By appropriating the notion of horizon by analogy and applying it to our perception of the world we can see a somewhat similar situation. We focus, for example, on a particular person whom we know or recognize or about whom we are curious. The more we see that person, think about her or look at her, the more we do so—tacitly, to be sure—by acknowledging that our person is not others we know or others we have seen against our daily horizon. We specify that person against the backdrop—the horizon—of all the people (indeed, all of humanity) that make up the human horizon. We may love that person, but we do so, again, against the greater capacity for love which is rooted in the human horizon itself.

Rahner insists that in human knowing and living two things go on at the same time: Our attention is focused on knowing or loving the other (person, thing in the world, etc.), while a broader, less clear awareness occurs. With that latter background of awareness we have a sense of the "bigger picture," but it can never be fully grasped or understood. The greater our expansion of knowledge or love, the more that preconceptual horizon deepens; we know and love against it. We do not fully grasp it. Because it cannot be fully grasped, it is always something more, something beyond. That is the basis for Rahner's famous affirmation that as beings in the world we are knowers and lovers against the large background of absolute mystery.

To use an analogy we have described in our chapter on silence: We hear music only against the background of silence just as we know and love against the background of mystery. Here is how one contemporary commentator on Rahner states it:

> . . . To find myself, to rescue myself from distraction and superficiality by allowing what is deeply true about myself to emerge into presence, is to find myself within this context— one that I cannot finally get my hands on, one that every deep drive for meaning and love indicates, and one which every thing speaks of but nothing finally delivers. Each thing which I directly experience points to this last and ultimate context by which it is finally to be understood and by which the world is finally to be integrated.[4]

If we think of horizon as the context for knowing and living, we can say that we are, to put it baldly, in touch with mystery in the living out of our lives. That perspective, especially when made explicit in a momentary flash or as a result of reflection, is the deepest experience of prayer because it flows from the open wonder at the mystery of the world itself. It is an experience which we all have had, but many of us do not name it as such. Those who name it best are the mystics and poets; when mysticism and poetry touch, it is named most elegantly. Just reflect on these random lines which come from some of our best poetry:

> . . . We are laid asleep
> In body, and become a living soul:
> While with an eye made quiet by the power
> Of harmony, and the deep power of joy,

We see into the life of things.
>   (William Wordsworth—"Tintern Abbey")

I long for the imperishable quiet at the heart of form.
>   (Theodore Roethke—"The Longing")

I cannot bring a world quite round,
Although I patch it as I can.
>   (Wallace Stevens—"The Man with the Blue Guitar")

The inability to "bring the world quite round" or the desire to see into the "life of things" or the "imperishable quiet at the heart of form" are all analogues for that mystery which encompasses the daily round of our existence.

I would like to underscore *daily round* for it is one of Karl Rahner's deepest convictions that it is, first and foremost, in the living out of our daily lives that we first touch on those profound realities which reflect the ultimate mystery which we call God. We may encounter God fleetingly with an intuition of beauty or in a moment of intense emotion or as a significant celebration since those privileged moments flash for us that sense of the awesome mystery against which our lives are worked out. That living out of our lives occurs not only at the individual level but, as Rahner insists throughout his writings, at the level of history, engagement with others, and in a definite time and space.

That "near to us" but "never fully comprehended" mystery is the reality which we call God. We further specify that ultimate mystery by name: Father, Mother, Lord, and so on. The name, however, never fully comprehends the mystery; it only approximates it. If we say "Father" (as we surely must do) but can visualize nothing in that name beyond paternity, we have put a parenthesis around mystery; we have encapsulated it and, as a consequence, have rendered that which is infinite, finite. We must never allow ourselves the illusion that we possess God. To suffer that illusion, is in fact, a way to miss God who always remains absolute mystery. God, as Martin Buber says, cannot be expressed; only addressed.

A further point: When we call on God by name—as we surely must do in the Christian Catholic tradition—we should remember that that naming is not "religious" in a manner which detaches itself from the full experience of being human. God, as the Bible makes clear, cannot be adequately or fully named; God is "the One who is." The further specificities which we add (e.g., Father, etc.) are meant to express the best impulses applied *analogously* to the One who ultimately is absolute mystery. As we will insist further on in this chapter, there are specific insights into the nature of the mysteriousness of God which the Christian tradition brings to an understanding of God, but they are not given to us (in revelation, for example) as something alien to or estranged from our own life. They may be mysteries (e.g., it is Catholic teaching that the triune nature of God, the Trinity, is an absolute mystery), but such mysteries are not repugnant to our reality as human beings. They are consonant with, or perfective of, our nature. Grace, Aquinas insists in a famous formulation, builds on nature and that grace includes the grace of God's self-revelation.

While the naming of God is often done in formal and hieratic ways in the church as we celebrate the liturgy or listening to the preaching of the church and so on, these namings resonate back to primordial realities of existence itself. That is why we can affirm and make our own the insight of Martin Buber:

> If you explore the life of things and of conditioned being you come to the unfathomable; if you deny the life of things and of conditioned being you stand before nothingness; if you hallow this life, you meet the living God.[5]

To more accurately name God is at the very heart of prayer.* To move from an articulate awareness of mystery to the calling out of "Abba" (see Gal. 4:4–6) is to deepen prayer just as the capacity to say "Our Father" and not exclude the notion of maternity deepens prayer.

Prayer at the explicit level of naming and saying is the making manifest and specific the feelings we have at those moments of perceiving undifferentiated mystery. It is to con-cretize—albeit inadequately—the ineffable and deep structure

---

* In this section, when I talk about naming God, I am referring to the use of titles for God; I realize that naming can also mean control (e.g., Adam naming the animals in the Book of Genesis), but that is a different matter.

of human existence itself. Seen at that level, then, prayer is not a turning away from reality or a bracketing of the everyday business of living but its celebration. It is, following Buber's language, a hallowing of life. Such prayer is a movement away from the particular, fleeting, and ephemeral to the universal; it is to move from the ordinary to the extraordinary. It is a direction in life where we can begin to grasp the deep significance of that which usually passes by our ken. In the development of that attitude (for, as we insist, it is first of all an attitude) we begin, like the great mystic Julian of Norwich, to see the divine in the particular:

> And in this he showed me something smaller, no bigger than a hazelnut, lying in the palm of my hand, as it seemed to me, and it was as round as a ball. I looked at it with the eye of my understanding and thought: what can this be? ... And I was answered in my understanding: it lasts and always will, because God loves it; and that everything has being through the love of God.[6]

Prayer and the Center

When we think of prayer as the gradual raising to consciousness of the horizon which is absolute mystery against which we all live, there rises in us a deep sense of grateful wonder which is a simple (yet complex) admixture of gratitude and adoration. In giving a name to that feeling toward which we attempt expression, we move more specifically to an entry into the language of prayer. For those who are pilgrims on the Christian way that articulation will reach for the language of the tradition especially as it is mirrored in the scriptures and the traditional prayer life of the church.

Prayer not only expands toward the horizon of existence; it also plumbs the depths of the self. People of intense prayer have always tried to come to grips with the deepest mystery of their own consciousness in relation to the infinite mystery which is God. That desire is at least as old as Augustine's *noverim me ut noverim Te* (I would know myself that I might know You) and as recent as the most contemporary exercises in contemplative prayer. In an age given to self-analysis and self-scrutiny there is always a danger point in such exercises and the dangers are obvious enough. If such going into the self is not managed with a sense of propriety and discipline, one can trigger reactions as variously unhealthy as morbid preoccupation with the self or naked self-centeredness. Genuine introspective prayer is not narcissism.

Listening to the quiet in the self is as old as Christian prayer itself. Its methods are various and its disciplines many. There is no possibility to write here a brief history of contemplative prayer, but we should at least note two things: (1) there is an intense interest in such exercises in the contemporary church and (2) many of the most creative efforts to provide us with a framework of contemplative prayer have deep roots in the Catholic tradition. Indeed, one could say that contemporary spirituality has sought out its roots assiduously in order to speak to the contemporary scene. The dramatic new writing on the Ignatian *Exercises* or on Franciscan spirituality and Carmelite contemplation are all witnesses to the strength of spiritual theology today.

One of the more interesting contemporary movements to enrich the practice of contemplation has been the development of the practice of "centering prayer" (the phrase is Thomas Merton's) popularized in North America by Cistercian spiritual writers like Basil Pennington. It is a prayer technique adapted to the needs of modern people, but it has its origins in the advice of an unknown fourteenth-century spiritual writer whose work *The Cloud of Unknowing* is now considered a great spiritual classic.

What is centering prayer?

Perhaps the best way to answer that question is simply to outline the steps for the practice of the prayer, as outlined by Father Pennington,[7] and then follow up with a few reflections.

(a) Find a quiet place (it could be one's room sacralized by the use of an icon or picture) and assume a comfortable posture. The idea is to get oneself into a place and position which are restful enough to find freedom from the more frantic pace of everyday activity.

(b) Quiet down with an act of faith as one enters into silence and the presence of God. At this stage one moves to the quiet center of the self, full of faith that we are in the conscious presence of God.

(c) In that silence we take up a resonant word of our own choosing (e.g., Jesus/Love/Abba, etc.) and repeat it slowly and persistently until we can "let go" of the word and remain in silence. Should our mind get busy or distracted, go back to the word until silence is found and centered once again.

(d) At the end of the prayer period (typically fifteen or twenty minutes twice a day) we slowly come back from the silence with the prayerful recitation of "The Lord's Prayer" or some other formula.

It would be easy, at first glance, to see centering prayer as nothing more than adaptation of TM (Transcendental Meditation) to Christian needs. Although there is some similarity of technique, such a view of centering prayer is too facile and reductive. In fact, centering prayer is a modern form of a prayer technique which is at least as old as *The Cloud of Unknowing.* While its direct roots are in that work, it should also be noted that the practice presupposes some very ancient theological notions: the idea of the indwelling of God; the notion that we can rest in God's presence; the acceptance of the belief that God's presence can be made explicit in our lives.

The purpose of centering prayer (and its contemplative analogues) is not to "reduce tensions" or give us respite from the hurly burly of everyday life as so many meditative techniques are touted as doing. Centering prayer is not a sacralized form of biofeedback. Its purpose is to give us a sense of God's presence in our life and at the deepest level of our personal existence. It is to actualize the religious belief that we are God's children; that God is near to us and loves us; and that we can live near to God's presence. Its purposes, then, are primarily theological and transcendental, not therapeutic and palliative.

Another aspect of centering prayer with deep roots in the Catholic ascetical tradition is the use of a word like "Jesus" or "love" as the instrumental focus of deep prayer. Again, it would be facile to compare that usage to the recitation of an oriental mantra (e.g., the Hindu *om*), but one can also trace the usage to a development which ultimately derives from the

ancient monastic practice of *lectio divina* which encouraged
the systematic and lifelong practice of appropriating the biblical
message into the texture of one's life. *Lectio divina* means
literally "divine or sacred reading," but it would be closer to
the mark to understand the phrase to mean "divine listening"
since the purpose of the practice was to absorb a text into the
awareness of life itself by constant reference to it and meditation
upon it. There comes a point where one is not simply remembering a text or ruminating over it; the text is now absorbed
into the personality not as a set of words but as part of the
outlook of living itself.

There has been a tradition of juxtaposing (sometimes invid-
iously) the active and contemplative life in the religious
development of Catholic Christianity. It is far more correct to
see those two aspects of the Christian life as complementary
to each other; as integral and integrating. Activity can become
mindless, and, what is worse, destructive. The gaping difference
between the saint and the activist is that the saint does not
"burn out." On the other hand, the church has always been
suspicious of a kind of quietism that lets go of all human
activity in favor of a passive and uninterested life of "rest."
Such quietism can turn, if unchecked, into a fierce hatred or
rigid depreciation of everything outside the confines of the
purified self. That kind of negative "spirituality" is alien to,
and incompatible with, the deep sacramental orientation of
Catholic spirituality which holds that as God created the world
he pronounced it "good." Furthermore, any spirituality worthy
of the name must be worked out in the arena of life and
humanity; we can never appeal to a spirituality which deni-
grates or emarginates the fundamental insight of the Incarnation: Divinity becomes flesh.

It is because the spiritual witness of those who write on
centering prayer reflects an awareness of the dangers of both
activism and quietism that one finds in that witness an
emphasis on the relationship between prayer and mission. Even
at the level of the prayer experience itself Father Pennington
writes of the value of "shared prayer."[8] Shared prayer is the
practice of friends, couples, groups, etc., praying together
("Where two or three are gathered in my name . . .") in order

to share their prayer experiences. In those mutual interchanges there is the natural growth of a sense of community with the concomitant bonding of those who participate in such communities of interest.

Beyond the intimate bonds of the prayer group itself (which always runs the risk of becoming a self-defined little "in" group of spiritual elites) one must insist that a prayer-ful life, of itself, should expand the human horizon of those who pray to a more Catholic sense of mission and purpose. While strains of the earliest contemplative tradition emphasized the "angelic" life as the goal of contemplation, that freedom from the desires of the body could not be seen—except as an exaggeration or an aberration—as a goal in itself. The authentic end of the life of prayer must include not only the perfection of the individual but also the strengthening of the community of belief and the world which awaits belief.

Whatever the complexities of the old debate over action and contemplation, the plain fact is that in the Catholic tradition those who have been the greatest exponents of prayer have also been the people who have left their mark on the age in which they lived. Is that not true of Charles de Foucauld who spent his mature years as a desert solitary in this century or Thomas Merton who spent thirty years in a rural monastery in Kentucky? In this regard I would invoke the authority of the great St. Teresa of Avila (I could also invoke, of course, the example of the other Therésè of Lisieux to make the point). At the end of *The Interior Castle* Teresa, after having discussed the penetration of the Spiritual Mansions in the ascent of prayer, invokes the two biblical figures who traditionally symbolize the contemplative and active life, Mary and Martha. Teresa writes:

> This, my sisters, I should like us to strive to attain: we should desire and engage in prayer, not for our own enjoyment, but for the sake of acquiring this strength which fits us for service. Let us not try to walk along an untrodden path, or at the best we will waste our time: it would certainly be a novel idea to think of receiving these ideas through any other means than used by Him and all the saints. . . . Believe me Martha and Mary must work together when they offer the Lord lodging, and must have Him ever with them and they must not entertain Him badly and give Him nothing to eat. . . .[9]

Prayer and the Church

Since our primary focus in this study is on the Catholic tradition, our remarks on prayer must conclude with some observations about prayer within that tradition. To this point we have done that only in a parenthetical manner. It is true, of course, that one may sense absolute mystery without being a member of the church (although in the church we learn to name that mystery), just as one can pray at the "center" of one's being without denominational allegiance. Both kinds of prayer, at first blush, lend themselves to individual effort or to a prayer life outside the church. Indeed, as the Second Vatican Council made clear in many of its pronouncements, the Spirit moves outside the visible boundaries of the church and grace is to be found there, not the least of which is the grace of genuine prayer. Nonetheless, we have alluded to the role of community in prayer and we now need to address a few words to that subject.

First, and foremost, we must remember that the church is a repository of prayer. By that I mean that not only does the church pray in time and space, but it remembers those who have prayed with conspicuous power just as it remembers the manner of their prayer. The church cherishes not only the treasury of faith but also the treasury of prayer. Its treasures include its liturgical tradition, its various religious families and their mode of prayer, its saints and mystics, its moments of creative and deep prayer.

In a recent collection of his work, published shortly after his death, Karl Rahner speculated on the spirituality of the future.[10] He was not emboldened to define that spirituality, but he did attempt to set out some of its characteristics. Two of them are germane to our discussion here: One is that whatever shape the new spirituality will take it will be connected in some "mysterious identity" with the past. Secondly, Rahner believes that new spiritualites will arise, not from individual virtuosos of prayer, but from small intense communities of spiritually mature persons.

Rahner's observations underscore a point that this work tirelessly makes: Catholicism's memory is a living reality which nurtures the present with the wisdom of the past. That tradition is a continuum, not a series of discrete points. Thus something like "centering prayer" is pertinent to an age which is sympathetic to things like TM or Zen, but "centering prayer" has, as its inspiration, a fourteenth-century treatise on contemplation which, in turn, has deep roots in an even older ascetical stratum. To be fully Catholic is, then, to sense both the exigencies of the present (i.e., the "signs of the times") and the resources of the past. By and large spirituality is not created anew like Athena from the head of Zeus; it develops from a constant source. That is not to say, of course, that there have not been new insights and formulations; it is to say that these fresh things build on a past.

If we think for a moment about the eucharistic liturgy, we can see more clearly the point we are trying to make. While the Eucharist has always been seen as the act of making Christ present in our midst, the modalities and forms of that making present have changed and evolved over the centuries. The liturgy described in the second-century treatise the *Didache* is not the liturgy of twelfth-century Cluny which, in turn, is not the liturgy of post-Tridentine Rome. In all of those instances the theological emphases are different; the interpretations of what the liturgy represented (as opposed to what it re-presented) were diverse; the "style"—community celebration, allegorical pageant, etc.—were wildly dissimilar. What is constant, of course, is the making present of Christ. To read any of the classic studies of the evolution of the Western liturgy (e.g., Gregory Dix's *The Shape of the Liturgy* or J. A. Jungmann's *Missarum Solemnia*) is to find a dramatic confirmation of that dialectic of continuity and change.

It is in the church, then, that we learn of prayer as a traditional act and experience that act in community. The bond holding together those who pray testifies both to the essentially communal nature of religion and to the need for a check against rampant individualism which can turn destructively narcissistic. It is well to remember that even the austere ascent of mystical prayer in a tradition like that of the Carmelites was learned in community. St. John of the Cross and St. Teresa of Avila spent a good deal of their time either reforming or founding contemplative communities. It is within community that enthusiasms are checked, experience passed on from master to learner, support provided, and concerns for others made manifest. That is true for the religious community in the same way that it is true for the parish or the church as a whole.

The communal character of prayer is ultimately rooted in the fact that the divine became human in the person of Jesus the Christ. At the very heart of the Catholic experience is the basic insight that we do not have to find God because God has already found us; God "dwells among us." For all the complexities, ambiguities, scandals, false starts, and timidities that one may wish to note in the church that fact of the Incarnation should remain the fixed point.

To view the world, ourselves, and others from the incarnational perspective is to have, in the first instance, the attitude of prayer prior to making that attitude a fact. The Catholic memory roots itself not only in ways of praying and people of prayer but ultimately in the person of Jesus, who teaches us to pray and prays with us in the community of belief as it unfolds in time and space. We may pray as individuals or as a corporate body, but ultimately what makes prayer social is that we pray in Christ. It is part of the complex reality of the Incarnation that we pray with Jesus as well as to him. "With Jesus" is at the heart of the communal nature of prayer in the church.

The old Christian doctrine of the "Communion of the Saints" is a useful summary of the social nature of Christian prayer. The old catechisms define the "Communion of Saints" as the bond existing between the Church Triumphant, the Church Militant, and the Church Suffering; i.e., the bond that exists between those who await salvation in purgatory, those who strive for it on earth, and those who enjoy it in heaven.* That common bond, Vatican II insists, responds to the deepest calling of the church and partakes "in a foretaste of the liturgy of consummate glory."[11] In that sense it is a salutary reminder

---

* The earliest formulas of this doctrine did not include references to the "church suffering." Communion of Saints originally meant the bond between the earthly and heavenly church. See Wilhelm Breuning, "The Communion of Saints," in *Sacramentum Mundi*, vol. 1, ed. K. Rahner et al. (New York: Herder and Herder, 1968), pp. 391ff.

that our prayer life in common does not merely exist in the present but also points to the future, i.e., it has an eschatological character.

At first blush the notion of the communion of the saints seems a rather grandiose notion. I have always been reminded of those late medieval and Renaissance paintings showing banked saints, yearning souls, and marching pilgrims shown in panoramic detail as they move away from the damned in hell. Such large concepts seem so far beyond the parameters of our own experience. Yet, visualizations aside, the doctrine does bring a fresh approach to the role of prayer in the church.

I have always been moved by the fact that the great anti-Nazi martyr Dietrich Bonhoeffer wrote his doctoral dissertation on this doctrine.[12] There is something almost touching in the fact the Bonhoeffer died alone, away from his Christian community, in a Gestapo prison when his primary theological interest had been in the bonds of unity as they were expressed in that doctrine which joins the church with Christ. Bonhoeffer's desire in that 1928 dissertation was to overcome Luther's sharp distinction between the visible and invisible church. Bonhoeffer wanted to highlight the intimate relationship of Christ to the church. Throughout his treatise he kept going back to phrases like "Christ existing as community" or "Christ existing as church." Using both the language and the ideas of St. Paul, he saw that being in Christ was the same as being in the church. From that Bonhoeffer went on to affirm "the presence of Christ in the church through time as a continuing revelation. So actually, a more appropriate term might be 'Christ revealed as the church' or 'Christ revealed as community.'"

In that early work Bonhoeffer was concerned to heal the perceived rift between the church as sociological reality and the church as a theological concept. His study had the merit of insisting on the church as a way in which Christ was "fleshed out" in the unfolding of history. If Christ's paradigmatic relationship to God was the "Abba" experience, then Christ revealed as community should provide the means to replicate that paradigmatic experience. At its best the church does precisely that.

There is a lovely custom in some parishes of having the congregation join hands as the "Lord's Prayer" is recited before the Kiss of Peace and the reception of communion. I find that symbolic gesture of immense moment; a sacrament-sign of the communion of saints in miniature. People join hands to pray in the words which Jesus instructed the first disciples when they asked him how to pray. The words of the prayer resonate with expectation both of the Eucharist to be received (should not the words "Give us this day our daily bread" be understood in that sense?) and of the future with the Lord ("Thy kingdom come") not only for those who live but for those who are with the Lord ("on earth as it is in heaven").

We have said the Lord's Prayer so often that it is difficult to fully grasp the rich significance of the words without a conscious effort. In that preeminent prayer of the church at that place in the liturgy there is a crystallization of a whole series of basic truths about the life of prayer and the life of faith.

We might further note that while the Lord's Prayer is set in the solemnity of the liturgy, its dynamic, like that of the liturgy itself, is toward the larger world. The opening petitions (Name-Kingdom-Will) foresee the reign of justice under God as the desideratum of the praying community. Commenting on the various discussions of the word *kingdom* (is it now? in the future? in process? in time and space? beyond this world?), Krister Stendhal writes;

> ... The very fact that the evidence for a clear answer to such questions is ambiguous and varied should perhaps teach us that the important point is not these—our clever analytical speculations—but rather our individual seeking of and praying for the kingdom.
> Whenever, wherever, however the Kingdom manifests itself it is welcome: in a healed body, in a restored mind, in a juster society, in a human heart that finds the power to forgive, in the faith and truth of a Canaanite woman, in the death and resurrection of the Messiah, in a new heaven and a new earth where justice dwells. . . .[13]

Those solemn affirmations of prayer in the liturgy sum up the faith of the community and give formal expression to it. In that sense, our community prayer (the liturgy) concretizes those moments—regular or spontaneous—when we pause to name the ultimate sources of our well-being. Prayers before meals, morning and night prayers, the quiet utterances we make on our knees or with bowed heads before the liturgy—these are all expansions and refinements of our prayer life in the church. To a surprising degree we turn to the language of the church for these prayers, but they are not merely rote rituals for that. They have their own signification. To say a hurried "Ave" or "Our Father" before bed has its own sacramental significance distinct from the energy we put into savoring the words of the formula itself. Even in our advertence we say something when we frame our daily round by the gestures and attitudes of prayer.

Those informal familial and personal prayers are extensions of the church's prayer life. Morning and night prayers parallel the offices of lauds and vespers just as prayers before meals have their roots in the various liturgical benedictions which go beyond Christianity into Jewish liturgical practices. In fact—and this has not always been clearly understood—the formal prayer structures of the church often spill over into the life of family and community just as the rituals and devotions of the family and community get absorbed into the church. When one attends a traditional Catholic wedding, for example, it is possible to see any number of gestures which figured in a familial society long before they were incorporated into the liturgical formalities of the church: the march of the bride, the exchange of rings, the words of consent, and so on.

A goodly number of common devotional and paraliturgical practices disappeared from Catholic usage in the wake of post-Vatican II events. This fact came to me most forcefully recently when a teenager, uncharacteristically early for Mass on Sunday, saw some women saying the rosary together in church and asked me what they were doing. That young man's question, a child, by the way, of observant parents, startled me for a moment until I realized that there was no woman in the rosary group who was under fifty. The recitation of the rosary is still a memory of the teenager's mother, but it had passed out of his own experience.

The gradual erosion of these practices is almost complete at least in this country. It may be that such exercises have gone through a life cycle and are exhausted or await rediscovery in new forms; one does see some recrudescence of interest in the rosary and some eucharistic devotions. The history of devotionalism is yet to be written, but there is no doubt that many devotional practices grow (and disappear) in tandem with theological developments. The "Stations of the Cross" are unthinkable except against the complex background of the medieval emphasis on the suffering Christ and the varied interests of the Franciscans in the Holy Land, and interest which goes back to Francis himself. The rococco effusions of Marian piety so common in the post-Tridentine period (fostered by Alphonsus Liguori, Louis de Montfort, etc.) received powerful impetus through papal encouragement of Marian maximalism in the last century; an encouragement which has been put on a more firm theological basis since Vatican II. We see an increased interest in popular religiosity as an expression of "religion from below" in the writings of the liberation theologians who have contributed much to a functional understanding of how such devotions mediated religious values important for the voiceless ones of the church. Newer forms of devotional life (small group prayer, Bible study, etc.) are now popular and tell us much about the preoccupations of the contemporary church.

All such efforts at a deepened prayer life ideally oscillate between the sources embedded in the memory of the church and the exigencies of the moment. The tension between those two poles promises vitality while the dissolution of the tension can result in atrophy or eccentricity. That is an important point. The most devoted members of the Catholic church are not immune from those enthusiasms which promise a panacea for the problems of the age or a means to totally revitalize the life of the church. Renovationist movements are always a part of the church's life; indeed, one could say that they offer a gauge to test the malaises afflicting a particular culture. Current movements like the Charismatic Renewal, Cursillo, Focolare, Marriage Encounter, and so on provide an edifying example of lay concern for the good of the church. No group or movement has "the" answer because there is no "the" answer. We wait in hope for the consummation of things while allowing for a diversity of religious experiences to play themselves out in the life of the church. They are all attempts at making concrete the promise of Christ to the world.

The very diversity of spiritual experimentation (which is, in my judgment, a very healthy thing) is one sign of the transition we are in as older forms of devotionalism fade away. Although ideally the liturgy should supply all the needs of the Christian, in practice that is not the case. One thing that seems clear in the history of spirituality is the impulse to diversify spiritual exercises for particular needs. Before the Second Vatican Council there was a common tendency to multiply the expressions of the spiritual life; one went to Mass, but if one were "devout," there was also mental prayer, the rosary, the making of novenas, various devotional practices, prayers to the saints and to the Virgin, and so on. At an abstract level this complex life was part of a unity. Consider this evocatively brilliant passage in which James Joyce describes the devotional world of Steven Dedalus after he leaves off his adolescent sexual explorations and returns to the sacramental life of the church:

> Sunday was dedicated to the mystery of the Most Holy Trinity, Monday to the Holy Ghost, Tuesday to the Guarding Angels, Wednesday to Saint Joseph, Thursday to the Most Blessed Sacrament on the altar, Friday to the Suffering Jesus, Saturday to the Most Blessed Virgin Mary. . . . His every day began with an heroic offering of its every moment of thought or action for the intentions of the Sovereign Pontiff and with an early mass. . . . His daily life was laid out in devotional areas. . . . The rosaries too which he said constantly. . . . On each of the seven days of the week he further prayed that one of the seven gifts of the Holy Ghost might descend on his soul and drive out of it day by day the seven deadly sins which had defiled it in the past. . . .[14]

That kind of intensive, specific, and highly schematized kind of prayer is now lost in the church for many people. Its comforts cannot be easily recaptured and its verities are hard to sustain. Contemporary spirituality is undergoing a sea shift. The very strong emphasis on contemplative prayer today (which may tend to obliterate the more iconic or imaginative forms of piety) may well spring from a new sensibility deriving from a loss of the more visual and naïve approaches to religious truths. Orientations in spirituality which are more horizontal (communion with others as well as the Other), more existentially rooted in the common experience of human living or derived from the shattering of human comforts by the radical nature of biblical categories, more reflective of the acceptance of faith as a search rather than a possession—all these tendencies make prayer today both an exciting challenge and a "problem." That challenge is both personal and ecclesial. Commenting on the rise of interest in contemplative spirituality, David Burrell has set out that challenge with such cogency that we will allow it to stand as a coda to this chapter:

> What Luther preached, ordinary events have brought about: there is no space left for the rote response of the "ordinary layman." One either walks the individual path of faith (nourished by community) or one blocks out the demands of consciousness today. The latter group will always be legion, of course, and one is ever awakened to find oneself sliding into its collective embrace. Here is where we feel most acutely the need for community, for it is invariably the witness of others which stirs us to recognition as well as shows us a way out.[15]

Points for Meditation

1. In your life would you consider prayer a matter of custom or cultivation? Another way of asking the question: Do you pray from habit or need?

2. Are there formal prayers which you especially cherish? If so, can you analyze why you find them so significant in your life?

3. Have you ever felt the need or desire for disciplined daily contemplative prayer in your life?

4. To what degree is the liturgical life of the church important for your own spiritual life?

5. Are there devotional practices which you regularly observe? How important are they in your life? How do they connect with your liturgical observances if at all?

6. What spiritual book—other than the scriptures—has been most influential in your spiritual development? What are its most conspicuous merits?

Notes

1. David Landes, *Revolution in Time: Clocks and the Making of the Modern World* (Cambridge: Harvard University Press, 1984). See also Paul Bradshaw, *Daily Prayer in the Early Church* (New York: Oxford University Press, 1982).

2. Thomas Merton, "Is the Contemplative Life Finished?" in *Contemplation in a World of Action* (Garden City: Doubleday Image Book, 1973), p. 345.

3. Peter Berger, *A Rumor of Angels* (Garden City: Doubleday Anchor Book, 1970), p. 57.

4. Brian O. McDermott, "The Bonds of Freedom," in *A World of Grace*, ed. Leo O'Donovan (New York: Seabury, 1980), p. 40.

5. Martin Buber, *I and Thou*, trans. R. G. Smith (New York: Scribner, 1958), p. 79.

6. *Julian of Norwich: Showings*, ed. Edmund Colledge and James Walsh (Ramsey, N.J.: Paulist, 1978), p. 183.

7. I have adapted material from Basil Pennington, *Daily We Touch Him* (Garden City: Doubleday Image Book, 1979), and the three essays by Fathers Pennington, Keating, and Clarke in *Finding Grace at the Center* (Still River: St. Bede Publications, 1978). See also *The Cloud of Unknowing*, ed. William Johnston (Garden City: Image Book, 1973), and, more recently, *The Cloud of Unknowing*, ed. James Walsh (Ramsey, N.J.: Paulist, 1981).

8. *Daily We Touch Him*, pp. 123ff.

9. St. Teresa of Avila, *Interior Castle*, trans. E. L. Peers (Garden City: Doubleday Image Book, 1961), p. 231.

10. Karl Rahner, *The Practice of Faith: A Handbook of Contemporary Spirituality* (New York: Crossroad, 1984), pp. 18–28.

11. *Dogmatic Constitution on the Church*, art. 51, in *The Documents of Vatican II*, ed. Walter Abbot (New York: Association Press, 1966), p. 84.

12. *The Communion of the Saints* (New York: Holt, Rinehart and Winston, 1963); see also William Kuhns, *In Pursuit of Dietrich Bonhoeffer* (Garden City: Doubleday Image Book, 1969).

13. Krister Stendahl, "Your Kingdom Come," *Cross Currents* 32 (1982) 261–62.

14. James Joyce, *A Portrait of the Artist as a Young Man* (New York: Penguin, 1977), pp. 147–48.

15. David Burrell, "Contemplation in Action: Personal Spirituality/World Reality," in *Dimensions of Contemporary Spirituality*, ed. Francis Eigo (Villanova: Villanova University Press, 1982), p. 156.

Selected Readings

The Classics of Western Spirituality. Ramsey, N.J.: Paulist, 1979–. Original texts of spirituality to be published in sixty volumes.

Edwards, Denis. *Human Experience of God.* Ramsey, N.J.: Paulist, 1983. Links common experience with the life of prayer. Concise and informative.

Hassel, David. *Radical Prayer.* Ramsey, N.J.: Paulist, 1983. An excellent discussion of contemporary prayer in an Ignatian context.

Merton, Thomas. *Contemplative Prayer.* Garden City: Doubleday Image Book, 1971. An important book by an acknowledged contemporary spiritual master.
Rahner, Karl. *Prayers for a Lifetime.* New York: Crossroad, 1984. Prayers composed by one of the century's great theologians.
von Balthasar, Hans Urs. *Prayer.* New York: Sheed and Ward, 1961. A classic study. Not easy to read, but filled with wisdom.

5

SACRAMENTS

From somewhere in my childhood—I think it was an elementary school catechism—I remember an illustration that showed a majestic Christ standing in the heavens with seven channels below his feet letting a liquid flow over a parched earth and its inhabitants. The illustration was meant to teach about the sacramental life of the church. There was Christ who was the source; the seven channels (each labelled) represented the sacraments; the liquid stood for grace (were we not always asking for God to "shower down" or "pour down" his grace?). The liquid image was a good one, refreshing parched and eager believers.

That concept of the sacraments stayed with me throughout my childhood and even—if the truth were to be said—colored my formal study of the sacraments when I was a theological student. When we read the old theological tracts on the sacraments, it was the seven sacraments we studied once the preliminaries were over. There is nothing wrong with that approach even though we now recognize that the term *sacrament* has a far wider application in the Catholic tradition than I was led to believe in my childhood. We now recognize that before the rise of a systematic sacramental theology in the middle ages the term *sacramentum* (Greek: *mysterion*) had a far wider meaning. Christ was a *sacramentum* (a visible sign of God's grace); the Fathers often called the church the "great sacrament." The term was used widely by the ancient church

114

to mean those visible manifestations of God's saving activity in the world. That is why St. Augustine, for example, could call Christianity itself a sacrament.

We also say that one of the characteristics of the Catholic tradition (English, Roman, and Orthodox) is its great emphasis on the sacramental. In the broadest sense of the term the church is sacramental to the degree that it believes—as it most emphatically does—that visible realities mediate the invisible reality of saving grace; that there are effective signs of God's power and presence in the world. To fully grasp that point is to understand something very typical about Catholicism as an observable social phenomenon. The supposed gaudiness and ritualism of the Roman Catholic tradition (as opposed, say, to the chaste simplicity of the reformed order of church life) is, apart from many cultural influences, a direct result of the deep Catholic conviction that transcendence can be, and most appropriately is, symbolized in and mediated through sensible realities. In everything from the simple act of making the sign of the cross to the complexities of the Byzantine liturgy or the intricacies of the decoration of a medieval cathedral one sees the Catholic conviction about the role of the sensible and tactile in religion. That tactile quality is patent in the traditional theology of the "seven sacraments" with its emphasis on what is called sacramental "matter": the pouring of water, the use of bread and wine, the anointing with oil, the imposition of hands, and so on.

The amount that has been written on Catholic sacramentality in recent years is staggering. The work of theologians like Regis Duffy, Bernard Cooke, and others is such that there seems little need to rehearse, even sketchily, a Catholic sacramental theology here. We have alluded to elements of that theology in different places in this work. It would be useful, however, to highlight aspects of what we will call the "sacramental view" of reality as it relates to different aspects of the Catholic experience. Such an emphasis might aid us in a closer grasp of two important truths which undergird a good deal of what is on these pages: (1) the sacramental view of reality, like prayer, is an attitude prior to its being formalized as a sacramental act or series of acts; and (2) an understanding of that attitude can aid us in deepening our grasp of the Catholic experience from a number of points of view.

For purposes of this chapter we will employ a rather generous understanding of the word *sacrament*. Richard McBrien, for example, distinguishes sacramentality in religion as a "finite reality through which the divine is perceived to be disclosed and communicated" and specifically as those finite realities through which God is communicated to the church and through which the church responds to God's self-communication."[1] We, of course, are more concerned with that more specific orientation by which sacraments are understood as sensible realities which put us in touch with (or contact with) God in Jesus Christ. I add "in Jesus Christ" because our understanding of sacrament must be differentiated from (even if there is room for) that more general sense—often found in the poets—of nature revealing a divine, hidden order.

Although we can say with some legitimacy that a nature poet like William Wordsworth is a "sacramental" poet, we wish to indicate that his kind of sacramentalism will be subsumed under the more focused idea of sacramentality within the consciously Christian tradition. To put the matter another way: We wish to discuss those visible signs in our world which help people of faith approach God through Jesus Christ.

In this insistence that a sacramental vision helps us to understand and approach Jesus who is the Christ I am not attempting to reconstruct a theory of exemplarism, i.e., that notion, common enough among some earlier Christian writers, which sees sensible signs as pointing directly to the revelation of divine mysteries. I would not argue, to cite an extreme example, that God put three leaf shamrocks on the earth to point to the mystery of the Trinity. My point of departure would be to insist that one can "see" the world from the stance of faith in such a manner that a deepened grasp of the faith is nurtured and the more profound the "seeing," the more patent the truth of Jesus who is the Christ becomes (truth = correspondence to reality).

If the sacramental vision is, as I would suggest, a basic attitude before it is a formalized act, then we should be capable of looking out to the world from the peculiar vantage point of faith and grasp the meaning of that faith as it "speaks back" to us about the rightness and richness of the faith experience. In that understanding of it, the sacramental vision is dialogical: We see in faith and what we see comes back to us as a re- velation ("a pulling back of the curtains"), which, in turn, deepens the faith we bring to that first meeting.

Sacramental vision is not to be construed as a fleeting insight or a flash of intuition (though we may well experience such insights or intuitions) but as what Eliade calls a "mode of being" in the world. It is a basic existential attitude which is given to us in an inchoate manner with faith and which can be cultivated and refined by a disciplined spiritual life into a greater and more perceptive maturity. Some rare figures—St. Francis of Assisi would be a conspicuous example—have this vision connaturally, but most of us aspire to it and only reach it through measured steps. In fact, one could argue that the slow development of the sacramental vision is nothing more than the maturation of the full spiritual life of a Catholic Christian.

As these pages will make clear, to develop a sacramental vision is, at the same time, to grow in prayer and concern for others. Like every maturation process it comes through slow incremental steps fitfully gained. In some ways those steps are easy to take (who, after all, could be a Christian and despise the beauty of creation?), but others seem contrary to our instincts and first impulses. That hard truth, however, should not surprise us. At the heart of the Gospel are striking paradoxes which must be puzzled out not as exercises in logic but in the concrete circumstances of life.

The Other as Sacrament

If we accept the ancient insight that Jesus himself is the primordial sacrament of Christianity (the visible sign of God- in the-world as a fleshly reality—as a person), it should be easy enough to understand that human beings, hallowed by Jesus, are, at their existential level, goodly creatures. Human beings, by that account, are signs of grace in the world both because they are made in the image and likeness of God and because their reality is also enhanced by reason of the Incarnation. In that light we should be able to see the hand of God in other people. At one superficial level, this is an affirmation which is easily susceptible to sentimentality. It does not require an overly sensitive soul to see transcendent beauty in the innocence of a child (and, to be fair, Jesus did himself juxtapose children and admittance to the Kingdom of God). The freshness of a child has its own natural appeal. Jesus, however, points explicitly to others who act as signs of his continuing presence in the world.

In the great eschatological discourse in Matthew's Gospel (25:31ff.) Jesus describes the coming of the Son of Man at the culmination of human history. He divides the "sheep from the goats" for salvation or condemnation with the judgment that they either did or did not feed him in hunger or clothe him in nakedness, and so on. When they inquire about the specifics of this charge, Jesus answers: "Truly I say to you as you did it to one of the least of these my brethren, you did it to me" (25:40). His answer to the condemned (25:45) is exactly the same as they are damned for their failure.

That passage has seized the Catholic imagination from its beginnings. One of the key tests for the Catholic saint was how closely the person could come to seeing the presence of Christ (i.e., Christ himself) in the most rejected of humanity. In the long history of hagiography a common *topos* was for the saint to serve some person in need only to discover later that it was Christ himself who was served. That happened to the penitent St. Christopher carrying the child across a swollen stream and St. Martin of Tours who divided his military cloak with a beggar only to discover in a dream that he had given clothing to Christ himself. The same sentiment is behind St. Benedict's admonition that "all guests at the monastery should be welcomed as Christ because he will say 'I was a stranger and you took me in' " (*Rule of Saint Benedict,* chap. 53). In my office I have a reproduction of a woodcut that Fritz Eichenburg once did for *The Catholic Worker*: a soup line of beggars with a profiled figure who is obviously Christ waiting for a warm meal.

Such examples could be multiplied *ad infinitum* since the idea of Christ in others is a leitmotif of Christian spirituality. I will content myself with only one specific example to make my point. About St. Francis of Assisi we know much, but we have very little autobiographical information from him. One rather precious autobiographical fragment that we do possess comes from his *Testament*. There is in that document a laconic but telling observation from his early life:

> When I was in sin, the sight of lepers nauseated me beyond measure; but then God himself led me unto their company, and I had pity on them. When I had become acquainted with them, what had previously nauseated me became a source of spiritual and physical consolation for me. After that I did not wait long before leaving the world.[2]

Leprosy in the time of Francis (as in the days of Christ) was seen as such a horrible disease that its victims were strictly segregated from society for life. In the days of Francis there was a distinct church ceremony—almost an echo of the taking of religious vows—for the separation of a leper from ordinary life; the leper was dead to the world of human social contact.[3] To embrace the leper, then, was to embrace one of the most alienated—and what is more important—and feared creatures on earth. Francis did not learn by hard effort to accept lepers. He explicitly says that God "led me unto their company." Francis, in short, was *converted* and in that conversion learned to see Christ in the lepers. This love for lepers, it must be noted, was not a form of "social service" but a sign that a person could love Christ even in the person of a leper. It is rather interesting that both Thomas of Celano's *Second Life* and St. Bonaventure's *Major Life* say that when Francis first dismounted from his horse to kiss a leper and give alms, the leper then disappeared from sight. Neither author draws out the implication of that story, but every medieval reader would have known immediately that the leper was *Christus absconditus*—a hidden Christ.

We have another example of that deep belief that the poor and abject are a sacrament-sign of Christ in the world in the work of Mother Teresa of Calcutta and her Missionaries of

Charity. Her work among the poorest of the world needs no documentation here since her work is known throughout the world. What does need some emphasis is her deepest conviction that service to the poor is service to Christ. Of the spiritual development of her Missionaries of Charity (both the male and female branches) she says a double conversion must take place. First, they must undergo that conversion of life which will impel them to serve the poorest of the poor in a life of vowed poverty, chastity, and obedience. Beyond that she demands a second conversion of heart rooted in a radical transformation of their lives seen as a total giving for others. The contemplative writer Basil Pennington has put it succinctly in writing about a visit with her in India:

> A second conversion must take place. He or she who wishes to profess the life of a Missionary of Charity must come to the profound spiritual awareness that to serve these least and most despised of God's children is to serve his very Son and this is a *great privilege.* It is the sense of privilege that accounts for the experience I had at the Vārānasī Home for the dying. There, the mystery of divine love and human transcendence lay patently before my eyes.[4]

The other is experienced in such circumstances not only as a sufferer but as one to whom we feel no natural affinity. Many of us, I suspect, would rather exert ourselves on behalf of the victims of poverty than on spending time with a particularly odious relative. The Gospel's injunction to love one's enemies, the Johannine dictum that one cannot love an invisible God when one refuses love to a visible brother, and other such observations in the New Testament are extensions of the example of Jesus who forgave his enemies and prayed for his tormentors. Those things, as recorded in the New Testament, are a challenge for us to do what we would naturally prefer to avoid: Love someone whom, in truth, we cannot abide.

That demand of the Gospel is the easiest to fulfill in the abstract: One loves an enemy who is safely at a distance and who is abstracted through a generalization (e.g., I really do love the Vietnamese communists). The real test, of course, comes when we are called upon to be civil to the irritating neighbor when we met over the fence by accident. In terms of sacramentality, however, it is the individual fleshed out in all of his or her unloveableness that makes the Gospel demand for love a true moment of grace. It is in that very real drama that we are called upon to show forth the forgiving love which is the demand of the Gospel.

In both the case of the wretched poor and the naturally hateful person it is immediacy and fleshliness that give sacramental significance to Christian love. St. Therése of Lisieux could claim in justice that she loved the whole world because her love was tested by living in a cloister under a neurotic superior who gave her no immediate cause to love her. We develop that peculiar kind of love which is Christian love only when we can love in the concrete and, when called upon, to love against our instinct. St. Thomas Aquinas says that natural love is an inclination to something (*inclinatio ad aliquid:* see *S.T.* I q. 60. 1.), whereas supernatural love occurs when that inclination is not there. Such love, to repeat a notion of Mother Teresa of Calcutta, demands a kind of conversion—a change of life—in order to experience it. The prospect of such a conversion is such a daunting prospect (most of the time I don't want to love people who irritate me) that it is a genuine grace to pray for such love since we always fear it may be granted to us.

When we understand the sacramentality of the other in that fashion and, at the same time, understand what it demands, we come closer to grasping the "hard saying" nature of the Gospel. We blissfully pray for our enemies in the formulas of the liturgy or manuals of piety, but rarely think about what such petitions entail.

It is not necessary, of course, that our love extend out only as an overcoming of antipathy. To deeply love someone—a spouse, a friend, a child, a parent—is, as the New Testament makes clear, a paradigm of divine love. To fully love someone for that person's sake is to imitate and mirror the "Abba" love which Jesus had for the Father. Some years ago I met an elderly gentleman who was the sole care of his wife, who was totally incapacitated by a series of strokes. She was confined to a wheelchair, incontinent, and incapable of speaking; she had sight, but there was little way of knowing how much mental function she had or to what degree she could hear and understand others. She was always clean, neat, and obviously well cared for by a husband who tended her needs night and day. I once asked him if he had ever thought of putting her in a nursing home permanently or for periods so as to conserve his own health. He told me that he would never do it as long as he had the strength to carry on; he added quietly, "After all, I love her. She's my wife." They are probably both dead now, but after all those years I have thought about that couple. His care and devotion were absolutely selfless; there was no way she could reciprocate his attention. His love was full and selfless. It was also something else: a sign-sacrament for a then young person who saw (and learned from) his love what love means. The good that that man did touched me and, in my writing about it, may touch others as his love still radiates in the world.

Most of us, I suspect, must learn to cultivate love until it reaches those plateaus where it can move to the level of the selfless and heroic. We begin with that love which comes to us connaturally; we almost instinctively love a child or a parent. That love may be tested by adversity as it frequently is in marriage or friendship. In certain circumstances we may be called upon to expand our love in a sacrificial manner with either in behalf of those who are close to us or because we feel called by the poor and despised of the world. In those slow, incremental steps of love we begin to "see" how the impulse of Christ leads us to a greater capacity for love. That is, at bottom, what spiritual growth and the imitation of Christ are.

The capacity for heroic Christian love is not only an extension of Christ's presence in the world. It also functions as a sign value and a pledge which insures the church's right to call itself Christian. The greatest credibility of the church comes not from the purity of its doctrine or the power of its institutions but the example of its saints. Figures like the saints demonstrate that the radical demands of the Gospel can be lived out; that the imitation of Christ is possible. These great figures, raised up in every age of the church's life, testifies to the vitality of the Christian message which the church preaches. The great saints, in short, serve both as an encouragement for others to do likewise and as a judgment on our own lukewarm response to the Gospel. In that way, the sign value of the saint serves both as a model and as a prophetic judgment.

The World as Sacrament

It has been a commonplace in the Catholic tradition at least as old as the Middle Ages that the created world is a sign/ sacrament of God. Medieval writers read about God in two books: the holy scriptures and the book of nature. Alan of Lille phrased it in a famous tercet:

> omnis mundi creatura
> quasi liber et pictura
> nobis est et speculum.

> Every created thing
> is for us a book, a picture
> and a mirror.

For the medieval person the words of the psalmist, that the heavens and earth proclaim the glory of God and the firmament reflects God's handiwork (see Psalm 19), were a literal truth. Not only could human reason discover the reality of God from an empirical observation of the world (as St. Thomas Aquinas insisted), but one could sense in the created order the hand of God as well as his purpose. The arguments for God's existence as set forth by St. Thomas and others advanced notions about the world's purpose and raised the issue of its cause. Those arguments—the famous *quinque viae* or fivefold way—were sophisticated and rigorously logical reflections which mirrored the less articulated medieval belief that the world was a harmoniously balanced wonder which reflected its creator just as surely as a beautiful and pleasing painting reflected the genius of the artist. If there was evil and catastrophe in the world, it could be explained by evil or malignant forces at work against God. After all, if a demented person defaces a piece of art, is it the fault of the artist? Thus St. Bonaventure, a contemporary of St. Thomas, urges those who would seek to find God to look first at the world:

Whoever, therefore, is not enlightened
  by such splendor of created things
    is blind.
Whoever is not awakened by such outcries
  is deaf.
Whoever does not praise God because of all these effects
  is dumb.
Whoever does not discover the First Principle
  from such clear signs
    is a fool.[5]

The sign value of the world as a springboard to such a part of the Catholic tradition that the First Vatican Council (1869) defined that it was a Catholic doctrine that human beings could come to a natural knowledge of God by the use of unaided reason. The council did not say that everyone did come to such knowledge nor did it affirm that it was an easy or common way to God; it did define that humans had the capacity for such knowledge. In fact, it is not all that common to meet someone who has come to a knowledge of God through the use of his or her reason alone; rarely do people argue themselves into belief or acceptance of God. If people come to a knowledge of God at all in that way, it is not usually through a strict dialectical process but through the much less schematic means of simply being awestruck by the beauty and complexity in the world around them.

Such a response of awe energized the poetry of the Jesuit poet priest Gerard Manley Hopkins, who in the last century wrote some of the most compelling poetry in the English language on the beauty of the world and the love of God. It was also a basic attitude for the English writer G. K. Chesterton (1874–1936), who often attributed his conversion to Christianity to the logical outcome of his lifelong wonder at the beauty and mysteriousness of creation. Chesterton understood the beauty of the world as a natural complement to the revelation of Christ. Thus, in his famous book *Orthodoxy* he wrote:

It was as if I had been blundering about since my birth with two huge and unmanageable machines, of different shapes and without apparent connection—the world and the Christian tradition. I had found this hole in the world: the fact that one must find a way of loving the world without trusting it; of being in the world without being worldly. I found this projecting feature of Christian theology, like a sort of handspike, the dogmatic insistence that God was personal and had made the world separate from Himself. The spike of the dogma fit exactly into the hole of the world.[6]

In the recent Catholic tradition the most systematic attempt to understand the world as a source and sign of God's working in the world is the theological vision proposed by the late Jesuit scientist Teilhard de Chardin (died 1956). For Teilhard, a Jesuit mystic as well as a theologian and paleontologist, the cosmos in all its vitality is an operative sign of God's creative energy in the world. Teilhard saw evolution, not as a scientific hypothesis only, but as *the* key to understanding the organic relationship between the divine and the world. Teilhard envisioned the world as coming out from God in a great evolutionary spiral as it reaches for greater complexity and greater unity. In that slowly evolving thrust of creation life slowly spreads over the geological world like a skin (the "biosphere" as Teilhard called it) until it was ready for the birth of mind which again spread another layer over the earth—a layer he called "noosphere." For Teilhard there was no reason to suspect that this increasing thrust toward complexification and perfection should end with the birth of mind. He saw mind as converging toward a higher perfection which, in the end of history, would coalesce in what he calls "Omega Point." That final skin would be the Christosphere. That perfection was the cosmic Christ of whom St. Paul speaks. The sorrows and limitations of the real world in which we live are the birthpangs of a world in ascent as it goes back to God, Omega Point.

Teilhard was convinced that the generations after him would despair of faith unless people could be taught that God was inextricably entwined with human effort and the arena of that effort which is the world. His view of the world moving to Christ was not simply a theological construct to marry science and faith. It was a bold view of reality which attempted to speak to modernity. In 1919, before he had done his great scientific research and after his experiences as a stretcher bearer in the Great War, Teilhard wrote some lines which he wanted to use as a guideline for constructing a new Christian apologetic:

> The God for whom our century is waiting must be:
> 1. as vast and mysterious as the cosmos.
> 2. as immediate and all-embracing as life.
> 3. as linked (in some ways) to our effort as mankind.
> A God who made the world less mysterious or smaller, or less important to us, than our heart and reason show it to be, that God—less beautiful than the God we await—will never more be he to whom the world kneels.[7]

Teilhard's view of the world is a magnificently commodious one both in its ambition to wed revelation and science and in its exalted view of christology. If there is a text which would serve as a touchstone for his view of Christianity, it would be the Pauline view of the cosmic Christ: "We know that the whole creation has been groaning in travail together until now; and not only creation but we ourselves, who have the first fruits of the spirit, groaning inwardly as we await adoption as sons, the redemption of our bodies . . ." (Rom. 8:22–23). Teilhard's approach is also suspect for many people. His peers in the scientific world found his mysticism "soft," while many church authorities found his theology overly optimistic and vaguely heterodox. From many scientists he found patronizing dismissals while from church authority he found censorship and suppression. None of his major theological works was published in his lifetime.

It is not for us to defend Teilhard's orthodoxy or his insights. That has been done by many able scholars. It is important, however, to take note of those aspects of his thought that emphasize ideas in the Catholic tradition which were undervalued but which contribute both to christology and to a fuller understanding of sacramentality, especially with reference to the world in which we live. For Teilhard, and thinkers congenial to him, there are two truths, densely interdependent, which deserve full theological reflection:

1. The created world is good precisely because it comes from the hand of God as pure gift. The world is not illusion (*maya*) nor is it eternal matter nor is it divine. It is created as a free

act by God and, in the act of creation, as the Book of Genesis makes clear, God pronounces that world "good." In the final analysis, all sacramental theology should begin with the biblical credo that the sensible world comes to us as a free gift of God who sees the world as good.

2. The order of creation and the order of redemption are intimately conjoined. That is the clear message of the prologue of St. John's Gospel in which the opening lines of the Book of Genesis are clearly echoed. In that beloved text of the Evangelicals (Jn. 3:16) the author of the Fourth Gospel says that "God so loved the world that he gave his only Son. . . ." World, in that context, can be understood in its most generous sense to include the human world and the world of creation itself.*

The clear message of both the above doctrinal statements is that it is in *our* world, created and redeemed, that the drama of Christ's presence is made manifest. The corollary of that truth is, of course, that we must take this world seriously and love it as much as God did. Our world is a free gift from God in the creative act and a grace-ful gift through the force of redemption.

To sustain and enlarge our sense of the world as gift and grace does not require that we contemplate it as object. The world is not, after all, divine. We do need, however, to accept the world with the gratitude characteristic of one who has been the unworthy recipient of a gift. This sense of gratitude is one which we have spoken of throughout this work, but it is so fundamental that it bears repeating. Our basic existential attitude—one absolutely fundamental for any true spirituality—must find its root in absolute gratitude. The "raw materials" for such a spirituality of gratitude are manifest in the liturgy where thanksgiving (eucharist) is completely fundamental. In the liturgy we have moments given over for gratitude which range from the particular (gratitude for the bread and wine which make up the eucharistic elements) to the general celebration of the Eucharist itself. The contemporary liturgical theologian Geoffrey Wainwright makes the point quite force-

---

* We should note, in passing, that "world" can stand for the powers which oppose the order of salvation in John's Gospel and, in those places, has a technical and quite different meaning.

fully in his observation about the circularity of liturgical gratitude:

> In worship we receive the self-giving love of God, and the test of our thankfulness is whether we reproduce that pattern of self giving in our daily relationship with other people. Of course, that test begins with our attitudes and behaviour as brothers and sisters in the liturgical assembly. . . . Liturgy appears once more as the focal expression of facts which embrace the whole of our existence.[8]

To learn to love the world in gratitude—to see it as a sign/ sacrament of grace—is not an easy thing to do. We live in the world as naturally and as unreflectively as we live in our own body. Not to have the world; not to live in the world: such a state is literally unimaginable. The very being of the world is, simultaneously, a given and, as Wittgenstein said, echoing Spinoza, an absolute mystery. It is part of growth in faith to move from accepting the world as a given and as background to a spirit of receiving it as gift. It is only with that cultivated sense of seeing the gift of the world that we can resist those terrible temptations that lure the unreflective person: the temptation to assume the world is ours and in that assumption begin to despise it; the equal temptation to fear the world as a trap and to yearn for the peculiarly Catholic heresy of "angelism" by which we see ourselves as trapped in our body and trapped in the world. In either case we deprecate the gift and, by extension, the Giver. How much more biblical and Christian it is to be "staggered by the stupendous marvel of existence—by the miracle of sunlight coming through a window, by the miracle of people walking on legs through the streets, by the miracle of people talking to each other."[9]

A cultivated sense of the sacramentality of the world and our sense of gratitude for it may prompt Catholics to make their contribution to those ethical issues raised by the misuse of the planet in this technological era. While a satisfactory theology of resources (an "eco-theology"?) has yet to be written, it does seem that there are some very basic notions in the Catholic tradition by which we can develop an attitude commensurate with the ethical issues raised by ecological concerns.

While the Fathers of the Second Vatican Council encouraged the development of the earth "so that it can bear fruit and become a dwelling place worthy of the whole human family" and called that great task part of the "design of God,"[10] it assumed, but did not spell out, an obligation to sense the world itself as part of God's plan—a world not to be abused or exhausted but one over which we are obliged to exercise stewardship and care.

The Catholic church has not been conspicuous in its leadership on ecological issues as such, but it appears evident that such a sensitivity should flow naturally from a genuine sacramental view of the world. That proposition is not unrelated to our convictions about the sacramentality of other persons. If we see the presence of God in others and in the world as well, then it follows that we cannot be indifferent to the plight of those who do not share the earth's bounty or who may lose it because it is mismanaged or raped through greed, sloth, or human indifference. A true sacramental vision must be such that it is aware of persons in the world not as atomic realities but as a network or skein of intertwined lives living on a single earth which is given to all for all. While we are obliged to see this specific person as a Christ bearer and the world as a gift given to us, we must also see this extension of God, not only as a discrete phenomenon, but as a wholeness which the Bible calls, simply, "creation."

Is there any particular merit in this sacramental vision which adds more to the love of nature or the love of our human fellows which is not enjoyed by those who express a similar love but who do not profess a need for, or interest in, the Catholic sacramental vision? It would be arrogant to deny that those who are "outside the pale" love less or reverence less either the world of nature or their fellow humans. However, I do think that the sacramental vision provides a kind of check or resistance to those ills often suffered by those who simply wish to do good. It provides a kind of realism which says that neither nature nor humanity should be viewed in a sentimental or abstract manner.

Such a vision demands that a person look with specificity and with a prior understanding that both nature and humanity are flawed. "A man loves nature in the morning for her innocence and amiability," writes Chesterton, "And, at nightfall for her darkness and cruelty. . . . Physical nature must not be the direct object of obedience; it must be enjoyed, not worshipped."[11] In the same fashion, the sacramental vision demands that we move from the abstract to the particular. We are not called upon to cherish humanity but to love human beings. Some people, for instance, have criticized Mother Teresa of Calcutta for not fighting to change the root causes of poverty and human degradation in the areas in which she works. That strikes me as an ill-placed criticism. Her vocation is to work immediately with those who are in need and as such she is working withing the sacramental vision of the church as she perceives it. Others may have another kind of call—a prophetic urge to tear down unjust structures or to rebuild at a megalevel. But the Gospel is well served by every believer who steps outside and begins to do good in the name of Christ.

Specific moments of encounter with divine reality as they are mediated through concrete realities are epiphanies of grace in which the presence of Jesus is made manifest. It is the making concrete of the reality of the Gospel. The incarnational theology of the Gospel not only hallows the world in which we live but gives full warrant to the notion that grace breaks through into our world. In the recognition of that "breaking through" we cultivate the sacramental imagination and, in that process, are faithful to the authentic Catholic faith in the sacramentality of human reality.

Sacraments and Ordinary Life

In the heyday of the liturgical movement in this country on the eve of the Second Vatican Council there was an idealized vision of Christian life as a sacramental and liturgical life. To thumb through old copies of *Worship* or *Jubilee* is to see a projected style of Catholic living harmonized to the rhythms and usages of the Roman liturgy. Such Catholics might recite an abbreviated breviary, perform paraliturgical rites at home, lobby for a "dialogue" Mass in their parish, mark the seasons with liturgical art, participate in Bible vigils or study groups, and so on. This idealized "style" of Catholic living owed a great debt to Western monasticism. That is not surprising since a good deal of the impetus of liturgical renewal came from monastic reformers both in Europe (e.g., the pioneering efforts which came from Maria Laach or Beuron in Germany; Maredsous in Belgium; Solesmes in France, etc.) and in this country (the Benedictines at Collegeville, Minnesota, being the preeminent center of liturgical renewal).

It is easy enough to patronize those rather romantic visions of Catholic life (as Garry Wills has done) now that the decidedly nonromantic realities of post-Vatican II liturgical reform have hit us, but one must insist that the instincts of those reformers were fundamentally sound. They rather fully understood the pressures traditional Catholicism felt in the face of modernity and they saw in a renewed liturgy a chance for a Catholic life which was theologically sound and which provided a sense of wholeness, integrity, and meaning for ordinary living. There was an equally strong impulse to focus spirituality on those essential foci of the Catholic tradition: the encounter of Christ in the scriptures and the Eucharist. It is more than a commonplace to say that the liturgical reforms envisioned by these reformers were accepted *tout court* by the Fathers of the Second Vatican Council.

It is only in the aftermath of the council and nearly after two decades of usage that we now realize how difficult it is to translate the vision of those reformers into a practical integrative style of life. In fact, there are those who question whether one can live in a manner envisioned by the liturgical reformers apart from some kind of communal structure such as that provided by monasticism or its variants.

It seems that there are two issues trying to emerge from such a vision. The first is that every age must learn to actualize a mode of living in which the word of God and the liturgy continue to shape one's life in its desire to be true to the following of Christ. It was easy enough to follow the cycles of the liturgy when living in a rural village with a church on the square. It is quite another thing for someone who lives in a city or in the suburbs where the church is just one more site along with those which cater to needs or provide a work space.

Not even architecture or town planning is integrated in modern culture as far as church life is concerned. Secondly, each age's difficulty in harmonizing daily life and the sacramental/liturgical life of the church seems uniquely difficult precisely because it is in our time that we experience our difficulties. Our problems are not matter for intellectual discussion alone; they are challenges to be met or acted on.

At the most primary level it is a question of religious consciousness and the need to develop it from a condition of latency. Those who are "practicing" Catholics are deeply involved in a sacramental mode of being at a level of complexity which is not often realized until one reflects on it. The very "automatic" practices of going to Mass, having one's children baptized, and so on are signs/acts of a way of life that is peculiar to those who so practice. It may well be that for the outside observer those signs/acts serve only sociological functions: "He goes to Mass or she sends her children to catechism lessons. They are Catholics." They may also be routine for the practitioner: "The kids will be baptized because we've always done that in our family." At this level, both for practitioner and for observer, the intrusion of personal reflection becomes important and potentially grace-filled: "Why do they make the effort at sending their kids to catechism?" "Why does our family always have children baptized?"

One may well say grace before meals as a habitual gesture (or to give good example to the young; it is the "right thing to do"). There is always the potentiality for that gestural act of habit to turn to something else. It may come in the form of explicit articulation ("we eat better than most folks in the world; that is a reason to give thanks") so that the act takes on a reflected meaning where before it was mere gesture. Such potentiality means that traditional usages, formalized acts of rituals, mere customs, etc., always have the possibility of having meaning infused in them.

The sign values of our religious gestures can be appreciated by recalling again the link between sacrament and time. By the performance of religious acts we signify that there are times (on Sunday, at meals, before retiring, etc.) that we wish to note by invoking an extraordinary dimension in our lives.

Those times are openings to grace. Some may object that this is the practice of religion at a rather trivial and microscopic level. I think not. All of us go through a day's activities according to rhythms which permit precious little time for reflection. When we stop—as I am now doing as these words are being typed—to think back on the day, we realized only then how crowded it is with ordinary and accustomed tasks which fill up the time. The sheer business of domesticity, child care, working for a living, relaxing, and so on is so much a part of the texture of my "life" that we cannot live spiritually on those privileged moments when God's presence comes to us unbidden. We may experience, unbidden, an onrushing sense of God's care in a time of euphoric happiness (or, equally, in a time of crisis), but we are also charged with transforming the ordinary. I think that a good place to start is with a reflective approach to those small acts of piety which tradition has given us. They are punctuations in the usual course of things that signify our faith in God.

The making concrete of the Christian life is not only something which I do at some private and privileged level. The sacramental attitude needs development and nurture both in a more conscious reflectiveness with respect to participation in the life of the church and in the larger world in which we live. Faith helps us to concretize Christ both by our membership in a worshipping community ("Where two or three are gathered in My name . . .") and as a presence in the world about us. The willingness to do that is a means of cultivating what sacramental theologian Bernard Cooke calls "Christ Meaning," i.e., the actualization of Christ in the concrete arena of life itself:

> By injecting the "Christ Meaning" into the different spheres of human experience and involvement individuals help change the significance of human life. They are a transforming influence: they are creative of a distinctive dimension of human history. Essentially, what they do is unleash in human awareness a knowledge of Jesus's Abba, a knowledge that has the power to revolutionize the meaning and the reality of human life, individual and social. To put it another way: these Christians introduce "uncreated grace" (that is, God in His self-giving) into the lives of people, so that those lives can be increasingly transformed, increasingly "braced."[12]

It is very easy for Christians to doubt the efficacy of their labors and their faith. What they do in a given parish or a given community can seem so meager against the complex background of the larger society. Cooke's point, however, is a fine antidote to such doubt. His thrust is to insist that in every small exercise of the witness of Christ there is an addition to the growth of the intrusion of Christ into the human. Every effort that a community (or an individual) makes to love rather than hate, succor rather than ignore, resist rather than accede, is in essence another eruption of the message of Christ into the neutral reality of life. To look at it from the negative side: Would we be better off as a people if we did not do what is done? Would we have a better social fabric if people did not cooperate with all those attempts to do the spiritual and corporal works of mercy? Surely not. The Gospel never promised a perfect or utopian world until the eschaton. What it does insist is that all things conspire toward an end the shape of which we cannot see. We are on the way, we are pilgrims, we strive toward a goal—all those images are redolent of effort, patience, persistence, and incompleteness. They are all attitudes, however, sustained both in faith and in hope.

To understand the making concrete of the "Christ Meaning" is also an aid in overcoming false dichotomies in the spiritual life or, to say it more positively, aids in integrating Christian life as a whole; Christian life as a mode of being in the world. There should be no sharp distinction between prayer life and sacramental life; between active life and the life of sacramental awareness. If we understand sacrament in a generous fashion as fleshing out "Christ Meaning" in the world, we see the truth of the patristic belief that Christian faith itself is a *sacramentum*. When we turn aside to pray in private, we make manifest a sign of God's presence just as surely as we do when we stand in public for reconciliation, peace, or to protest injustice. Those acts are not contraries; they are of a piece.

Finally, a sacramental attitude demands (indeed, it presupposes) a healthy and robust love for the world in all of its beauty and delight. It is an attitude which sees real value in good art, in friendship, in the world of nature, in culture, in play. The Catholic tradition has an ample tradition which encourages flight from the world, solitude, and self-denial. Those impulses are neurotically unhealthy if they do not somehow integrate that flight and self-denial is somehow linked to the world's goodness and not its evil character. When asceticism is an expression of hatred or disgust or despair, it is a poisoned asceticism. A pamphlet used by the Trappists of Gethsemani to inform potential novices puts it bluntly: "If you do not like people, the monastery is no place to go. If you hate the world this is no place to come. . . . We like it if you notice rain, feel the wind, hear the birds, smell the soup. We like you to be aware, not asleep; alive, not dead; in touch, not gone."

In a recent historical study of (and apologia for) Christian asceticism Professor Margaret Miles concludes that any form of asceticism in the Christian tradition (and there have been some) which are at odds with the "Christian affirmations of the human body in the doctrines of creation, incarnation, and resurrection" must be rejected out of hand as being incompatible with the totality of the Gospel.[13] Miles further notes that we are better served by using the word pair flesh/spirit rather than body/mind. The biblical categories of flesh/spirit better reminds us that we must recognize ourselves as having a connection to the source of life (i.e., spirit) and, as a consequence, a necessary resistance to being concerned with the "flesh" in an obsessive or addictive manner. She writes:

> Such objects, good in themselves, become "too dear" in that the person becomes attached to them instead of to the source of life and being. They become addictive. Because they are created things they owe their being to the generosity of the creator, they cannot provide the infinite life and satisfaction for which human beings long. We are addicted when we refuse to recognize that we demand of these objects what they cannot provide. We need to recognize that forcing them beyond their capacity to give devalues them, and that we must continually be frustrated by their inability to give us greater life.[14]

Miles is speaking in that citation of sex, power, and possessions, but her point has wider application. It is a healthy aspect of the sacramental vision. It aids us in seeing the desired equilibrium we must seek between being in the world (i.e., in the flesh) and not overcome by it. Such an existential attitude creates a reverence for balance, a sense of gratitude for creation, a perception of the deep meaning of the Incarnation, and, finally, a focus on the not-yet reality promised by the Lord.

That point deserves some added emphasis. There is no contradiction between a sacramental vision of life and the Gospel demands for asceticism as long as one keeps two things in mind: the goodness of creation and its distinctiveness from God. Those two facts can be subsumed under the general truth that this good world is not God. We are called upon to love the world, live in it, enjoy its fruits, celebrate its beauties, treasure its bounty, and extend its largesse to others. Only when a fixation on the world as an ultimate value instead of a sign of ultimate value predominates in a life does a conflict enter into the life of a Christian.

This truth can be manifested in different ways in a person's life. Some are called to radically reject the world as a sign of a greater value. The radical poverty of the Gospel incarnated into the life of a Christian can serve as a prophetic witness against the materialism of the world and as a testament to the enduring value of God, the only absolute. Let it be noted that the rejection of the world, in that case, is not a rejection of evil but a rejection of a good in order to pursue a higher good. In such instances the asceticism of the person who feels such a call reminds others both of the beauty and of the goodness of the world and of values that transcend that goodness and beauty.

Others may not be called in such a radical fashion. What they may be called on, however, is a greater sense of detachment either as an act of heroic love for others (e.g., I will live simply so that others may share the largesse of the world instead of destitution) or as a curb for inordinate preoccupation with limited and limiting goals in life. It is that impulse which, as Raimundo Panikkar has written, helps the truly spiritual contemplative to overcome those temptations so peculiar to modern culture: no to "the power of the big" and yes to intimacy; no to the temptation to triumph and yes to a life of contentment.[15] In those conversions there is always a sense of what we possess and what we must not be possessed by.

That delicate balance of affirming sacramentality and a respect for asceticism is not simply a matter of intellectual discrimination; it comes only through "seeing" and that openness to mystery which we call "prayer." It is only then that we grasp simultaneously the world and God's presence *under* it as the foundation and sustainer of all reality. That level of consciousness is contemplative prayer at its healthiest. In those moments sacramentality, asceticism, and encounter fuse into one. It has been best described in a classic work on prayer:

> When we contemplate the word of God, we must let ourselves be gripped by this primary truth, namely, that the whole compact mass of created being we are so familiar with sails like a ship over the fathomless depths of a wholly different element, the only one that is absolute and determining, the boundless love of the Father. . . .[16]

It is at that level that the rightness of the sacramental vision becomes not only clear, but nourishing.

Points for Meditation

1. To what degree has your sense of sacramentality been enlarged beyond the traditional formulations of the "seven sacraments"? Do you see Catholicism as essentially a "sacramental" church?

2. Are there special moments, acts, scenes, and so on in your life and memory which have had a powerful sacramental quality for you? Can you recall some moments in your formal sacramental life (e.g., at Communion, in penance, when marrying, etc.) that have been peculiarly special for your own spiritual formation?

3. What would prove to be an extreme test of your ability to sense Christ in another person? Could you see yourself working for the extremely ill or handicapped or neglected as an act of Christian living?

4. Can you provide some further reflections on the relationship of Christian faith to ecological concerns?

5. Under what circumstances, if ever, has the world manifested the "glory of God for you"?

6. Is Bernard Cooke's notion of "Christ Meaning" useful? How do you think you have (or could have) applied it in your life?

Notes

1. Richard McBrien, *Catholicism*, vol. 2 (Minneapolis: Winston, 1980), p. 732.
2. From *Omnibus of Sources*, ed. Marion Habig (Chicago: Franciscan Herald Press, 1974), p. 67.
3. On this ritual and other matters pertaining to leprosy, see Arnaldo Fortini, *Saint Francis of Assisi*, trans. Helen Moak (New York: Crossroad, 1981), pp. 206ff.
4. Basil Pennington, *Monastic Journey to India* (New York: Seabury, 1982), p. 4.
5. From "The Soul's Journey into God," in *Bonaventure*, trans. Ewert Cousins (Ramsey, N.J.: Paulist, 1978), p. 67.
6. G. K. Chesterton, *Orthodoxy* (Garden City: Doubleday Image Book, 1959), p. 79.
7. Pierre Teilhard de Chardin, *The Heart of the Matter* (New York: Harcourt Brace Jovanovich, 1978), p. 212.
8. Geoffrey Wainwright, *Doxology: A Systematic Theology* (New York: Oxford University Press, 1980), p. 422.
9. From a newspaper column by G. K. Chesterton, quoted in *The Man Who Was Orthodox*, ed. A. L. Maycock (London: Dobson, 1963), p. 170.
10. From the *Pastoral Constitution on the Church in the Modern World*, art. 57, in *The Documents of Vatican II*, ed. Walter Abbott (New York: Association Press, 1966), p. 262.
11. *Orthodoxy*, p. 77.
12. Bernard Cooke, *Sacraments and Sacramentality* (Mystic, Conn.: Twenty-Third Pubns., 1984), p. 235.
13. Margaret Miles, *Fullness of Life: Historical Foundations for a New Asceticism* (Philadelphia: Westminster, 1981), p. 156.
14. Ibid., pp. 157–58.
15. Raimundo Panikkar, "The Contemplative Mood: A Challenge to Modernity," *Cross Currents* 31 (1981) 261–72; esp. pp. 268–69. That same argument is pursued in Panikkar's *Blessed Simplicity: The Monk as Universal Archetype* (New York: Seabury, 1982).
16. Hans Urs von Balthasar, *Prayer* (New York: Sheed and Ward, 1961), p. 36.

Selected Readings

Cooke, Bernard. *Christian Sacraments and Christian Personality*. New York: Holt, 1965. A dated, but still valuable contribution.

Ganoczy, Alexandre. *An Introduction to Catholic Sacramental Theology*. Ramsey, N.J.: Paulist, 1984. A good survey of European trends in sacramental theology.

Guzie, Tad. *The Book of Sacramental Basics*. Ramsey, N.J.: Paulist, 1982. A handy book on sacramental theology in relation to liturgy.

Martos, Joseph. *Doors to the Sacred*. Garden City: Doubleday, 1981. Good but uneven historical study; irritating in its lack of notes.

Schillebeeckx, Edward. *Christ the Sacrament of the Encounter with God*. New York: Sheed and Ward, 1963. A classic study. Still very useful.

6

STORY

There is a popular tendency to think of religion in general and Catholicism in particular as a set of propositions (dogmas, creeds, statements, etc.) to which we either give or fail to give our assent. Now, it is true that every religious tradition encapsulates its faith in statements since that is one of the basic modes of human discourse. To set forth a clear statement about a religious position does invite one to clarify his or her own intellectual commitment. To inquire if someone believes if the cosmos makes some kind of sense is to inquire about a profoundly religious notion which stands at the heart of most religious expression. We do not usually get questions framed in such a basic and compelling way. Recently a chance acquaintance cornered me at a faculty reception to ask how I could possible be against birth control. I had not even brought the subject up, but because I had been introduced facetiously as the "token Catholic" in the department, the question seemed pertinent to my interrogator. I really did not want to get into the nuances of *Humanae Vitae* over coffee, so I used the old professorial ruse of saying that the issue was a very complex one and, um, would you care to try one of these delicious cookies? The alternative was a very unconvincing discourse on something that would appear unintelligible except against the far larger story of Catholicism itself.

It is not unfair to ask about one's position on this or that religious or moral position, but it rarely seems as profitable as the far more basic and illuminating question: How does faith shape the trajectory of one's life? Or, more basically, how does one's faith make a difference? To ask that question is to ask, in somewhat different terms, about one's story. If I were able to tell my story, my questioner might then be in a position to grasp why I might even consider the question of birth control one worthy of discussion. Without my story an interest in the topic might seem either dogmatic or antiquarian or perverse. Questions of value, especially questions of religious value, rarely escape the autobiographical.

There is a keen scholarly interest in autobiography today. From the discussions of that topic one thing stands out rather clearly: Autobiography as a genre is very hard to distinguish from fiction. Unlike a diary autobiography is written after the events of one's life and not coterminous with them. The writer looks back on a life, imposes order on it, and either consciously or unconsciously chooses those elements in life which provide a framework and a direction to that story. Autobiography results from selection and judgments of omission; as such it is a literary invention and a philosophical construction. It is for that reason that Roy Pascal has argued[1] that almost all great autobiography is a kind of theodicy, i.e., a justification of God's dealing with a human life or, less dramatically, a tacit assumption that one's life has a shape and direction.

Human story is a crucial ingredient for the understanding of Christianity. We have the gospels, for example, because people were witnesses to the power of Jesus over their lives. The gospels echo with their celebrative worship of Jesus, their remembrances of him as his story was told in their communities, and as an act of witness for those who were not yet in that community. Story was a form of witness; the post-Easter promise of the Spirit which was to make the early church a witness in Jerusalem, Judea, Samaria, and finally, to the ends of the earth (see Acts 1:8) shaped that story into the form which we now possess. This story was to act as a witness of those who had experienced Jesus as the Christ as well as a promise of what this experience could mean for others.

This sense of witness—this telling of the story—is a very complex one. It involves *my* story as an individual living in the late twentieth century as well as *our* story which is the long story of the tradition of the Christian community. Those stories, in turn, intersect with that of Jesus and our desire to be faithful to what he is and what he represents. One of the reasons why the Catholic tradition treasures its saints is because their lives illustrate the many ways in which the story of Jesus the Christ is absorbed into the living fabric of the church. The memory of the stories of the saints not only illustrates the perennial force of the Jesus story, but serves as an exemplary tradition to show how that story is deepened in the course of time.

True autobiography begins in Western culture with the *Confessions* of St. Augustine written in 397–98 A.D. Augustine's story and his reflections on that story (especially in Book X of the *Confessions*) have exerted an enormous influence on religious thinking in the West. Peter Brown has noted that it is almost impossible for us today to sense how strangely that book must have looked to its first readers.[2] It was not simply a history or a memoir but, as the very title says, a *confession*. The confessional character of the book must be understood at a number of levels. It was a confession of faith in God (*confessio fidei*) and, as such, was addressed to God in prayer. It was a confession of Augustine's sinfulness as a "late lover" of God and, as such, was self-revelatory. Finally, it was a confession of praise to God who graciously shaped Augustine in grace, gave him the truth, and saved him. It was, in short, not Augustine's story so much as a story of God working in Augustine.

As one reads the first nine books of the *Confessions* it is clear that Augustine wrestled with two fundamental problems in his life: the problem of finding intellectual satisfaction for his questing mind and the desire for some surcease from his driving lust. Like many of us, Augustine came to grips with his intellectual problems long before he made peace with his moral ambiguities. We see his early love for the pursuit of wisdom kindled by a reading of Cicero's now lost *Hortensius.* We follow his gradual disenchantment with the Manichees; his debt to the writings of the Neoplatonists; and the decisive influence of Bishop Ambrose of Milan who taught him how to read the scriptures with a "spiritual eye." Yet, along with that

intellectual pilgrimage toward Christ there was another problem: Augustine confesses that his lust for women had gone
beyond habit; it "became a necessity." One aid in the resolution
of that problem was, of course, the example of his friends and
the story of Anthony and the other desert ascetics. Finally, in
a dramatic scene, Augustine is converted. The autobiographical
portion of his story ends with Augustine in the port city of
Ostia awaiting ship to return to Africa to begin his new life.

The *Confessions* initiates a tradition in Christianity by which
people tell their own story in tandem with the story of God to
witness to the power of God over their lives. The sum of those
stories is the living tradition of the church. The centrality of
those stories derives from the innately human impulse to tell
them. They are part of what has been called the narrative
quality of experience. John Shea, who has written widely on
story in a Christian context, makes the point tellingly:

> People are natural narrative beings. They love to tell the stories
> of the experiences that were important to them. Few people
> have the discipline to stay at the "basement level" of interpre-
> tation that the story as story provides. . . . We supply a cognitive
> interpretation along with the narrative line. At this stage the
> attitudes and outlooks in the retelling process are explicitly
> articulated.[3]

Father Shea's point rings true to experience. Quite often
when we tell someone a story, we not only narrate the "facts"
but also try to convey some meaning or some point to the
story. What is true of common experience is all the more true
in religious story. When we narrate our story or that of Jesus,
it is not merely to recall the facts but, somehow, to convey
meaning. That meaning may be drawn out explicitly or it may
be implicit in the nature of the narrative itself. In either case
it is there as a humming bass note giving shape and meaning
to the whole. It is for that reason that the telling and retelling
of my Christian story as well as ours carries with it insight
into the Jesus story since it is against that story that we
measure the meaning of our own. All of our stories, in short,
are the variables which orbit around the constant of the Jesus
story.

My Story

Being faithful to Karl Rahner's insight that theology should begin in anthropology, we begin with the individual historical person in the church and ask: How does this individual tell his or her story, for what purpose, and to whom?

It is clear that there is no simple answer to that question. People tell their stories to a variety of persons and for a variety of reasons. They witness to their belief; they justify who they are and why they act in a certain way; they attempt to persuade or convince; they try to sort out who they are at a time when things get muddled; and so on. There are strong ecclesial motives for the telling of stories. From John Henry Newman's *Apologia Pro Vita Sua* in the last century down to the present day there has been a torrent of books explaining why a person has joined the church (or left it); what the faith has meant in a person's life; or, in these unsteady days after the Second Vatican Council, why one remains in the church despite the turmoil of the times or how one has accommodated to a changed expression of religious living.

For the most part these stories involve public persons. The readers of such accounts are motivated, at least in part, by a desire to know why a person of such eminence is or has become a Catholic Christian or how a religious position has shaped a life. In the hands of a sensitive and reflective person the telling of a story of faith can deeply influence the lives of others. The enormous, worldwide success of the late Thomas Merton's *The Seven Storey Mountain* (as well as his other writings; Merton rarely wrote a book which was not to some extent autobiographical) can be explained only by the fact that Merton, though he was a monk, was a quintessentially modern person whose personal life and pilgrimage were so entwined that they shed light on the human condition for a wide spectrum of modern people. Merton, as Elena Malits has persuasively argued, brought to modern theological consciousness the legitimacy of the quest for self-identity. Sister Malits writes:

> He reintroduced and legitimized the use of "I" in religious inquiry—not just the "I" that represents the individual ego asserting various opinions and making certain claims but also

the searching, probing, receptive, loving "I" that passionately seeks to discover God in the self, in every person, in the whole of creation. The literary context for articulating this quest for and by the true self is, of course, autobiographical narrative.[4]

Merton's autobiographical narrative made him, despite his Trappist hiddenness, a public person. Everyone who is a Catholic Christian—whether public person or not—must ask at one time or another how faith in Jesus Christ either affects or fails to affect the conditions and shape of one's life. At moments in life that question is thrust upon us whether we want it there or not. At times of crisis one cries out, or is tempted to cry out, against the silence of God. At the stages of personal growth inevitable questions of religious commitment arise: What does my inherited childhood religion have to do with my impending marriage or the education of my children or my choice of vocation or the future direction of my life? This conjunction of faith and "my" story becomes critical when there is dissonance or conflict: How does one balance faith and lifestyle (a burning issue for gay Catholics today) or faith and occupation (can I be a conscientious Catholic and work in a weapons factory?) or faith and social behavior (how do I handle my affluence?). In all of these instances what one thinks of one's life stands over against the story of Jesus and the imperatives that flow from that story.

The tensions between these two stories have been institutionalized in the practice of "confession" in the sacrament of penance. It hardly needs to be said that in the contemporary church there has been a fresh approach to an understanding of the sacrament of penance. The vexatious scholarly problems raised by recent research in the sacramental theology of penance need not detain us here. We simply note the conclusions of scholarship by recalling that the sacrament of penance has had a long development in the church and that the notion of the private confessions of sins is only a part of that development, and a late one at that.

For our purposes I want to understand the idea of "confession" in a general way: to stand for those silent or articulated accusations of unworthiness which we make at the beginning of the liturgy when we are invited by the celebrant to "recall our sins to mind" or in those communal penitential rites now more common or in the private act of confession in the sacrament of penance. The wider latitude available to us in the church with respect to confession of sins (we can even think of such activities in the context of spiritual direction) is clear with still more creative options possible. A contemporary sacramental theologian has written:

> . . . The classical private confession is no longer seen as the only possible way to sacramental reconciliation and ethical development; and still less is the aspect of a judicial monologue in the process of reconciliation considered to be the central aspect. The key word "dialogue" takes on in this area as well a central importance; the discussion, the process of reconciliation, which develops between penitent and priest, is characterized by co-operation, a mutually personal dialogue, a kind of "concelebration." And there are some attempts, in theological discussion, to consider a possible renewal of "lay confessions" with an adaptation to the modern situation.[5]

Confession is a kind of storytelling if it manages to go beyond the old habit of merely cataloguing a dreary list of weekly peccadilloes. Such a confession is, at its best, an attempt to scrutinize one's past life in painful honesty in order to see how life is unfolding with reference to Christian commitment. This scrutiny may be done in the context of the sacrament of reconciliation or it may simply be an exercise in spiritual growth. In either case the old practice of the "examination of conscience" is retained, not as a search for sin as much as an attempt to assess the state of a person's life. It is an attempt to say who one is at a certain juncture on life's way.

The silent moments of self-examination and self-accusation which preface the liturgy of the church are regular opportunities to take stock of one's life since the previous time when the community gathered for worship. They are moments which can be—and often are—perfunctory pauses because we are so accustomed to them. It may well require some disciplined reflection* to shape them into something which carried freight

---

* The reader might see here why a discussion of silence is so crucial for the cultivation of spirituality. Disciplined reflection is difficult apart from an appreciation

in our lives. Part of the responsibility at these times may require the pedagogical efforts of the celebrant as well as the attentiveness of the worshipper. That these first moments of the liturgy are squandered is largely the result of insufficient pastoral preparation.

It may happen that a person will see in those reflections elements which require clearer articulation and explicit utterance. The formal sacrament of penance—with its confession of sin and its rite of reconciliation—is a way to concretize those parts of my story which I wish to excise in order to find a fuller community with the church and a firmer sense of reconciliation with God. The sacrament of penance is structured both for ecclesial reconciliation and for surcease from remorse. The fact that such an act is done in a formal, articulated, and ritual fashion corresponds to that deep need we all have for formal recognition of healing the breach. We want to shake hand with those with whom we have quarreled just as we want to hear from those we may have wronged that it's "o.k.—forget it!"

We should also note that along with the weekly round of the Sunday liturgy there are also marked times of the year in which we are urged to think about our stories with some intensity. In the weeks before Christmas (Advent season) and, especially, in the forty days of Lent which precedes the Easter season we prepare for the feasts with a period of self-examination, penance, and a heightened sense of expectation. Because these seasons prepare us for feasts of renewal (they honor both birth and rebirth), we are urged to renewal. Lent is par excellence the penitential season—the time when we most explicitly recognize our failings in order to be "born again" in the paschal mysteries of the resurrection of Jesus. On Ash Wednesday in the liturgy we ask God to "bestow sight to the darkness of sinful eyes" while "bringing us the blessing of forgiveness." In that sacred time of Lent we are urged to take stock in order to begin again. Lent can be seen as the intensification of the

---

of the positive value of spiritual silence. The lack of pastoral direction on the role of silence in the liturgy is to be regretted. For all the recent discussion of silence in spirituality there is little reflection on its links with the liturgical observation of silence.

process which we follow in the liturgy each Sunday. Silence, time, and story come together in a compressed and urgent manner in such periods.

Self-examination, self-accusation, and confession are part of the sacramental rites of reconciliation whose ultimate goals are forgiveness and restoration of amity. We should also recognize, however, that such acts, not necessarily in their liturgical or ritual context, are also part and parcel of that wider growth in Christ which we call "spiritual perfection." There is a long tradition in Christian theology going back into the patristic period which views the progress of a person's prayer life as a series of incremental achievements or stages. The mystical literature of Christianity is replete with images marking ascent. The early Christian writers loved to allegorize and spiritualize the image of Jacob's ladder (see Gen. 28:12ff) as a mysterious sign of spiritual growth. St. Bonaventure in the thirteenth century wrote what many believe to be the paradigmatic medieval treatise on mysticism using as his central notion the idea of ascent. In Bonaventure's title (*The Soul's Journey to God*) we have the image of a journey or a pilgrimage leading up to God after the manner of an ascent.*
In the next century, making ample use of Bonaventure's ideas, Dante depicts himself (who stands for every Christian person) journeying to God through descent and ascent. Indeed, it is possible to read *The Divine Comedy* as a great poetic gloss on the three traditional stages of the spiritual life: purgation (of sin in the *Inferno*); illumination (of the intellect and will in the *Purgatorio*); and union (with God at the apex of the journey in the *Paradiso*).

Dante's great poem may be seen as the expressive summit of medieval Catholicism's understanding of the journey of the soul on the road to perfection, although the theme would be pursued in further centuries as books like St. John of the Cross's *The Ascent of Mount Carmel* witness. For all its complex richness, however, Dante's poem is in the final analysis a story—or, perhaps, given its impact, *the* story—of the Christian pilgrimage complete with the necessary stages by which people

---

* Bonaventure wrote his treatise while living in retreat on Mount Alverna in Tuscany (Italy) where St. Francis of Assisi received his stigmata in 1224.

ultimately find the center and meaning of their life. For all its fundamentally medieval trappings Dante's poem embraces in a large and capacious fashion those two fundamental poles of the pursuit of Christian perfection: knowledge of the self and, through that knowledge, knowledge of God. It is not accidental, I think, that one of the most compelling stories of that search in the modern period, Thomas Merton's *Seven Storey Mountain*, should borrow its title from Dante's *Purgatorio*.

Not all our religious stories are today imagined as an ascent. In an age when the notion of God "up there" and us "down here" has less currency we are more likely to think of our stories along horizontal lines as a quest or a pilgrimage or a journey. This is a notion not alien to Dante (who ends his journey after the vision of God in the *Paradiso* with the image of a pilgrim who has finally arrived at his destination), but the idea has more power for us today. In a study of modern stories of quest[6] (and they are numerous) Mary Jo Weaver has argued that even those secular journeys in literature where the journey involves the discovery of the self, there are certain structural and metaphorical similarities which echo the more ancient spiritual journeys. Both the modern and the ancient journeys are concerned with the loss of the autonomous self; both deal with a sense of displacement which the old spiritual writers called "the dark night of the soul"; there is a spirit of urgency in undertaking and completing the journey; and, finally, a feeling for the intimacy of community as a counterbalance to the restrictions of the individual ego.

To think of "my" story in relation to the Christian one is to think of how the Gospel becomes a part of us and what we are as a result of it. The impulse to tell stories today with greater urgency may spring from our own need for assurance about the power of the Christian story today. We would like to think that the stories we tell somehow guarantee the strength of faith. There is an apologetic value in hearing of the great lives of Christians. The stories of the saints both ancient and contemporary not only edify; they reveal to us the strength of the Christian story to shape and mold us even in these days.

Many of us, however, are not "great" Christians; we know it and, alas, we underestimate our story. I say "alas" because the very texture of every human life is so complex and layered that its story discloses unique riches both about the character of that individual existence and about that existence as enriched in faith. Catholicism insists on the fact that each individual is uniquely precious because each of us is made "in the image of God" and because each of us is to be called to be a child of God. That process of spiritual growth is not of a piece. It is as varied as the human experience itself. Those stories which arise from such spiritual settings are valuable and largely untapped resources for religious insight. I would make my own the remarks of David Tracy in this regard:

> The story each person *is* discloses a human possibility that otherwise might go unremarked. The classic stories disclose the meaning of a life lived in the grip of a classic possibility: real tension and struggle, the lived actuality of hope, tragedy, resignation, fulfillment, justice, love. The particular focus of the fundamental questions in the situation often receive more disclosure from some classic story than from other modes of reflection. . . .[7]

"My" story, then, is not only a confession of failure but a narrative of quest and achievement. It is also a story of disclosure: that illumination which shows the depth and significance of being grasped by faith. It is a story recounted not only to the confessor or the spiritual director; it is a story told to the self and to the community. That story is a small story in that it is my own, but like everything else in the tradition it resonates and gives form to that larger story which is the tradition itself.

Our Story

Our collective story is the tradition of Catholic Christianity as a living memory shaped in history. That history, as exemplified in the standard textbooks, seems clear enough in its widest outline. Generations of historians have attempted to narrate the great events of our past using the dates, movements, and makers of movements as the watershed moments which gave shape to our collective story. That narrative history cannot, and should not, be denigrated or underestimated. In this latter part of the twentieth century we still must wrestle with what the Council of Chalcedon said about Christ in the fifth century just as we must attempt to fully grasp the sea shifts which occurred in our sensibility at the time of the Council of Trent or the French Revolution or the Second Vatican Council. To be ignorant of those events is to be ignorant of who we are today. But that story does not tell all.

We do not possess a history of the Catholic tradition; we are building one. That construction takes place at two distinct levels: the retrieval of the forgotten past and the shaping forces of the present seen as happening.

When we look back on our common history, we tend to look back selectively, i.e., through the lens of our own experience and our own prejudices. Until very recently we seldom looked at women in the tradition. We paid passing tribute to those who were just too important to be ignored (e.g., St. Catherine of Siena or St. Teresa of Avila), but by and large church history was a male enterprise told almost exclusively by males (quickly: name a female church historian who wrote a generation ago) for males. That situation is rapidly changing today as women attempt to retrieve their story in the church. That story is, of course, part of our common tradition, but it is only now being discovered and articulated.

In our search back through the memory of our tradition we get a better sense of who we are as a people at this moment. It is a story not only of the great but of the many whose names we no longer have. The history of the church in the United States, for example, is a relatively short history; it is a fascinating saga and one that is well documented. What has not yet been told with vigor and clarity (even if we somehow know it in our guts) is the mostly anonymous tale of those who were the grit and stuff of the American Catholic experience. That story—our story—would have to include our immigrant parents who built the first urban parishes; the legions of nuns and religious who taught children, sheltered the abandoned, and nursed the sick; the forgotten parish priests who ministered to largely despised congregations of immigrant working class families. The very tone of the American church was forged out

of that rich brew of anonymous sacrifice. It is a microcosm of
the larger reality of the church, but in its unromantic reality
it is particularly our story. We are only now beginning to hear
of it.

Beyond the recapture of that story—which is the story of an
institutional and empirically retrievable church—there is that
other, more difficult, tradition of the evolution of our spirituality; the collective account of the pursuit of the *imitatio
Christi*. It is the story of our saints, not of our doctrines; of
people, not of ideas. The study of the saints (hagiography) is
such a bewilderingly complex field of folklore, mythology,
legend, and fantasy that it is easy to forget that when one
stands back from its complexity there is still the possibility of
detecting the diversely rich styles of the pursuit of Christ in
particular moments of space and time.

For the past decade or so I have been thinking about and
writing on saints and paradigmatic types in the Catholic
tradition.[8] That extended meditation has convinced me that
there is a pressing need for a study of saints using, as a basic
hermeneutic, a focus on the *imitatio Christi*. One approach to
that study would be to raise the simple question: How, and in
what ways, have our paradigmatic figures responded to the
challenge of intensifying Christian identity? How had this
search responded to, and been a shaper of, that person's culture
and history? Such studies would enrich our christology immensely not only at the theoretical, but also at the pastoral
and spiritual, levels. George Tavard, who has made a similar
suggestion with reference to the tradition of mysticism, sees
this issue clearly. He writes:

> But rare seems to be the author who regards the witness of the
> mystics as a valid and valuable resource for the explanation of
> Christ as the center of a permanently contemporary experience.
> Indeed, the thesis of Dietrich Ritschl, that the proper context
> for theological reflection should be the contemporary experience
> of *Christus praesens* has found little echo. The presence of
> Christ has been seen, in recent christologies, as a presence in
> societies, a social presence, rather than a presence within the
> self, a spiritual presence apprehended in the inner life.[9]

Our story of the *imitatio Christi* would not be only of

archaeological interest; it would aid us in understanding how the different foci in the tradition have contributed to the complex reality of Christ that we have inherited today. We cannot think of Christ as the creative word in the same fashion as the Byzantine *Pantocrater* tradition or imagine Christ in his humanity as did the early Franciscans, but both those traditions—as well as many others—have contributed to our grasp of Christ today and still linger in our collective memory.

We cannot escape the historical accretions of our story. It is around us in even the most common experiences we have. Each week when I am at Mass in our local parish, I see a large crucifix over the altar in the sanctuary. It is not a particularly distinguished piece of art. My guess would be that it was carved in one of those numerous ateliers in the Tyrol which supply the religious goods houses of this country. Nonetheless there is a lot of compressed historical sensibility in that carving. The fact that the cross has a corpus on it says that its inspiration does not come from the Eastern tradition which bejewelled its crosses and displayed them without a corpus to emphasize the triumph of Christ over the cross. The carver's emphasis on the "five wounds" derives from an iconography that goes back to the medieval emphasis on the physical suffering of Christ, an emphasis provided largely by the Franciscans (who had the model of the stigmatized Francis himself as an inspiration). The swirling loincloth of Jesus has just a hint of the baroque to it, while the *V* position of the arms of Jesus echoes the classic depictions of the crucified Christ which come out of the tradition of the Spanish tradition of Velasquez. In short, that Christ who appears to a congregation in the 1980s reflects a long accumulated history, told by the memory of artistic tradition, which reflects, in turn, certain changes in the way people thought about and imagined Christ—ways which became valid enough to enter the long memory of the church.

One basic idea that can be learned by a meditation on the styles which can be detected in that parish crucifix is this: Our religious sensibility today is not totally our own; our sensibility as expressed in art, books, persons, and events is polyvalent. The central figure of Jesus Christ cannot be detached from, or viewed in isolation from, the weight of two millennia of reflection and memory. For that reason all of our religious discourse is densely derivative. To understand that and, in turn, to the degree that we recall our tradition we see more of the riches which have been contributed to our drive to penetrate the meaning of the Gospel.

There is some merit in preserving the past as past, but there is the danger that preservation can turn into mummification. If our tradition is to be more than an attic of spiritual relics, it is crucial that we appropriate that tradition as a living memory. To do that demands a constant reference to the past with the questions of the present. We look at stained glass windows depicting the martyrs of the past with their emblematic instruments of torture. We look at those wheels, gridirons, and swords with an understandable degree of detachment. How different our reaction would be if we saw figures in jeans and sweaters who carry with them modern equivalents of torture and humiliation: electrodes, truncheons, mind-altering drugs. We remember the martyrs of the past, but the martyrs of today are as vibrant in their faith and as tortured and humiliated as those who lived in Roman or Elizabethan times. A contemporary martyr like the late Archbishop Oscar Romero (who was shot to death while saying Mass in El Salvador) or the young women who were murdered in that same unhappy country stand in a noble tradition whose memory is now confined to the images of stained glass or plaster. The contemporary martyrs allow us to understand that we are not dealing with remembered history but actuality.

It is worth noting that a recalling of the shared memory of the past keeps us in some state of equilibrium during unsettled periods like our own. Many Catholics seem shaken by the spasms and convulsions of contemporary change. To them the placid traditional culture of Catholicism seems shattered beyond repair. History teaches, however, that the past is not as placid as it appears when viewed as hindsight. The Catholic tradition has always experienced a tension between its sense of continuity and its impulse for change. We do not see that clearly because we are in the midst of our change and feel it at our heel. Only the sensitive and informed historian can recreate for us the perilous condition of the church in the fourteenth century or the despair in Catholic Europe at the fall of the Papal States. Similarly, now that we have canonized him both ecclesiastically and historically, it is difficult to remember that a Thomas Aquinas and much of what he stood for was, in his day, considered revolutionary and dangerous.

The point is this: The experience of being a Catholic today seems uniquely difficult mainly because it is the single experience which we have. Our experience, however, viewed in the larger framework of the flow of the tradition should give some perspective—and one would hope—some serenity about the state of the church as it is actually encountered. At the same time, the reappropriation of the church's memory emboldens us to look for the new with both anxious anticipation and equal serenity. The temptation of the extreme right is to freeze the tradition of the church like a fly in amber in some given past golden age (with an equal demand for only a Tridentine Mass, only a scholastic understanding of the sacraments, only a juridical approach to church polity, etc.). This ossification is as unfaithful to the Catholic experience as that of the extreme left which would jettison the entire past for an experience which is accessible only if it is "now." The Catholic sensibility accepts the past not as baggage to carry along but as potentiality to be utilized in the very act of remembering. That sense of the tradition is the one which is most faithful to those dynamic metaphors of growth and movement which characterize the contemporary church. We are a remembering people who are on pilgrimage, which is to say that we are a people who know from whence we come and where we are going, but at the same time we know that we have not yet arrived.

It has been a commonplace to speak of a development in doctrine since the 1844 publication of John Henry Newman's pathbreaking *Essay on the Development of Christian Doctrine.* We should keep in mind, however, that it is not only doctrine that evolves, that gets clarified, and rethought. There is an evolution in the Catholic experience itself. I do not experience the realities of the faith in the same fashion as did my forebears anymore than I experience those realities in the same way as a contemporary Pole or Argentinian. There has been a development in religious iconography, style of life, national expression, spiritual modes, and so on. If there is an evolution in our approaches to prayer, community living, witness, and so on (and there surely is), it is an evolution precisely because it takes as its starting point the long memory of the church which witnesses both to what is useful and to what must be relegated to history. The long memory of Catholic tradition provides a seedbed for the growth of new ways of being a Catholic Christian.

A final note: Part of remembering our story is to recollect those things which we have either forgotten or repressed. Any tradition as old and variegated as ours will do what we as individuals will do, i.e., conveniently forget or gloss over or put a "good face on" that which is unpleasant or threatening. Free from any obsessive self-laceration it is both possible and crucial to keep alive the underside of our memory if only to serve as an admonition and as a warning for the present. We are better off as Catholics today to the degree that we are unflinching in our acknowledgement of those moments in our past when we have compromised with the powers of the world, used the cross as a banner for war, turned our back on others who had a right to our concern, insisted on rules which crushed or alienated our own.

That darker story also must be told as a direct obligation of Christian responsibility. The Second Vatican Council, perhaps to atone for the church's earlier reticence and resistance to any internal criticism, stated as a principle that the laity and the religious have not only the right to free inquiry and free thought in the realm of the sacred sciences (which would surely include our history), but also the freedom to "express their minds humbly and courageously about those matters in which they enjoy competence."[10] The unnecessary "humbly" rankles a bit; but the principle is crystal clear.

There is another way of forgetting in the Catholic tradition which goes beyond glossing over those nasty popes or venal bishops. One can gloss over, collectively or singly, those in the church who are not in a position to have their voices heard. Today we see vigorous attempts to recall all that which has been forgotten. One of the most conspicuous of those attempts has been the drive to recover the Christian story of women.

At its simplist, feminist thought has been concerned to tell the women's story.

Nothing has brought this forgotten dimension of our tradition home to me with more force and clarity than a simple observation made by Elisabeth Schüssler Fiorenza in the introduction to her compelling work on women and Christian origins:

> In the passion account of Mark's Gospel three disciples figure prominently: on the one hand, two of the twelve—Judas who betrays Jesus and Peter who denies him—and on the other, the unnamed woman who anoints Jesus. But while the stories of Judas and Peter are engraved in the memory of Christians, the story of the woman is virtually forgotten. Although Jesus pronounces in Mark: "And truly I say to you, wherever the gospel is preached in the whole world, what she has done will be told in memory of her" (14:9), the woman's prophetic sign-action did not become part of the gospel knowledge of Christians. Even her name is lost to us. Wherever the gospel is proclaimed and the eucharist celebrated another story is told: the story of the apostle who betrayed Jesus. The name of the betrayer is remembered, but the name of the faithful disciple is forgotten because she was a woman.[11]

The anonymity of that true disciple may stand as a shorthand symbol of all the forgotten women in the church. If we have neglected that story in the past, we must make amends today. There are those who would argue that to be concerned with such issues is a species of "trendiness." I think otherwise. It seems to me that the unfolding of the Catholic tradition is a drive to flesh out the full meaning of the Incarnation of Jesus in time and space. That "fleshing out" does not come easily. Indeed, as we look back over the centuries of the unfolding of the tradition, we see very slow increments of understanding and insight. It took us centuries to understand the true horror of slavery just as it takes centuries to purge out a spirit of antisemitism from the church. I would like to think that the slow growth in the humanization of the Gospel story is, at the same time, a slow growth—borrowing from Teilhard de Chardin—in its christification.

If today there is a stirring among women to make actual the words of St. Paul that in Christ Jesus there is neither male nor female, then we must see the current activity of feminism in church matters as a "sign of the times" (see Chapter 2). To say that such stirrings (and today they are far more potent than mere stirrings) are unsettling is to miss the point. The basic question is whether this movement (and many like this one) represents another small step in the christification of the church. If it is, then we must not only accept it, but work for its full potential. It is from such steps that the tradition becomes more Catholic in the fullest sense of that term.

The Jesus Story

Throughout this volume we have constantly turned to the questions of how Jesus the Christ bridges history so as to make contact with contemporary experience in the church. We have discussed the hearing of that original event as it is proclaimed in space and time; we have considered its ritualization in community; we have sought out the ways in which it is made applicable for lives both individual and social. In all of these considerations we have made constant reference, actual or implied, to the story of Jesus in relation to our story. In that sense this whole work is concerned with the story of Jesus. So, this part of the chapter has been written already; it simply lacks systematic codification.

It remains for us here to insist a bit more explicitly on that person Jesus who, as the theologians say, gave us the concrete expression of what God is like. Whatever the transcendent context of our life may be and however we experience it, we likewise affirm in faith that both that perceived life and its transcendent significance find their fullest meaning only to the degree that they are like the life of Jesus in some manner. The appropriation of that transcendental horizon in our particular life develops to the degree that we can affirm the basic New Testament credo that Jesus is Lord.

The first thing that we might note here is that at a certain basic level the story of Jesus is a simple one in the sense that it orbits around those things which are elemental in existence. When we look at the gospels with wonder, unfettered with either the pretensions of scholarship or the prejudices of the past, we find in Jesus a certain spare quality and a certain elemental vision. Jesus spoke of the gritty details of daily life. In that speaking he reached for that which is easily observable and responded to it with something akin to poetry. His basic concerns were with pain, frustration, anguish, death, human hurts, hunger, thirst, aspirations, the need for justice, and the desire for beauty in life. His language was free from abstractions and rich in metaphor, simile, and example. He told stories to make a point, to unsettle his hearers, to raise an issue. He reached for the visual things: fields, workers, the temple, crowds, food, the humble swirl of the masses, the unnoticed widow or shepherd. Still, as a poet, he saw those things with a freshness and an immediacy that created an urgency which has not paled. As James Mackey has written:

> The same stuff of existence is all around us, land and sea, cattle and fowl and fruit trees, bread and wine, oil and energy, and people. And the Spirit which Jesus breathed into a dying world is still present in books and buildings, in lectures and rituals, and above all in patterns of living and in people; still pointing to the invitation issued in every existing thing and event, and enabling us to respond.[12]

Even the death of Jesus is not alien to our existence and its experience. His death, degrading though it was, resonates in our minds and imaginations because of every terrible, unjust, wasteful death we know about. We see that death in every abused child, abandoned mother, victim of war or famine or official injustice.

The simplicity and the resonance of the Jesus story break down, of course, in the fact of the resurrection: that Easter faith which proclaims that Jesus was raised up by God "on the third day." The working out of the implications of that Easter faith is central to the Christian life. It is crucial for the Jesus story. When the Acts of the Apostles (see 10:36–41; 13:23–25; and the short kerygmas like Rom. 1:1–4; 1 Cor. 15:3ff.) sets forth the short credo of the early church about the resurrection, it is, as it were, the statement of a charter by which the future story of Jesus develops (and will develop) both in its complexity and in its relevancy. Frans Jozef van Beeck writes apropos of Acts 10:

This short summary of Jesus's life clearly has a triple agenda. The first one is to state that the telling of the story is a testimonial invocation warranted by the resurrection. The second one is that the life of Jesus was a climactic journey, marked by goodness to others and struggles with the powers that be, and ending in final rejection followed by divine vindication. Third, the implication for the church is that the story of Jesus provides her with a programmatic parallel to her own life; the story becomes the charter for the church's imitation of Christ.[13]

It is out of that triple matrix which van Beeck outlines that we can affirm the story of Jesus as significant story. In the resurrection faith of the church, then, we have the legitimacy to tell the story of Jesus not merely as historical memory but as reality. In that telling we have the charter for the church and its essential mission. Since the resurrection story posits a *more* to life than the extension wrought by death, we can see that the ordinariness of life becomes enriched with potentiality and promise. Life takes on a thicker texture so that we can express our life not only as something being lived now, but as something which has a thrust to the future.

The paradox of the Jesus story is that it ends with a beginning. We follow his life through the crucifixion which seems to mark off the trajectory of a life—attractive though it was—of failure. The fact of the resurrection then "bends back" to give that life new meaning and a new significance. The current of biblical scholarship which sees much of the Gospel story as a product of the resurrection faith of the early church may not only be expressing a conclusion of scientific exegesis but an insight of genuine theological richness. It gives a deep faith meaning to the Jesus story as we have it in the gospels.

There is, then, in the Jesus story a central sense of renewal and retrieval. What Jesus did and said had meanings for its own time and in its own right, but acquired new textures and applications in the light of his triumph over death. In the listening to the Jesus story we look back and we look forward. It is in that dual movement that we find the link between the Jesus story and those two stories which we have discussed earlier in this chapter. We look back on our personal story as an act of purifying remembrance and as a preparation for looking forward. It is for that reason that we have insisted that the confessional part of penance (and confession conceived of in the widest possible sense) must be seen not as something new but as a graced possibility for the new; another moment of *metanoia*—conversion. That, of course, underlies all of the classic strategies of self-scrutiny from Augustine's introspective confessions to the Ignatian particular examen to the current interest in journal keeping, spiritual direction, and so on. "Confession" must not be seen in isolation from the direction of one's spiritual life broadly conceived.

This sense of the story of the self in tandem with our communal story and the story of Jesus cannot be relegated to a kind of ego-centered experience. One of the great insights of contemporary theology is its insistence that such a rigorous examination of the self in relation to the story of Jesus should result in a "bad conscience" with respect to the plight of the poor and the alienated of the world. We cannot privatize our religious development. That point has been made throughout this work, but it bears repeating. It would be one of the worst manifestations of "me" religion to think solely in terms of my perfection, my advancement, or my salvation. We are part of a larger story and without that story our own is insignificant and inauthentic.

It may be that we pass from "guilty conscience" to an actual encounter with those who cry for help. We may not have the privilege of working in the barrios of Latin America, but even in our limited middle-class life we find people who are enslaved by drug dependency or women who are abandoned or children who need direction or aid. Those opportunities are always around us. To reach out to those people is also part of the development of our spirituality. It is an integral part of it. Denis Edwards has written:

> ... Such moments of encounter can be truly times of grace in our lives, times when we are given the mysterious gift of knowing the Holy One in this person before us.
>
> In the encounter with the poor we learn something about life, about what it is to be a man or a woman, about our stance before God. There is something, a Word of God, that can be heard only from the "little ones" of the earth. The living contact

with the poor brings us to a sense of our own poverty and of our common humanity.[14]

Our common story—the history we are in process of making—is central to this enlarged sense of social meaning in the construction of our life story. It is from the memory of the church that we receive cautionary tales, seek for models of being, look for clues for fleshing out our desires to change bad conscience to encounters, and sense solidarity with the communion of believers which exists both in time and in space. When we have a sympathetic conjunction of my story and the common story which is our story and the story of Jesus, we are deepening the meaning of the word *Catholic* in a full and rich manner.

Points for Meditation

1. Have you ever tried to reconstruct your life in faith by a systematic reflection on those "graced moments" which led you to where you are today as a Catholic Christian?

2. What most edifies you and discourages you about the Catholic tradition?

3. From what in the tradition have you most benefitted in your own life? Which models and heros/heroines have you derived most benefit?

4. If you were to tell a single story from the larger story of Jesus as a summary statement of what he means for you, which story would you choose?

5. What story about yourself would you like to tell to those closest to you which would give some sense of the place of your faith and your life as a Catholic Christian (or a searcher after faith)?

Notes

1. Roy Pascal, *Design and Truth in Autobiography* (Cambridge: Harvard University Press, 1960). For other studies, see Lawrence S. Cunningham, "Religion and Autobiography: A Bibliographical Note," *Horizons* 5 (1978) 211–14.

2. Peter Brown, *Augustine of Hippo* (London: Faber and Faber, 1967), pp. 158ff.

3. John Shea, *An Experience Named Spirit* (Chicago: Thomas More, 1983), pp. 106–7. For a theology of story Father Shea's earlier work is important: *Stories of God* (Chicago: Thomas More, 1978) and *Stories of Faith* (Chicago: Thomas More, 1980).

4. Elena Malits, *The Solitary Explorer: Thomas Merton's Transforming Journey* (San Francisco: Harper and Row, 1980), p. 155.

5. Alexandre Ganoczy, *An Introduction to Catholic Sacramental Theology* (Ramsey, N.J.: Paulist, 1984), p. 122.

6. Mary Jo Weaver, "Quest for Self/Quest for God," in *The Bent World: Essays on Religion and Culture*, ed. John R. May (Chico, Calif.: Scholars Press, 1981), pp. 177–90.

7. David Tracy, *The Analogical Imagination* (New York: Crossroad, 1981), p. 275.

8. Lawrence S. Cunningham, *The Meaning of Saints* (San Francisco: Harper and Row, 1980) and *The Catholic Heritage* (New York: Crossroad, 1983).

9. George Tavard, "The Christology of the Mystics," *Theological Studies* 42 (1981) 561. The book Tavard refers to is D. Ritschl's *Memory and Hope* (1967).

10. *Pastoral Constitution on the Church in the Modern World*, art. 62 in *Documents of Vatican II*, p. 270.

11. Elisabeth Schüssler Fiorenza, *In Memory of Her: A Feminist Theological Reconstruction of Christian Origins* (New York: Crossroad, 1983), p. xiii.

12. James P. Mackey, *Jesus: The Man and the Myth* (Ramsey, N.J.: Paulist, 1979), p. 261.

13. Frans Jozef van Beeck, *Christ Proclaimed: Christology as Rhetoric* (Ramsey, N.J.: Paulist, 1979), p. 345.

14. Denis Edwards, *Human Experience of God* (Ramsey, N.J.: Paulist, 1983), p. 79.

Selected Readings

Baum, Gregory, ed. *Journeys*. Ramsey, N.J.: Paulist, 1976. An anthology of autobiographical essays by contemporary Catholics.

Dunne, John. *Time and Myth*. Garden City: Doubleday, 1973. A profound meditation on personal story and spirituality.

Navone, John. *Tellers of the Word*. New York: Jesuit Educational Center, 1981. An attempt to develop a theology of story.

Pelikan, Jaroslav. *The Vindication of Tradition*. New Haven: Yale University Press, 1984. An evocative meditation on the value of tradition and its memory.

Wiggins, James, ed. *Religion as Story*. New York: Harper and Row, 1975. An uneven but useful collection of essays.

7

PERSONS

In writing to the church at Corinth, St. Paul catalogues a short list of ministries which the Corinthians know:

> God has appointed in the church first apostles, second prophets, third teachers, then workers of miracles, then healers, helpers, administrators, speakers in various kinds of tongues. . . . (1 Cor. 12:28)

I said that this was a "short list" because elsewhere in the New Testament there are other terms to designate other offices and roles for persons in the church. There are both those designations for the collectivity of believers (e.g., a royal priesthood, the household of the faith, the saints, etc.) as well as ministries such as deacons, *episcopi*, presbyters, and so on. In the early development of the church the designation of personal and collective roles for persons in the church took on the look of a bewildering catalog: widows, martyrs, ascetics, confessors, monks, nuns, hermits, *conversi*, catechumens, exorcists, lectors, *fossores*, acolytes, subdeacons, prelates of various stripes and degrees. Behind each of these designations there is a whole freight of historical meaning and development as the church designated certain defined roles for people or, conversely, people defined certain roles for themselves. They are roles which filled a need for the work of the church in a given time.

We see such roles still being created and/or suppressed today in the name of the church's mission. In my own parish there are official or quasi-official roles for people which simply did not exist when I came here twenty years ago: readers at the liturgy; eucharistic ministers; married deacons; a woman chaplain to the hospital sick who serves as an extraordinary minister of the Eucharist; etc. We also see the emergence of another reality which, borrowing from a larger social phenomenon, has been called a "Catholic knowledge elite"—those clerics or (more frequently) laypeople who function either in church bureaucracies or close to them who offer themselves as people with skills and/or knowledge as journalists, strategists, lobbyists, commentators, and so on. Their views of the church and its mission may run from the extreme right to the extreme left, but their purported right to advise the church comes, not from ordination, commission, or religious virtuosity, but from their possession of useful knowledge and professional skills. In my home town they labor as professional journalists, as spokespeople for the local dioceses to the state legislature, as social workers, and as university professors.

Many people in the history of the church who have enjoyed special vocational designations have filled either functional positions (their office was needed for this or that purpose) or positions which were seen as part of the church's essential makeup (the episcopacy or the priesthood) or because of some charism that was seen as coming from grace as in the case of the nun or ascetic. All such offices, however, appeal to some theological justification derived from the mission of church life to cherish and proclaim the Good News—the Gospel. Under certain circumstances this or that person functions so well and with such clear reference to the church's mission that those persons take on a paradigmatic value or symbolic value which both enhances their role and provides indications for others as to how it should be fulfilled. That role, of course, is tied to that special elite in the history of the church whom we designate as saints.

Saints have many and varied roles in the total context of the church: they act as conduits of grace: they function as penitential surrogates: they are intercessors. Beyond these traditional designations, however, they also act as paradigms for others. The church, in effect, singles out some individuals and says to them that they are models to emulate or against which one may measure the seriousness of the Christian life. This "singling out" is done with varying degrees of success. In the case of patron saints, for example, St. Apollinia is protectress of dentists not because of her orthodontic skills but because her pagan tormentors tore out her teeth (on reflection, not a very reassuring choice), while St. John Vianney is patron of parish priests because he was a zealous pastor and parish priest.

When the church singles out a person for his or her paradigmatic qualities (by canonization, for instance) or when people in the church instinctively honor such a person even without official warrant (as they surely do in the case of a Dorothy Day or Thomas Merton or Teilhard de Chardin), the implied warrant for that recognition is the insights that such a person's life provides for one's own personal spiritual development. The life of Dorothy Day gives us clues about the blend of deep traditional piety and radical social activity; the late Archbishop Romero's life and death give the ring of contemporaneity to the venerable title of "martyr"; the late Pope John XXIII demonstrated how peasant simplicity, shrewd political and religious insight, and the trappings of power could coexist without corruption. As Karl Rahner has written, it is the role of the saint to teach us that even *in this way* one can live as a Christian.

The paradigmatic person keeps a foot in the past and the present as he or she looks to the future. The link to the past permits us to see the person as identifiably Catholic. Presence in the here and now exemplifies the adaptability of the Catholic memory to the exigencies of the changing cultural situation of human history. The look to the future is an act of faith (at times, a heroic act) in the strength and permanency of the Christian life in this or that form.

In this regard, some remarks of Raimundo Panikkar are pertinent. Speaking about monasticism, Panikkar has argued that the monk (in the sexually inclusive sense) is a universal religious archetype not because everyone is called to the monastery but because one way to fulfill the task of being truly human must take into account monkhood. His point is both subtle and simple: The monk is not the paradigm of human life, but it is one valid way of being fully human. Obviously, one easy way to be a monk is to join a monastic group, but we should not mistake such groups or institutions for the values which they were erected to protect. Monasticism finds its "locale" in monasteries, but the monastic dimension of life is far wider than their locales:

> Inasmuch as we try to unify our lives around the center, all of us have something of the monk in us. This center, by virtue of being a center, is immanent to the human being; but, at the same time, by virtue of being as yet unattained, it is transcendent. We should bear in mind that we are not speaking of any specific monastic institution, in any specific religion, but rather of the anthropological dimension. Monasticism is not a specifically Christian, Jaina, Buddhist, or sectarian phenomenon; rather it is a basically human and primordially religious one.[1]

Panikkar, then, argues that the monk provides an insight into the meaning of being human in a religious way. It would appear that one entry point into an understanding of the Catholic spirit would be to inquire into the values of those paradigmatic figures in the church who crystallize certain "types" and ask what values such persons reflect. To do that fully demands that we take into account the historicity of that person's life and then seek at a deeper level to uncover what values might enrich our own contemporary situation. We need to approach such figures with pertinent questions. To borrow from Andrew Greeley's language about doctrine: We need to ask questions which respond to a new agenda rather than an old one.[2]

In a somewhat analogous fashion we can ask "new" agenda questions about paradigmatic persons in the church. In the broadest fashion the questions are not why the church venerates saints, but what values does such a focus on saints derive from such a veneration? We inquire, in that fashion, about the appeal of a St. Vincent de Paul or why St. John of the Cross influenced so many people with so many diverse agendas or why, in our time, Charles de Foucauld could attract so many people to what appears on the surface to be such an arduous lifestyle.

This is a very broad topic and one that cannot be satisfactorily dealt with in detail. As an issue, however, it is richly pertinent to our lives. One's Catholicism is closely bound up with its representative pantheon. In the reformed tradition—just to provide a stark contrast—official honor is paid alone to those biblical figures who are inseparable from the notion of *scriptura sola;* it is a visible contrast to the Catholic tradition.* Catholicism widens that plane to take into account saints, canonized and uncanonized, as well as other religious virtuosi (monks, nuns, religious, etc.) who "specialize" in an intense life of Christian spirituality and service. Those figures can serve in the words of David Tracy as "classics" of the Catholic experience: "Beneath all our necessary suspicions of, even destruction of the sentimentalizing, mythologizing, hagiographical "lives" of the saints, lies the power of these lives to disclose their singular truth: the truth of a life lived on the wager that only the paradigmatic is real."[3]

Mary as Symbol

Some years ago the Lutheran theologian Wolfhart Pannenberg observed that whereas christology is the developed reflection on a historical event (the Incarnation), mariology is a developed reflection on a response to that event. As such, Mary's significance for Christian theology is more in the realm of symbol than in history.

A long look at the Catholic tradition would seem to bear that out as a fair generalization. Popular Marian piety, religious iconography on Mary, even doctrinal formulations over the centuries derive either from the demands of orthodoxy (e.g., the definition of Mary as *Theotokos* at the council of Ephesus in the fifth century derived from christological, not mariological, speculations) or to express certain symbolic truths which are pertinent to the spiritual life of others in the church: Mary as symbol of the church; Mary as Virgin Mother; Mary as Servant; Mary as the symbol of the *anawim;* Mary as New Eve; etc.

Devotion to Mary is an ancient and characteristic part of the

---

* Like all generalizations, this is only *mostly* true; the paradigmatic tradition in the Reformation is conspicuous in such things as Foxe's *Book of Martyrs* or the Reformation Monument in Geneva.

Catholic tradition. Already in the third century, before the era of persecution was over, we see depictions of Mary holding the Christ child in the catacombs of Domitilla in Rome. A century earlier Justin Martyr was writing about Mary as the New Eve in order to expand and give a sense of symmetry to the Christ/Adam pairing of St. Paul. By the time of Christian emancipation in the fourth century there was already in place a developing mariology and a liturgical cult dedicated to the Virgin. That tradition would nourish a strain of Catholic religiosity which would erupt into major manifestations in periods like that of the Gothic cathedrals to post-Tridentine (and anti-Reformation) devotionalism. That mariological spirit would reach its apogee with the twin definitions of the Immaculate Conception in the last century and the doctrine of the Assumption in 1950. Only the more integrated mariology of the Second Vatican Council (the treatise on Mary was put into the context of the dogmatic constitution on the church rather than publishing it as a separate document as some of the fathers wished) would rein in the more exuberant forms of mariological speculation.

The persistent phenomenon of marilogical devotion (however much it has been attenuated today) is a hallmark of the Catholic tradition. It can be seen as one fundamental way in which the church has used a person to symbolize what it sees as the blueprint for a relationship with Jesus. In that sense it is central to an understanding of the church as it comes to grips with its central purpose as guardian and disseminator of the Christian mysteries.

At the same time it should be recognized that all of mariology cannot be explained simply by recourse to the founts of revelation. Its origin in historical Christianity must be understood, at least in part, in the light of the Mediterranean world's reluctance to give up the feminine element in religion as it confronted the patriarchal religion of the Bible. It would be a vulgar reductionism to equate Marian devotion to the cult of the pagan *Terra Mater* or *Magna Mater*, but it would be fatuous to deny that it was from the humus of pagan religious ideas and practices that Marian devotion took nourishment. The evidence is palpable. A church name like that of Santa Maria sopra Minerva in Rome can stand as a shorthand description of what I am saying: the church of St. Mary was built over a shrine to Minerva, but at the symbolical level the Virgin triumphs over Minerva. Anyone who has walked through a museum in Italy looking at Roman religious statuary and then the Christian painting collection gets the point quickly. Mary supplanted the pagan goddesses.

That is not to say, however, that Mary became a divinity or a demidivinity in the Catholic tradition even though certain excesses of devotionalism would seem to warrant such a conclusion. What one can conclude, however, is that Christianity in its Catholic formulation was often experienced in feminine terms even when all the necessary theological distinctions were firmly in place. The observations of Elisabeth Schüssler Fiorenza seem quite correct to me:

> Even though any Catholic school child can explain on an *intellectual theological* level the difference between the worship of God and Christ and the veneration of Mary on an *emotional, imaginative, experiential* level the Catholic child experiences the love of God in the figure of a woman. Since in later piety Jesus Christ became so transcendentalized and divinized that his incarnation and humanity are almost totally absorbed into his divinity, the "human face" of God is almost solely experienced in the form of a woman. The cult of Mary thus grew in proportion to the gradual repatriarchalization of the Christian God and Jesus Christ. The Catholic tradition gives us thus the opportunity to *experience* the divine reality in the person of a woman.[4]

That is a positive assessment of Mary; it underscores a traditional element which is fundamental to an understanding of her place in Catholic piety. True to her powerful symbolic energy, however, Mary has become in our own time a symbolic lightning rod for all manner of dissatisfactions, both of the right and the left, in the church.

A good deal of the modern interest in Mary has been seen by many scholars as a direct repudiation of the modern world. Marian manifestations ranging from the definition of the Immaculate Conception in the last century to the many apparitions of Mary at places like Fatima in Portugal, Knock in Ireland, La Salette and Lourdes in France have been interpreted as a sign of the church's intransigence with the post-Enlightenment spirit of European culture. It is as if the church was saying to the modern world that the sacred does break through to the human plane; that the truly pious (inevitably unlettered peasants who were even the butt of clerical skepticism) still hold extended colloquies with the dramatis personae of salvation history; that the church can still resist the blandishments of a liberal view of religion, the pretensions of the modern secular state, and the irreligious forces of modernity. It is not accidental that the salutary warnings of Fatima were much concerned with atheistic communism and godless political behavior.

In an earlier era like the Gothic Age most Marian piety came from the genuine folk piety of the laity, but in the modern world it has been the papacy, battered both by the liberalism of the Risorgimento, the inroads of modernism, and the crumbling hegemony of the older claims of Western Christian culture, that has most energetically promoted Marian piety. That has been true of every pope since Pius IX, and with a Slavic twist, is powerfully true of the current pontiff, John Paul II. His devotion to Mary (his motto is *Totus Tuus*—"All for Thee," i.e., Mary) is inexplicable except against the background of the Polish understanding of Mary as the "Queen of Poland." She is a symbol of the unity of *Polonia* and, in its recent history, a powerful countersign to the pretensions of the communist state. Mary as energizing symbol is, and has been historically, a symbol of unity and resistance. George Hunston Williams, one of the best interpreters of the Polish pontiff, has written:

> Marian shrines are numerous in the countryside and in the mountains. In the devotion to Poland, martial and maternal feelings intermingle. Poland is felt to be both fatherland and motherland, although the Pope uses the latter designation almost exclusively. The whole of his land is the Garden of the New Eve, Queen of Poland.[5]

Those expressions of piety and devotion, no matter how extravagant they may seem to some ears, are well within the bounds of Catholic orthodoxy. They are national expressions, culturally based, of basic truths about Catholic mariology. To

see the full force of Mary's symbolic role as a conservator of
the status quo or as critic of modernity it is helpful to look
briefly at those groups at the fringe of right wing orthodoxy
who use the Virgin as a rallying point for resistance to modern
trends both in and outside the church. One extended example
might help.

In the early 1970s a New York housewife, Veronica Leuken,
began to report a series of apparitions of the Blessed Virgin
Mary after the tragic death of a teenage son. The church
authorities were not sympathetic to her claims and have been
noncooperative with respect both to the claims of Mrs. Leukens'
devotees and the devotional offshoots which surround the
visionary. Despite such official resistance the devotees of the
"Bayside apparitions" (named for the area of Long Island, New
York, where they occur) remain enthusiastic and faithful. What
is most interesting about the whole phenomenon is the content
of the revelations which Veronica Leukens reports.

According to a book compiled by a promotor of this group,[6]
the Blessed Virgin Mary, in her talks with Veronica Leukens,
has commented on—and this is only a partial list—the following: the evil of rock music groups, the loss of Latin in the
liturgy, communion in the hand (against); altar rails being
removed from churches and kneeling for communion (in favor);
priestly resignations (they will never get to heaven); the liturgy
as a meal (heresy); the scandalous behavior of modern nuns;
the lack of discipline in seminaries; immodest clothing; Masons
and ecumenical religous groups (against); the decline in the
use of traditional sacramentals like scapulars, holy water, and
so on. In other words, the Bayside revelations are a veritable
shopping list of conservative grievances against the post-
Vatican II church. The more sensational claims of the revelations include the firmly held conviction that the real Pope Paul
VI was held as a prisoner and that an imposter took his place
in the final few years of his life and that Pope John Paul I was
murdered by a cabal of Vatican intriguers (also a claim made
by a tendentiously silly book published in 1984). To give
ominous weight to the veracity of the revelations it is often
noted in the circles of Bayside that Veronica's pastor, who
regarded her as a hysteric, died suddenly and unexpectedly.

For the alienated Catholics of the right Mary is a prophetic figure calling the church back to fidelity and away from the traps of modernity. Mary as revealed at Bayside is a symbol of alienation and dissatisfaction. She serves that same function for many on the left, especially those who have analyzed her role from a feminist perspective. Often it has been alleged that the deep antifeminine element inherent in Christianity has been mitigated somewhat because of the deep-rooted devotion to Mary in the Catholic tradition. That argument is rejected as unsatisfactory by a number of feminist thinkers. Writers ranging from popularizers like Marina Warner to academic scholars like Rosemary Reuther have argued that the cult of the Virgin has been too much in control of a patriarchically organized and controlled church who have manipulated Marian imagery for its own ends. A woman who is exalted as "Virgin Mother" is a woman who, while fulfilling the unique role of child bearer, is, at the same time, "dephysicalized," i.e., Mary's sexuality is neutered by a systematic reduction of emphasis on those aspects of femininity which seem to threaten male, especially celibate male, power: physicality, eroticism, sexuality, and the energies which flow from those functions. Furthermore, these scholars argue, far too much emphasis has been placed on Mary's submissiveness ("Thy will be done"), her domesticity (the Holy Family), and her passivity.[7]

As a consequence of the above critique some feminist scholars and writers simply dismiss Mary as an irrelevant contemporary religious symbol. Others, most notably some scriptural scholars, have begun a massive reexamination of the scriptural data in order to recover Mary's place in the faith of the earliest Christian communities by a detailed study of those highly theologized images of Mary in the New Testament. If there is one area where older and newer, more radical views, coincide, it is in the conviction that the Marian texts of the New Testament carry with them a deeper meaning than is first apparent by a too simplistic and surface reading of the text.

That new scriptural orientation dovetails rather nicely with the work of contemporary liberation theologians who write about the symbolic power of the person of Mary from two perspectives: One is the role of Mary in the popular religion of the poorest persons like those pilgrims who so assiduously visit the shrine of Our Lady of Guadalupe in Mexico and the other is the symbol of Mary as representative of the righteous poor who, in God's good time, will triumph over powers of oppression and gain the justice promised to them by the good news of the Kingdom ("He has put down the mighty from their thrones, and exalted those of low degree," Lk. 1:52–53). Mary then becomes a symbol, not of passivity, but of open-ended hope, consolation, and potential power for the powerless of the world. Harvey Cox, in his recent study of post-modern theology, has come to appreciate this side of folk religion; apropos of the power of the Virgin of Guadalupe and her cult he writes:

> A poor person, she inspires the hopes of all those who believe that God is preferentially present in the lives of the disinherited. An echo of a pre-Christian goddess she reminds us of the larger and older family of faith of which ours is a part. A victim of clerical manipulation, she recalls the destructive role churches have often played in perpetuating injustice and in robbing the dispossessed of their most valuable symbols of identity and hope. It is hard to imagine a more potent symbol for that *fuerza* from the edges and from the bottom which must ultimately create both the theology and the religion of the post-modern world.[8]

The Silent Ones

The historically conditioned emphasis on the church as a hierarchical one has made it inevitable that a theological truth should also turn into a sociological one. If the visible church is conceived as a pyramid with the pope at the apex and the laity forming the baseline, it is natural enough to think of the pope as higher, which, in vulgar parlance, easily becomes better. The papacy is not insensitive to the possibility of that shift and, as a consequence, has abrogated to itself the title of "servant of the servants of God" and uses the symbolism of the pope washing the feet of twelve poor men (never women!) on Holy Thursday to indicate that the pope's office does not exempt him from that humility and lowliness exemplified by Christ. Despite such symbolism the notion of higher and lower has deep roots in the Catholic tradition. The large-scale attempt to root out clericalism from the church, for example, is an attempt to retain the role of the ordained minister without the concomitant status of cleric as better. Despite such attempts such class distinctions still exist. The sad nature of that division was bluntly summed up by the odious Monsignor Talbot (Cardinal Manning's "man" in the Vatican and an implacable foe of Newman) in the last century. Commenting privately on Newman's argument about the role of the laity in the formulation of doctrine, Talbot said crisply that the duty of the laity was to "pray, pay, and obey."

Class distinction in the church reflected, historically, the more general class distinctions in culture as a whole. For example, it would have been natural enough for a feudal society to understand the church in the same fashion as it understood civil society: a rigidly hierarchical structure with aristocrats and plebeians in a proper and ascending place, the lower owing fealty to the higher. While bold speech (parrēsia) and prophetic utterance might be recognized as coming from God—and, thus, a Catherine of Siena could chide a pope for lack of zeal or a Bernard of Clairvaux could warn a potential pope about dangers to his soul from the office—such utterances were regarded as extraordinary departures from the norm. While popes might come from peasant stock (as did both Pope Pius X and John XXIII in our day) and saints from the lumpenproletariat (Benedict the Moor was born a slave; Martin de Porres was an illegitimate mestizo; Benedict Joseph Labre a beggar), these must not be seen as normative. Careful researches have shown that most canonized saints came either from what we would call the middle class or the upper classes.[9]

The tensions of class and rank have always been a part of the church and probably will always be there in one form or another. Today, for example, in a prosperous church like that of the American one, the tensions show up not so much as conflicts between clergy and laity as they do between knowledge elites and the nonelites, i.e., the "people in the pew."

With that sociological admission in mind we must also insist that there are theoretical and evangelical resources to resist the more egregious and damaging of those class distinctions as well as a mandate rooted in the Gospel to do so. We begin with those basic articles of belief which are at the root of the Catholic faith: All are sinners; all have been called to salvation;

anterior to the service of ministry is the vocation of being followers of Christ; the paradigm of the early church as a pilgrimage and a way open to all who wish to be part of the people of God; the universal need for repentance. Together with those bedrock doctrines are compelling reasons which spring from the church's call to evangelize: Class and rank pervert or stall the church's mission; the church loses insights into its own message when it refuses to hear those who do not enjoy privilege for reason of sex or status or lack of access to the power of advanced cultures. All of these factors allow, indeed demand, that the forgotten of the earth be heard and, what is more, shape the character of the church's presence in the world.

Before we entertain distinctions (however valid) between clergy/laity or "more perfect states" of life or lay/religious, there is the fundamental theological fact that all share equally in the redemptive work of Jesus Christ. The Second Vatican Council's insistence on the notion of the "people of God" provides a horizontal view of all humanity called to Christ. From that perspective there is not only no distinction between male or female or Gentile and Jew but none between pope and peasant or cardinal and working class woman: "As members, they share a common dignity from their rebirth in Christ. They have the same filial grace and the same vocation to perfection. They possess in common one salvation, one hope, and one undivided charity."[10]

From that conviction, forcefully restated in our century by the Second Vatican Council, those silent ones in the church— the women, the church of the non-European world, the minorities—have seen that horizontal view of Christianity as an affirmation of their rights and as an obligation to speak for them. While it is common to see that speaking out as nothing more than a torrent of carping criticism, it is much more than that. Those who have felt neglected, ignored, or oppressed in the church itself now possess the warrant in the post-Vatican II church to speak for their rights in the church. This is as it should be; if it brings some dissent and shrillness into the halls of Catholicism, it is a small price to pay for the long-range benefits which will accrue from openness.

As one whose religious upbringing came on the eve of the

council (I was a theological student in Rome when Pope John announced his intention to convene the council), there was nothing from my early experience which would lead me to think about "rights" or open speech with respect to church matters. I was taught only to think of obligations. The events of the past two decades have quite simply shattered my complacent view of Catholicism as a comfortable subculture which caters to my spiritual needs while providing me with a worldview which is consistent, not irrational, and comprehensive. The voices of those who have been long silent in the church have radically changed my notions of what the church is and what it should be. My suspicion is that this is not an experience unique to myself. What has happened, simply put, is that we have *learned*. The voice of the silent ones is not only prophetic but instructive.

That point requires emphasis. The voice of the silent ones in the church is not simply a voice of criticism demanding this or that reform. It is, above all, a *teaching* voice. The church possesses, but is not in full possession of, the revelation of Jesus who is the Christ. In its long history it both cherishes and tries to deepen its understanding of that revelation. It does that both by responding to heterodox proposals about that revelation (as Newman argued in his studies on the development of dogma in the last century) and through the "breakthroughs" of those people of prayer, reflection, and Christian action who have extended the meaning and application of the Christian faith.

Today, more eloquently than ever, people of good will in the church learn from the great swelling of wisdom coming from those neglected women religious, layfolks, peasant activists, reformers, martyrs, and heros/heroines who in the past seemed to be merely background for the writing of church history. Today they have found their voice and they teach the church hard lessons.

What is their message? What do we learn?

First, that we have to "desanitize" the ordinary ideological reading of the Gospel which has permitted us to see Jesus as only a slightly more idealized version of our own best self. However difficult it may be for us to learn that lesson within a tradition whose art, architecture, theology, devotionalism, and habit have dwelt on high christology, we need search for and take account of the Jesus whom the silent ones see: the Jesus who travelled in bad company. This is the Jesus who had prostitutes for friends, who was a thorn in the side of the religious and social establishment, who rejected the *bien pensants* of his day, who was a disturber of the peace, and, let us be reminded, a convicted felon who spent a night on death row before a public execution.

The silent ones remind us that Jesus said some very tough and unpleasant things: that if a poor person demanded a coat, we should add something to that demand; that those who hurt us badly should be forgiven; that one had to give up, not a good deal, but everything to be fully worthy of him. The silent ones, in short, tell us that at the heart of the Gospel is not only sweetness and light, but disappointment, sorrow, sacrifice, the cross—and the hope of triumph over all these things.

This reading of the Gospel does not demand that everyone who is a Catholic must turn into a radical activist or a rigid sectarian resisting the world. What it most emphatically does mean, however, is that we must be open to the challenges which the signs of the times bring us. Part of that willingness to read the "signs of the times" is the implied openness to listen to what those of a different color, sex, disposition, or social class have to say when they make a claim on the Gospel as part of the people of God. A radical reading of the Gospel imposes simple yet profoundly difficult tests on our faith: can we love and affirm those to whom we ordinarily show, at best, indifference, and, at worst, open hostility? Can we stretch out beyond what we are and what we want to embrace, not only the discomforts of the Gospel, but its promise of the cross?

It is pertinent, in this regard, to recall that those figures who have so lucidly incarnated the meaning of the Catholic experience in our time have been those who have best illustrated that reading of the Gospel. Whether it be a missionary reaching out to the poorest of the poor or the Little Brothers and Sisters of Jesus living contemplative lives in our worst modern urban deserts or Jean Vanier providing community for the mentally and physically handicapped or a Perez-Esquivel laboring for human rights in Latin America or those unknown saints in the gulags and prisons of the world, the message is the same: the love of Christ compels and the compulsion is beyond that which, by nature, we are ready to accept.

Those are heroic acts for the sake of the Gospel. There are others who live quieter, less spectacular lives, who bear burdens in the church which seem to fly in the face of justice: those who are divorced and remarried who are denied the sacraments; those who cannot approach the altar as servers (much less as priests!) for reasons which are misty at best; those who are condemned to bear children, rather than having the choice of doing so; those who perceive the morality of the church as moralism and find, not acceptance, but pariah status. Many of these silent ones have raised their voice in protest and, in turn, have seen their protest patronized or ignored. They have the right to demand: Are we not then part of the people of God if we are homosexual? Does Jesus have nothing for use if we limit our families? Are we outcastes in the faith? Are we, to locate the issue more historically, the heretics, Muslims, and Jews of today? If there is a commission in Rome for the atheists and unbelievers, why not one for the divorced and remarried?

Do not miss my point. I think I can understand why Rome resists the notion of women priests (although I do not agree) and I am not unsympathetic to the dilemmma of the late Paul VI when he penned *Humanae Vitae*, just as I understand the formidable tradition which mitigates against easy acceptance of homosexuality (as opposed to homosexuals). The church, by definition, is traditional and conservative: It is supposed to hand down and to protect. Nor do I believe that its resistance to the new cries of the silent ones (who are no longer silent) is always self-serving and done in bad faith. What, as an essentially conservative Catholic, I must resist, however, is a rigidity and hardening which mistake an imperfect grasp of the cultural scene for an eternal verity. If the history of the church should teach us anything, it should teach us that we had best listen. When we did not, the church suffered disorder and disaster.

There is a time for silence and a time for speech. To understand that notion of timeliness we might turn again to that paradigmatic person who opens this chapter: Mary. She is the speaker of few words at Cana or the keeper of her thoughts or the silent one at the foot of the cross. That silence, however, is not the silence of passivity, timidity, or from "knowing her place" (although in the deepest sense of the term she did know it). When she was impelled to speak at length, she did with words framed in the cadences of the Old Testament prophetic tradition. It is not accidental that the Magnificat is an *Urtext* of the liberation theologians. That great hymn (Lk. 1:47–55) resounds with the heroines of the Hebrew pantheon who came before her (compare, for example, her hymn with that of Hannah in 1 Samuel 2). It is set out in a series of polarities: a lowly maiden who will be praised by future generations; the overcoming of the mighty and the exaltation of the lowly; the fulfilling of the hungry and the rejection of the rich.

In that great hymn, put into the mouth of a woman by the inspired writer, one finds the paradigmatic program for the silent ones who are not forgotten or overpowered; rather, they are empowered. One can see, in the long iconographical tradition of the church, the same picture of Mary: the one who is a silent sufferer at the foot of a cross or as a pierced heart or a sufferer of seven swords; in traditional feminine roles as mother or nursing a child; in theologically symbolic roles as symbolic of the church; and, finally, as the bearer of wisdom or the mother of the poor and forgotten as she is as the *mestiza* of Guadalupe.

Church authorities have not been slow to understand the power of Mary's symbolism in the church. They insist on the right to authenticate and control manifestations of her cult and developments in depictions of her. They have been the champions of her "official" cult. They ward off anything that would give rise to departures from orthodoxy. A little known example might suffice to make the point.

One specific, and little noted, aspect of Marian symbolism might be cited as emblematic of the official church's concern with the suggestive power of such symbolism. From the late nineteenth century into the early twentieth century there were some tentative attempts to depict Mary as a priest. Both Pope

Pius IX and Pius X approved the use of prayers describing Mary as a priest. Those first moviments toward such a description were quickly halted. The approved prayers were suppressed. A decree of the Holy Office (issued in 1913; promulgated in 1916) forbade the use of images of Mary showing her in liturgical vestments. In 1927 the same Holy Office voiced official displeasure at an article in an obscure Italian clerical journal (*Palestra del clero*) which attempted to justify such a devotional usage. These bans effectively cut off such probes of Mary as priest.[11]

The notion of Mary/Priest developed from rather rococco speculations about the doctrine of Mary as coredemptrix and, as such, are theologically deficient. One can speculate, however, that the Holy Office might have seen the development of such an idea and such an iconography as a threat to the prescribed role for women in the church and the absolute masculine domain of sacerdotal roles in the church. The suppression of that kind of devotionalism, in short, was a hedge against any erosion of the received character of the priesthood.

The "Mary/Priest" episode, in many ways of minor significance, does illustrate the potential power of imagery and reaction to it. The entire issue of the "Mary/Priest" paradigm brings with it a number of unarticulated questions: If Mary is so exalted in the Catholic tradition (she is, among other things, the patroness of priests), why cannot she claim the dignity of the priesthood especially in light of the fact that modern theologians were pressing her claims to be a coredemptrix, a mediatrix of all graces, and queen of heaven? Is there, behind all of the theological objections, an ideological basis for such resistance? If so, is that not a microcosm of such ideologies in general? It is an issue which demands exploration.

The Person as Epiphany

That strangely tortured philosophical mystic Ludwig Wittgenstein once said to a friend that to be religious meant, not talking about religion, but leading a different kind of life. He then added: "It is my belief that only if you try to be helpful to other people will you in the end find your way to God."[12]

It would miss the point to dismiss Wittgenstein's *mot* as a "works" oriented notion of religion by which human goodness leads to God of itself. What that passionate student of Augustine, Tolstoy, and Dostoevsky had in mind, I think, is the conviction that the experience of God is inconceivable apart from that cultivated sense of forgetfulness of self which permits one to love widely enough to know God through the exercise of love and charity. Understood in that sense, his observation is not dissimilar to those sayings in the New Testament which strike the same chord: "He who says he is in the light and hates his brother, is in the darkness still" (1 Jn. 1:9); "Religion that is pure and undefiled before God and the Father is this: to visit orphans and widows in their affliction, and to keep oneself unstained from the world" (James 1:27)

The lesson to be drawn from the above is that there can be no strict vertical relationship between an individual and God which omits or precludes a concern for others. *Solus cum Solo* (alone with the One) is indeed a motto of the life of the monastic ascetic. It would be a perversion—indeed, it was for some ascetics—to understand that in a narrowly restrictive way. Why individual spiritual writers have emphasized the virtues of solitude, detachment, silence, and withdrawal as essential components of the Catholic ascetical tradition, these virtues cannot be understood in an atomistic and detached manner.

The basic point to emphasize here is that the life of contemplation and withdrawal in the church—even in its most severe eremetical forms—is a charism of the church. Such a life is understandable and legitimate only to the degree that it is integrated into the larger community either as an option for one who feels called to such a life (the church benefits the individual) or as a witness to certain values found in the Gospel or as a countersign to the "world" (benefit the church gives individual or community). It is not, and should not be so conceived, an elitist and self-defined exercise for the self alone. The various forms of religious life, either in community or in solitary existence, advance both "the progress of their own members and the welfare of the body of Christ," as the Second Vatican Council noted.[13]

What is true of the contemplative is equally true of others in the church. It has been charged by conservative critics that so much emphasis of late has been put on neighborly or horizontal love that contemporary Catholicism has lost a sense of the transcendent relationship with God. It seems fair to charge that certain enthusiasms unleased after the council did seem to reduce all Christian activity to social action or "this worldly" religion. However, those experiments, bold and naïve, can be seen as symptomatic of an impoverished spirit of horizontalism generated by the devotional individualism of post-Tridentine spirituality. Granted the partial justice of such critiques, it still seems unimpeachable that the religion of Jesus demands that those who follow him must live close to the experience of others.

That movement out to the other seems implicit in the very missionary character of the church. From its beginnings in the Pentecost experience the church has been quick to speak to the world in an intelligible voice (see Acts 2) in its proclamation of the Good News. If at certain periods in church history missionary activity was barely distinguishable from specific sociopolitical ends, it is equally true that the history of missionary expansion in the church is a monument to self-forgetting love and a profound desire to make the Gospel known to everyone on the earth.

Today the missionary enterprise of the church attempts to mediate between the desire to give the Gospel "to the world in this generation" and the goal of being a simple presence amid the world's religions or their secular counterparts. The former desire runs the risk of triumphalism and the latter, passive defeatism. The more authentic statement of the church's missionary activity whether understood as "foreign missions" or evangelization of one's own culture would be a *via media* between those two extremes. The eminent missiologist Walbert Bühlmann writes:

> Undoubtedly, a certain increase is needed so that the church can be a sign. But the decisive element is precisely the character of being a sign, a quality, the power to radiate light; it is not quantity, which can degenerate into a sluggish mass, sedentary and self satisfied. According to modern theology, the mission

of the church is not to secure the salvation of "souls which would otherwise be lost" or to bring the greatest possible number into the church as the ark of salvation; rather it is the aim of building up the church as a sign of salvation for all and of gaining new witnesses to the grace of God always working in the world.[14]

That sign presence in the world, whether conceived of as aggressive pastoral work or a more contemplative presence, roots itself in a deep faith in the power of the Gospel. Such a presence is also strikingly dialogical with its faith in the sign value of human presence. The witness is *there* and by his or her life it is proclaimed that there are certain deep values to be shared with others. This sign-presence is not—or, at least, should not be—identified with any spirit of religious imperialism or religious aggrandizement. The missionary presence is a sign of the love of Christ and that sign should ideally say: What you are is good and a result of God's presence in the world; to your being and your goodness there is something (Someone) who increases, deepens, and expands your humanness. In that dialogical stance the message of Christ and its bearer comes together as one sign-presence. The missionary (and I am thinking of that term in the broadest possible sense) makes the Gospel palpable and real by the dual office of interiorizing and manifesting the Gospel to others: "So let your light shine before others. . . ."

If one were able to step outside our world and view it as a whole, we would have to say that the Gospel is present over the globe not as an abstract tissue of ideas or even institutions but as hundreds of thousands of presences which reveal a variety of Christian impulses through a variety of apostolates. The corporal and spiritual works of mercy are worked in many and varied ways. Each of the persons who see that as a life's work extends the church both in time and in space. This wide skein of evangelizers and missionaries (of which we are a part) are epiphanies and sacraments of the reality of the Gospel being lived out. This skein is an epiphany of the living Christ.

It is important to see the church in this fashion so as not to reduce the message of Christ to abstractions. It is all too easy to talk about the need to evangelize the world and forget that such a task is not done at a global level but by the millions of specific presences, bound together in faith, who live in specific places in particularized ways. Recently I had occasion to visit the motherhouse of a large congregation of sisters to visit an elderly high school teacher who now lives there in retirement. As we toured the house, of which she was so obviously proud, I could not help but watch the retired sisters and think of the thousands of children they taught, the equal thousands of sick they nursed, the years that some of them spent in lands far from their own—witness they gave for the values of the Gospel. Who could possibly compute the good that these women (so unjustly patronized or mocked today) did under circumstances which were difficult and, at times, unjust. They, along with the rural parish priests, the mothers who cared for ill children, the missionaries in jungle or desert, the social workers in the cities of the world, the ordinary people fighting for a decent life, the activists who seek to elevate people, the preachers and catechists, the bureaucrats and the lay brothers, and others like them, seldom are seen or heard of, but they enflesh the church and its message in concrete sign-presences.

It has been a venerable theological notion to see the local community as a microcosm of the church as a whole; the *ecclesia* reflected in the *ecclesiola*. It is not inappropriate to focus at even a more specific level: the committed individual as a more specific representative of the same reality. Hans Urs von Balthasar has written that there is a tradition which can be traced back to the early church father Origen describing the "dispossessed soul" as an *anima ecclesiastica*; a "churchly spirit."

By free consent to grace (and von Balthasar sees Mary's *fiat* as a paradigm of what he is speaking about) one accepts the role of being-for-one-another. In that role the person gives back to the world everything that is received in grace and faith. In that self-giving the person bears within himself or herself the "form" of the church, not as a sociological reality, but as an enfleshment in the world. Von Balthasar writes:

> Whoever consents to this divine form of life, to a life in which from the outset one abandons all claims to possession in favor of the other; whoever offers for the other's disposal everything

which belongs to him, including that which is most private and apparently most immediate, of such a person the God of love disposes in all truth and effectiveness for the benefit of his brothers and sisters.[15]

We have insisted throughout this work on the basic Catholic insight that Christ's presence is *mediated* to us: his word through the scriptures; his presence through the Eucharist of the gathered community which is the church; his presence through the *ecclesia*. These forms of mediation, in turn, are reflections of the great act of mediation which is the Incarnation; the Word made flesh. To those acts of mediation we now add the mediation of Christ through persons. Christ seen as the hidden presence of the poor and abused of the world and Christ mediated through those *animae ecclesiasticae* who, in selfless love, give back everything they have received in grace.

These various forms of mediation are not discrete realities; they interpenetrate in a dynamic and incremental fashion. We receive the word of God and the person of Christ in the church's worship life. That reception shapes and changes us in such a fashion that we can "see" the world outside ourselves in a new and different fashion. In that "seeing" we move out to the world and, in turn, the world "sees" the vision of the Gospel. We receive through mediation and, in turn, mediate the Gospel.

That task of mediating the Gospel to others through our personal appropriation of the grace of Christ is basic to being a Christian. It is the making present of the body of Christ in a full manner; it is the "filling up of those things lacking in the body of Christ" of which St. Paul speaks. It is for that reason that we put such an emphasis on the notion of person. Every person has a basic dignity as a child of God; every Christian who extends the dignity of the human person by reaching out in love is a preacher of the Gospel and an actualizer of the immanent Kingdom of God.

The location of the presence of Christ in the human person has been a leitmotif of the teachings of Pope John Paul II from his inaugural encyclical *Redemptor Hominis* down to his most recent statements. His "personalism" is not merely philosophical but deeply rooted in his understanding of the ramifications of incarnational christology. On topics ranging from abortion and capital punishment to nuclear war and the condition of the working class the pope turns time and again to the bedrock truth that our redemption has been worked out on the plane of the human person; that the Word took flesh and dwelt among us.

It has been the argument of this chapter that the individual person (and its corporate representative either in church or in society), before he or she is denominated by class or distinction, has an inalienable dignity by reason of the redemptive grace of Christ. Furthermore, we argue that we both possess that "Christic" quality in ourselves and are urged to see it in others, most specially in those who, at first glance, seem unlikely sources for finding the sense of Christ. It is central to the Catholic experience—witnessed to in its saints and its insistence on the presence of Christ among the "silent and poor ones"—that our faith be one that reaches out to others in care and love. We are called upon to do that in the context of living out our lives not as extraordinary and occasional moments of charitableness or altruism. The balance between our life with God and with others is not to be seen as two compartmentalized facets of existence but as the balance of harmony. Using the classic christological vocabulary, we can say that our task is to be a person who fully integrates our human nature with the gift of divine filiation. That is what is meant by being called to be children of God. As usual, Karl Rahner saw the issue clearly and stated it with passion and lucidity:

> All divine vocations, however they may be thought of, are summons, vocations, to complement the descent of the eternal God into flesh. They are always vocations to earthly ordinariness and death, vocations to believe in the light shining in the darkness, to actualize love that seems to go unrewarded and unrequited, to enter into solidarity with the poor and the "shortchanged"—the brothers and sisters of Jesus Christ who are anything but the elite, and seem rather to belong to some hideous, mass produced humanity. Only through the performance of this task as a mission to "those below" does the Christian really accomplish his or her radical surrender to God's incomprehensibility as a beautifying surrender through faith, hope, and charity. Otherwise he or she remains locked up in the prison of his or her own selfishness.[16]

Points for Meditation

1. Is there a person(s) who best exemplifies what the Christian life is for you? What particular values and virtues have they mediated to you for your own spiritual growth?

2. Is the catalog of saints pertinent to your spiritual life? Which of the saints would you single out as being most instructive for your sense of Catholic Christianity?

3. Can you sort out your own feelings and ideas about Mary and Marian piety in the life of the church and in your own life?

4. To what degree do you feel a need, arising from your own progress in the spiritual life, to embrace the "others" of the world?

5. Which person(s) would most challenge your concept of Christian love?

6. Can you articulate your own understanding of how love of God/love of person(s) coincide? should coincide?

Notes

1. Raimundo Panikkar, *Blessed Simplicity: The Monk as Universal Archetype* (New York: Seabury, 1982), p. 15.

2. I borrow from Andrew Greeley, *The New Agenda* (Garden City: Doubleday Image Book, 1975).

3. David Tracy, *The Analogical Imagination* (New York: Crossroad, 1981), p. 384. I have pursued the notion of saint as paradigm in my book *The Meaning of Saints* (San Francisco: Harper and Row, 1980).

4. Elisabeth Schüssler Fiorenza, "Feminist Spirituality, Christian Identity, and Catholic Vision," in *Womanspirit Rising,* ed. by Judith Plaskow and Carol Christ (San Francisco: Harper and Row, 1979), pp. 138–39. See also Elizabeth A. Johnson, "The Incomprehensibility of God and the Image of God Male and Female," *Theological Studies* 49 (1984) 441–65.

5. George Hunston Williams, *The Mind of Pope John Paul II* (New York: Seabury, 1981), pp. 48–49.

6. After completing some essays on Mary in a book of art entitled *Mother of God* (San Francisco: Harper and Row, 1982), I received an unsolicited copy of *Our Lady of the Roses* published by Apostles of Our Lady, Inc., in Lansing, Michigan, from which much of the information in this section is gleaned.

7. This is basically the argument of Marina Warner's *Alone of All Her Sex* (New York: Knopf, 1976).

8. Harvey Cox, *Religion in the Secular City* (New York: Simon and Schuster, 1984), pp. 260–61.

9. See, among many others, Alexander Murray, *Reason and Society in the Middle Ages* (Oxford: Clarendon, 1978), and Donald Weinstein and Rudolph Bell, *Saints and Society* (Chicago: University of Chicago, 1983).

10. From the *Dogmatic Constitution on the Church,* art. 32, in *The Documents of Vatican II,* ed. Walter Abbott (New York: Association Press, 1966), p. 58.

11. I have taken most of my information on this topic from the treatise on mariology in *Sacrae Theologiae Summa* (Madrid: Biblioteca de Autores Cristiana, 1956), pp. 447ff.

12. Quoted in Rush Rhees, ed., *Recollections of Wittgenstein* (New York: Oxford University Press, 1984), p. 114.

13. From the *Dogmatic Constitution on the Church*, art. 43 in *Documents*, p. 73; See also: Jean LeClercq, "The Contemplative Life and Monasticism in the Light of Vatican II," in *Aspects of Monasticism* (Kalamazoo: Cistercian Studies, 1978), pp. 17–44.

14. Walbert Bühlmann, *The Coming of the Third Church* (Maryknoll, N.Y.: Orbis, 1977), p. 145.

15. *The von Balthasar Reader*, ed. Medard Kehl and Werner Löser, (New York: Crossroad, 1984), p. 228.

16. Karl Rahner, *The Practice of Faith: A Handbook of Contemporary Spirituality* (New York: Crossroad, 1983), p. 207.

Selected Readings

Brown, Raymond, ed. *Mary in the New Testament.* Ramsey, N.J.: Paulist, 1978. Fundamental essays from an ecumenical perspective.

Gustafson, James. *Christ and the Moral Life.* New York: Harper and Row, 1969. Christ and personhood in an ethical context.

Küng, Hans. *On Being a Christian.* Garden City: Doubleday, 1976. Important study by a controversial writer.

Schillebeeckx, Edward. *Ministry.* New York: Crossroad, 1982. A new and radical look at offices in the church.

Tavard, George. *Women in the Christian Tradition.* South Bend: Notre Dame, 1973. A historical study.

8

CATHOLICITY

The word *catholic*, from the Greek, means "pertaining to the whole" and, by extension in religious usage, "universal." The word *catholic* is not found in the New Testament except for one use of an adverbial form of the word (Acts 4:18) with the meaning of "totally." It is first used by Ignatius of Antioch, in the early part of the second century, to describe the church. For Ignatius the term *catholic church* means the church taken as a whole as opposed to this or that particular Christian community. According to Hans Küng, that meaning remains attached to the term *catholic* until near the end of the second century.[1] By then, and certainly early in the third century, a new meaning becomes attached to the word *catholic:* the Catholic church (i.e., the entire church) as opposed to this or that dissident group of believers. In that way Catholic began to mean orthodox in opposition to those sects or movements which were heretical and/or schismatic.

In the fourth century two important developments occurred which added new meanings to the word *catholic.* In 380 A.D. the emperor Theodosius declared the Catholic church to be the official church of the Roman Empire. The official church of the empire, then, was called "Catholic" and it alone was to enjoy the protection of the law and the patronage of the state.

In roughly the same period St. Augustine of Hippo began to think of the term *Catholic church* as meaning the geographically diffuse body of believers as opposed to small heretical groups like the Donatists. Catholicity began to be thought of in terms of numerical strength and geographical representation. The best formulation of that understanding of catholicity is the formula of Vincent of Lerins (died 450 A.D.?): The Catholic faith is that faith which is held always, everywhere, and by everyone (*semper, ubique, et ab omnibus*). Thus, catholicity is a notion which also has close ties to the idea of Christian unity. Catholicity, then, includes the idea of orthodoxy, the fullness of the church, the unity of faith, and its presence in the world. It is in that sense that we must understand the use of the word in the creed when we speak of the church as "one, holy, catholic, and apostolic."

With the advent of the Protestant Reformation an element of polemic began to surround the word *catholic*. The early reformers insisted both on their right to the use of the word as well as on their membership in the Catholic church by using the word as it had been historically understood in the creed. Catholics (we cannot avoid the descriptive use of the word) insisted that they alone had a right to use the term and rejected the Protestant claim to catholicity. The Catholic church was a visible and identifiable reality which had the essential characteristics (*notae*) of the church founded by Christ (unity, holiness, catholicity, and apostolicity) and that church, in the peremptory words of the Catechism of the Council of Trent, which alone possessed those *notae* was "the Catholic church whose head is the Roman pontiff."

With the hardening of the religious polemic over the centuries the word *catholic* eventually became a creedal word for Protestants, but it became both a descriptive term and a theological category in the Roman church. In popular usage Catholic meant not Protestant or—confusingly enough—Eastern Orthodox. That is the common usage today. There has been some attempt to retrieve the term *catholic* as a more precise theological term by speaking of the universal church (embracing Catholic, Orthodox, Reformed) as the "ecumenical" church since *ecumenical* means pertaining to the whole inhabited world, with the term *catholic* reserved for the descriptive usage designating a particular tradition within the large ecumenical church.

We cannot leave off these preliminary remarks without

mentioning the use of the notion of catholicity in traditional apologetics. Catholic controversalists and polemicists made an argument which, with variations, went something like this: If Christ founded a church which would endure until the end of time as the vehicle of his salvific will, then the church should be identifiable in history as the one which manifests that continuity *semper, ubique, et ab omnibus*. Now, the argument continues, it is only the Catholic church which can plausibly claim such a continuity and such a universality of witness. Catholicism alone has the spatial extensity, the numerical quantity, the cultural variety, and the temporal continuity to claim ancestry back to the New Testament times and the New Testament promise. I remember from my high school days a large graph chart with vertical lines representing time periods from 33 A.D. down to 1950. Horizontal lines designated the foundation times of the various churches. On that chart Roman Catholicism started in 33 A.D. and grew fatter (the thickening of the line represented population of the denomination) as it approached and finally touched 1950. The next line—if memory serves—was the Orthodox church beginning in 1054 (the year of the East/West schism), while the little lines beginning in the sixteenth century (e.g., Lutherans, Calvinists, etc.) seemed significant only if they were compared with the miniscule blips given to the nineteenth-century sects (Mormonism, Christian Science, etc.) who hardly showed up at all.

That chart, a crude polemical tool, originated from a far more complicated line of argument used, for example, by St. Robert Bellarmine (1542–1621) in his controversial writings against the Protestant reformers. It received its most sophisticated usage in the formulations of John Henry Newman in the last century. In the *Apologia Pro Vita Sua* Newman recounts how his early studies of church history led him finally (and painfully) to reject his previously held notion that the Anglican church, of which he was an ordained member, somehow preserved the historical continuity of the ancient church along with the genuine reforms of the Reformation. It was a chance reading of a line from St. Augustine which destroyed Newman's notion of Anglicanism as the middle way (*via media*) between Rome and the Reformation churches. Augustine argues that an early heretical group with which he was contending (the Donatists) were not good men because the world judges them (*securus judicat orbis terrarum*) for cutting themselves off from the larger unity of the church. Augustine's lines struck Newman very forcefully. He saw the Anglican church (to say nothing of the Reformers) as being in the very same position: cut off from the ancient church: "By those great words of the ancient father, interpreting and summing up, the long and varied course of ecclesiastical history, the theory of *Via Media* was absolutely pulverized."[2]

The destruction of the *Via Media* did not, of itself, lead Newman to Rome. As Owen Chadwick phrased it, in Newman's view the early Fathers indicted the Anglicans for schism, but they indicted Rome for error.[3] He still believed in the catholicity of the Anglican church at this period with the notion of catholicity meaning, very broadly, continuity with the apostolic and patristic church of antiquity. When that belief began to erode, Newman was on his way to Rome. For Newman the church of Rome was the present inheritor of the tradition of the apostolic and patristic church.

Newman's insight into the continuity of the Catholic tradition was for him both a powerful personal revelation and and polemical tool. The other side of this traditional apologetics was an appeal to the church's catholicity of vision and its position as a metanational reality. That kind of apologetic affirms Newman's idea that the church is a seamless tradition that runs through history and a tradition flexible enough to encounter, accept, and transform all that is good in human culture. The most persuasive statement of that aspect of catholicity by an older apologist is found in Karl Adam's *The Spirit of Catholicism*, a work that had a long and powerful influence in the decades after its publication in 1924. One could read Adam's entire book as an exposition of catholicity as transformer of the human in culture. For that reason alone this now unread classic deserves a rereading. We can get some sense of the flavor of Adam's apologetic from this not untypical passage:

The church is not one society or one church among many

others, nor is she just a church among men; she is the church of men, of all mankind. . . . The interests of the church have never been subordinated to purely national interests, nor has the church ever put herself long in bondage to any state. . . . All peoples, each with their special aptitudes, are her children and all bring their gifts to the sanctuary. . . . This is the true conception of the Catholic church. It is a great, supra-national tidal wave of faith in God and love of Christ, nourished and supported by the special powers of each nation and of every individual man, purified and inspired by the divine spirit of truth and love.[4]

There is much to be learned by a meditation on Catholicism as a tradition and catholicity as a theological concept. As a concept for persuasive apologetics it seems woefully deficient and is largely abandoned today. As an apologetical tool it relies on an exact identification of Catholicism with the historical Christian tradition going back to the time of the New Testament. It assumes that the Catholic church is that reality. The Second Vatican Council, however, in an extremely celebrated passage, does not affirm that Catholicism is the church of Christ; it says that Catholicism *subsists* in it.[5] Furthermore, recent advances both in historical research and in historiography have taught us that the notion of a single, organic, unfolding, undifferentiated spiritual reality called the "Catholic church" is, historically speaking, a simplification of a much more complex reality. Finally, and this has been recognized for some time, an argument based on ubiquity and numbers is a very treacherous argument to advance. To say that the Catholic church is "true" because it is the most numerous or the most widespread would be a little like saying that Marxism is the "truest" economic system because it is so numerically represented and so widespread over the world.

Still we are left with the word *catholic* and the accepted reality which we call the Catholic church and a concept of a Catholic tradition. Because the concept of catholicity does not yield a persuasive apologetic does not mean that the concept is vaporous or, worse, noxious. Even as stern a critic of the apologetic use of the concept "catholic" as Hans Küng recognizes the distinctive reality of Catholicism as something quite distinguishable from "Protestant" or "Reformed." In his massive *On Being a Christian* Küng proposed to inquire about Catholicism as a "basic attitude" which, in the concrete, centers around continuity in time of faith and the continuity of the faith enduring in all disruptions (tradition) and to the universality in space of faith and the community of faith embracing all groups (against Protestant radicalism and particularity—which is not to be confused with evangelical radicality and congregational attachment).[6]

Küng writes as a theologian who is, both by instinct and by training, an ecclesiologist. He explores Catholicism both from that angle and from the angle of his own developed christology. We can also take another tack and consider that "basic attitude" of which Küng speaks as simply a religious worldview or a religious sensibility. We often speak of "Catholic" novelists or "Catholic" countries, but rarely do we inquire if that adjective tells us something more than the novelist's faith position or the predominant religion of a certain country. Is there something peculiar to, and identifiable with, a sensibility which is Catholic? The answer to that question has broad implications because it touches on the very essence of what it means to be a Christian who further says "I am a Catholic." It is that something "further" which we need to explore.

Catholicism as Memory

At the conclusion of his comprehensive study of Catholicism Richard McBrien singles out three theological foci as central to the distinctive character of Catholicism.[7] They are sacramentality, mediation, and communion. These foci are closely related.

Sacramentality is to be understood in the broader sense as visible realities which transmit (mediate) the presence and power of God in Christ. In that broad sense of sacramentality we underscore a basic Catholic conviction which is that our awareness of God is always mediated through tangible realities: The world itself reflects the glory of God; God's definitive revelation comes through the *magnum sacramentum* which is Christ; Christ is made present through other visible realities: the church, the sacraments of the church, and all those other signs which the church uses—everything from the sign of the cross to stained glass windows—to remind us of the presence of Christ in the world. This insistence on the sacramentality of religion helps explain the very tactile and visual quality of Catholicism. It is a religion which has a deep traditional sympathy for art, sculpture, ritual, drama, display, celebration, feasts, processions, and so on.

This mediated sacramental life does not exist in some free-floating state. The sacramental experience of God in Christ does not happen in the same way that a poet experiences the power of nature: through the individual encounter or solitary experience unique to that poet's life and sensibility. Catholic sacramental life, while it touches this or that individual, occurs in the larger framework of the community. The memory of Christ, the making concrete his presence, the liturgical celebration of his mysteries, the application of his mercies to the world—all of these things happen now as they have happened in history because there is a community which treasures and passes on these things. That community* is a tradition, i.e., a community which "hands down" the collective memory of its experiences with Christ; the key function of the Catholic community is to recall the words of the apostle as being words of their own: "I received from the Lord and, in turn, passed on to you" (1 Cor. 11:24).

The fact that the Catholic community is a community of tradition—a community which passes on and hands down—means that it is, by definition, a conservative community. We should add the cautionary observation that a conservative tradition which "hands down" is, nonetheless, a dynamic tradition; one great temptation of the conservative tradition is to mummify rather than to conserve.

The conservative character of a traditional community helps us to get a better understanding of catholicity. To be a Catholic is to live in communion with those who are our own contemporaries as well as those who "have gone before us and sleep the sleep of peace." To be Catholic is to take responsibility for

---

* I am not insensitive to the fact that this community is a special kind of community with its salient character being provided by its Petrine office. I shall treat that central characteristic of the Catholic community elsewhere in this book.

our past as well as the present and the future. I always regarded it as a deeply moving thing to hear, in the old Roman canon, the mention of the names of the martyrs, male and female, of the Roman church. That liturgical litany of remembrance was recited not only as an act of intercession but as an act of memory and an affirmation of the bonds between the earthly and heavenly church: that sense of standing in solidarity with the past which is, through grace, present. To be a Catholic is to be a member of a family with a very long memory. We always are learning more about that family from the members of the family and its memories.

This strong sense of traditional communion serves as a strong antidote against that radical individualism (the worst fault of contemporary fundamentalism) which insists on the unique character of every individual experience as the criterion for religious authenticity. A sense of traditional communion ought also to provide a strong sense of bonding with others in that tradition; a *catholic* (universalizing) sense of fraternity and solidarity. It is not poetic license or mere sentiment which leads the church to use organic metaphors of human bonding to describe itself: people of God; people of the Way; pilgrim people; Body of Christ; and so on. To be a Catholic is not to negate individuality except in the sense of individuality as radical and self-serving centeredness. "I want to do my own thing" is a very un-Catholic rule of life.

Because the Catholic tradition is a conserving tradition, it carries with it a long list of experiences which it has tested over the ages and found to be Catholic. It is in that conserving and testing that we approximate the meaning of Catholic as "pertaining to the whole." Within the core structure of obedience and fidelity to Christ there is a wide plurality of options open to those who seek after Christ. Outside the Catholic tradition religious sensibilities are satisfied by a range of diverse ecclesial options. Those who prefer silence and austerity might gravitate to the Society of Friends while those who seek a more emotional outlet for religion might belong to the Assembly of God, and so on. The Reformed tradition provides denominationalism to satisfy the complex needs of religious seekers.

The Catholic tradition has allowed different sensibilities to thrive within its community. It has been said that the Catholic answer to the Protestant tendency to fractionalize into differing sects or denominations was to permit the founding of different religious orders.[8] There is some truth in that observation. Religious orders do not exist solely to shelter those who take vows and wish to live within their walls. They also serve as instruments for the propagation of particular devotional or spiritual approaches to Christian growth. Indeed, some religious orders were founded with the primary aim of spreading a particular form of devotion. When one surveys the wide range of religious orders in the Catholic church (there was an old joke that even God didn't know now many orders of nuns there were), one cannot but be struck by the wide diversity of their emphases and style of life. For those people who have a taste for the austere and the other-worldly there is the eremetical tradition of the Carthusians, the common life of the Cistercians and Benedictines, and the institutionalization of desert spirituality in the Carmelite tradition. There is the stable life of the Benedictines and the vagrant mendicancy of the Franciscans for, in the lovely words of Chesterton: "What Benedict stored, Francis scattered." There is the intellectual tradition of the Jesuits and Dominicans and the humble servant orders like the Brothers Hospitallers or the Sisters of Charity. The vividly sensual piety centered on the passion of Christ has inspired religious orders like the Passionists, the Stigmatines, the Society of the Precious Blood, as did the extravagant mariology of the post-Tridentine world (e.g., the Montfort Fathers). It is interesting today that religious orders of women often advertise for recruits today and in their advertisements indicate whether they are "traditional" or "modern," indicating how the religious orders adapt to the sensibilities of the age. The recent ascendency of Opus Dei in the church (at the expense of the Jesuits, according to the current journalistic wisdom) is another indication of how religious sensibility is expressed within religious congregations.

That wide-ranging diversity is not peculiar to the diverse religious orders. One sees it at every level of church life. A look at even an unexceptional parish will prove the point.

I have before me the weekly bulletin of the parish church I

attend, a parish which is excruciatingly typical of American suburbia: roughly five to seven hundred, mostly white middle-class families, served by a parochial school, a rectory, and a convent with a very tiny contingent of nuns. In the bulletin I note the following: a Cursillo announced for the weekend; a Bible study group which will meet at the rectory; a short course on Christian prayer to be given by the pastor during the Lenten season which is nearly upon us; the daily recitation of the rosary by a group; an upcoming retreat for teenagers in the parish; a meeting and communion breakfast for the Holy Name Society; weekends planned for "Marriage Encounter" and no-tice of a forthcoming "Engaged Encounter"; a desire expressed to form a new prayer group (presumably a charismatic one). These events, added to the life of the parish as supplements to the normal sacramental, liturgical, and pastoral ministry of the parish, reflect a wide—but hardly atypical—menu of spir-itual possibilities. Some of them are modern; others venerable; some American in origin, while others are imports from abroad. They reflect very traditional practices like the rosary and certain post-Vatican II enthusiasm like the Bible study groups. Some are rather staid carryovers from the "old days" (e.g., the Holy Name breakfasts), while others play to the contemporary desire to blend spirituality with group dynamics and experien-tial religious expressions (Cursillo; Marriage Encounter). I am also sure that some of these activities are lay-inspired and simply accommodated for by the pastor of the parish.

What keeps all these devotions and movements (for some-thing like Cursillo is far more than a devotion) from "spinning off" into sectarian enthusiasms is the larger Catholic umbrella which gives them both legitimacy and theological cogency. The connection of a particular devotion to the larger Catholic tradition allows that devotion to play its part in the life of the church and to either develop as the tradition develops or pass into disuse.

The rosary is a good example of what I mean here. The rosary began in the Middle Ages as a counting device for those who said a set prayer (usually the *Pater*) for each of the psalms sung by the choir monks who could read. Eventually this practice of the "poor man's psalter" was given a Marian tone to it with the prayers being the traditional *Ave Maria.* When the rosary took its set form, it became an immensely popular and widespread devotion in the Catholic church. At a certain popular level it was almost a symbol of being a Catholic. Almost overnight in the world after Vatican II the rosary fell into disuse among younger Catholics. One sees now, however, a renewed interest (if only a flickering interest at the present) in the rosary but with some different emphases. Some see the "mysteries" of the rosary as the focal point of the exercise and emphasize the meditations on these mysteries as central to the devotion. That emphasis, of course, reflects the contemporary orientation to the Bible. Others see the possibility of using the rosary, with its insistent repetitions, as an aid to meditation by considering the rosary as akin to the use of a mantra in other religious traditions. This, of course, is close to the Orthodox practice of the "Jesus Prayer" and the "rosary" which is used to keep count of the repeated invocations of the Jesus Prayer itself. In both cases what one sees is that an old devotion, springing from a definite period and a definite culture, is now being modified by the influences of a different time and a different culture. That, at its deepest level, is what the Catholic tradition should always be doing: keeping our memory while remaining open to new ways to treasure it.

I have said that the Catholic tradition is, of necessity, conservative because it has the task of remembering and handing on that memory to others. I should like to say a few more words about the "conservative" function of the tradition because, at least in some influential circles, the notion of "conservative" conjures up images which either please or enrage.

Some people glory in the term "conservative." They see conservatism in the church as a single standard against the relativism of the contemporary world. They adopt as their own the motto of the late Alfredo Cardinal Ottaviani: *Semper idem*—"always the same." At its most rigid that kind of conservative impulse incarnates itself in groups like the Catholic Traditionalists with their fiddleback chasubles, their old Latin liturgy, their rigid rejection of any ecumenical gestures, their obsessive anticommunism, their love affair with the political right; their readiness to drum out dissidents and to wield the interdict and ban of excommunication.

For those of the Catholic left, the past is past and without pertinence to the present needs of society or the church. For them to conserve is to evade. In the years immediately after the Second Vatican Council we saw some peculiarly virulent forms of "now" religion. Many semiprominent clerics, religious, and activist layfolks seemed infected with a sort of intellectual AIDS; they were susceptible to every crank idea, fad, enthusiasm, and movement which the zeitgeist threw out for public consumption. We had the sight of clerics solemnly endorsing everything from gay rights to vegetarian pacifism in the name of the Gospel. The Catholic tradition should be broad enough to absorb these enthusiasms and sort out what is worthwhile over the long run, but the curious quality of the religious left was their rigid dogmatism; their conviction that their politics, their "lifestyle" (how I loathe that word!), their approach to spirituality, are the correct ones. The arrogance of the radical left was roughly comparable to the rigid ignorance of the radical right.

There is some evidence that both the radical right and the radical left are assuming their proper place in the Catholic spectrum, i.e., peripheral obscurity. But the "balancing out" of postconciliar Catholicism does not mean that we are going back to the "good old days." The plain fact of the matter is that we are in an era of a radically new religious consciousness which came about as a result of the Second Vatican Council. There is no more likelihood of returning to the older religious consciousness than there is of our returning to a pre-Einstein understanding of science.

In the course of this work we will speak often of this shift in religious consciousness. One point needs to be said here with respect to it: Newness does not mean a loss of the old; it simply means that the older tradition of knowing is seen from a different angle or a different perspective. John W. O'Malley has discussed this shift in Catholic consciousness in two articles which can only be described as seminal.[9] He has set out the "newness" which has entered the church as a result of the experience of the Second Vatican Council. However convulsive that change may have been, O'Malley bids us recognize our continuity with the past (I would call that continuity our "catholicity"); he concludes his study in this fashion:

> No large institution will overnight transform its paradigm into something entirely different; no institution ever continues over a long period of time to operate wholly on the same paradigm, especially not an institution so deeply embedded in human culture as the Roman Catholic church. The persistent Catholic impulse to reconcile "nature and grace" is, when raised to the level of social institutions, an impulse to reconcile the church with human culture in all its positive dimensions—with sin excepted and the gospel affirmed. In that sense the Council, for all its daring, moved solidly in line with the Catholic tradition. The Church is fully incorporated into human history, and changes that take place there deeply affect it. That is what the Council saw, and that perception is perhaps its best legacy. That is what it means to belong to a Church that, as the Council insisted, is truly a pilgrim in this world. That is the continuing challenge of the Council to us all.[10]

The great challenge in being a Catholic today is to somehow remember the tradition of the past and use that memory for the present exigencies of our life and culture. To do this with some sense of responsibility requires that we not only ask the right kinds of questions, but that those questions be framed with some sense of the memory of the church. The questions are as numerous as they are complex. They range from questions about the nature of belief itself to issues of ecclesiastical polity. It should be noted, however, that many questions which seem to be issues of mere ecclesiastical concern are, in fact, questions which deeply delve into the area of theology and fundamental belief. It would hardly be possible to trace out such questions, but a random sampler of two issues—both of which claiming a fair amount of both official and popular interest—might give us some sense of how tradition, theology, as well as current cultural pressures, are involved. I shall use, strictly as examples, two questions of some currency: the issue of clerical celibacy and the question of the church's relationship to the poor of the world.

Celibacy

If current trends are any indicator, the West is going to have a clerical crisis over the issue of celibacy in a very short time. Just scanning the Catholic papers in my study for the past few weeks, I see articles about the legitimacy of seminarians "dating" as part of the "discernment" of their vocation (this in a large Northeastern diocese which has closed its seminary and had one candidate for the priesthood in 1983) and an article about the decline of Catholicism in Puerto Rico being blamed both on the aggressive nature of fundamentalistic recruiting and on the alien nature of a fast diminishing celibate clergy in a culture which puts such a high premium on family life. These random examples from the Catholic press are both the tip of the proverbial iceberg; nobody in the church denies that.

Married priests may help answer that impending crisis (it will surely do so in those parts of the world where celibate values are so alien as to appear almost perverse) in a concrete fashion. Legislation, however, permitting a married clergy, will not necessarily address the deeper issues which must be faced: What values has a celibate clergy served in the history of the church? If celibacy is abolished (or marginalized), will we lose some value which we have possessed? Does the erosion of celibacy as a perceived value merely serve as a symptom for a more profound shift away from an eschatological to an incarnational faith? How will we maintain a sign of "not being of the world" in the future? That question has profound ramifications for the future shape of the religious life, the sexual character of the priesthood itself, the notion of ministry and its role in the pastoral life of the church.

The point upon which I insist is this: When we make a change of moment (say, of some usage like celibacy) which has a long tradition behind it, we need ask what value that usage may have possessed and whether there are other ways of expressing that value. This is not a counsel of timidity; it is a counsel of catholicity. It is obvious that long-standing usages, simply because they are long-standing, have no value beyond their mere antiquity. They may well have validity in their sign value.

Rich Church/Poor Church

To speak of the church and the question of economics is to enter an area of discussion which is both complex and passionate in its partisanship. A good deal of the subject issues around the very complex issue of poverty. To my mind the term *poverty* is one which is fraught with theological evasion and conceptual confusion. In the first place—and I will simply state this apodictically—I find the current discussion about "religious poverty" in the religious orders an obfuscation and evasion. The simple fact is that no vowed religious in this country (in the West in fact) lives a life of poverty in any meaningful sense of that term. To speak of religious poverty strikes me as a simple misuse of common language. What most orders mean by religious poverty is, in fact, *simplicity of life*. That notion, by the way, is a great value for our society and religious orders would do the world a service to shift their thinking to creative ways of simple living as a countersign to the materialism of the age and cease discussions of "religious poverty" which is an affront to the poor.

Secondly, poverty is a term which is very relative. In North America poverty is relative to a very high standard of living; i.e., the poor of my city would be indescribably wealthy by the standards of the African Sahel. The relativity of poverty has always had a certain acceptance in Christianity ("the poor you always have with you"), but destitution (the word I would use for those who live at a level of want that makes life inhumane) quite rightly brings down prophetic wrath and indignation. To keep people destitute is to deny their humanity. That seems to me an unimpeachable Christian fundamental. For people in our culture to be homeless is simply intolerable from a Christian point of view and something must be done. *How* to do that *something* is quite another issue.

What has puzzled me for a long time is to think of ways in which we as a church can close the gap between the destitute and those who are not destitute (i.e., to make the rich church/poor church one church). That gap is so patent and horrible that something needs be done by the church and that something must be profoundly radical. By "radical" I do not mean radical in the political sense but as *root commitment* to action *when we know what to do.* Whatever we do must be done in fidelity to both simple justice and Christian charity. The current debates at the level of political theology strike as generating more heat than light. It may be that there are no grand schemas which will be useful beyond setting the moral limits and demands for justice and charity.

In the interim we must foster every effort rooted in our tradition, from small intentional groups to large movements, to confront the injustice in the world. It may seem simplistic— I do not think it is—but the prescription that every Christian step outside and start doing good seems eminently sensible to me. The church, with its widespread organization at the grass-roots level, seems ideal for the kind of hands-on, direct involvement with the problems of injustice in the world. Every parish ought to foster small groups of Gospel-minded people who will work steadily at the injustices and hurts in their area. To do that is the first step in the raising of consciousness about the larger problems of the world. The person who helps with a Vincent de Paul soup kitchen in this country will not be indifferent to the pictures of refugees which appear on television.

It may be objected that such a program is a "drop in the bucket" or, more strenuously, that it is a kind of false consciousness which does not get to the radical issues underlying poverty and destitution. It is a salve for a middle-class case of bad conscience. I think that unfair as a judgment, no matter how often I hear it. That it is a small step may be true, but its purpose is to energize and convert that "silent majority" of good Catholics who could care less for the slogans of liberation theology or the spirit of democratic capitalism but who do have wells of good will which could be tapped for the benefit of the world. What I am suggesting is that we try to think of ways to engage the energies of that group of Catholics, the largest group in the church, whom we call the "middle class" and who are more often than not ignored or patronized by the academic and professional Catholic. To reach out to them to do justice would be a very Catholic move.

In both of the examples which I used above I insisted that we think of what the church possesses in her memory and in actuality while we, at the same time, watch the "signs of the times." Behind that insistence on my part is the profound conviction that the Catholic tradition has profoundly important resources to be mined for the good of humanity. They need to be called up, examined, modified, and put to use. Some might argue that this is too provincial a view; that the church is too narrow a vehicle for the needs of the modern age. To that we can only offer a counter argument of action rooted in faith. For the person of faith—for those who have not given up on the church—its catholicity is a promise, not a reality. As a promise it offers "new things and old" as does any good householder. The "old" is its memory; the new is its faith and openness to the future. In those two elements resides its catholicity.

Catholicity as Openness

In *The Road to Wigan Pier*, his great report on the poverty of the working class in the England of the 1930s, George Orwell wrote the following:

> The most immediately striking thing about the English Roman Catholics—I don't mean the real Catholics, I mean the converts: Ronald Knox, Arnold Lunn *et hoc genus*—is their intense self consciousness. Apparently they never think, certainly they never write, about anything but the fact that they *are* Roman Catholics; this single fact and the self-praise resulting from it form the entire stock-in-trade of the Catholic literary man. But the really interesting thing about these people is the way in which they have worked out the supposed implications of orthodoxy until the tiniest details of life are involved. . . .[11]

Orwell, not very sympathetic to Catholicism in general, here protests a certain insular smugness which he detected in the Catholic literary culture of his day. He was right on target. G. K. Chesterton, one of my favorite authors, cannot be exempted. There is in some of Chesterton's writings (especially in his apologetic writings) a sort of hearty bullying combined with a dogmatic dismissal of any other point of view. Such arrogance represents Catholicism at its narrowest.

Flannery O'Connor once said that the abiding sin of Catholicism is smugness. She had in mind the rather tightly segregated and self-righteously satisfied American Catholicism of a generation ago. To be a Catholic in my youth was not merely to be a member of a church; it was to live in a complete and vividly distinct subculture. To a surprising degree my family defined itself through the church: We were educated there, we socialized there, we worshipped there, we spent our spare time there, we attended movies only after the church gave the o.k., we never went to other churches, and the highest aspiration a young person could have was to give one's life for the church or, in lieu of that, marrying in the church. One of the reasons that I have always viewed fundamentalist Christianity with a tolerant eye (e.g., the operation which Jerry Falwell runs in Lynchburg, Virginia) is because, *mutatis mutandis*, it is so similar in tone to the Catholicism of my youth: the same love/ hate relationship to the world; the same obsessive concern with sexual purity; the same desire to show that "our" people can get advanced degrees; the same defensiveness; the identical anticommunism and conservative politics; the same clannishness; and—the same smugness. Culturally, it is Catholicism without beer.

It is not my desire to either praise or damn the insular Catholicism of my youth; had I the space, I would probably praise more than I would damn. American Catholicism was simply one regional variation of the church as a whole. By and large Catholicism was an institution shaped by reaction. The modern church was formed in large part by its reaction against the rise of the modern secular state, against the postcritical thought that was normative after Kant, against the modernism which developed from that and the triumph of science in the last century. The Catholic counter strategy was simple and effective: Draw the wagons in a circle and fend off the barbarian marauders; excommunicate modernists and Marxists; keep science at arm's length; construct a substitute culture. That culture—"Catholic culture"—was constructed out of revival of the *philosophia perennis* of Thomas Aquinas, a profound nostalgia for the Middle Ages, a need for order and authority, and a loathing—with some good reason—for the values of modernity.

Such a culture was Catholic only in a very restricted sense.

It drew on a very narrow range of human experience and, despite its lip service to modern culture, hedged itself in by various and sundry means. That Catholic culture—dreamed of by Newman in the last century, proclaimed by Christopher Dawson and Jacques Maritain in our own—was largely insular, inbred, or fatuous.* At worst it was suffocatingly smug as James Joyce so convincingly described it in his fiction:

> ... Lately some of their judgments had sounded a little foolish in his ears and had made him feel a regret and a pity as though he were slowly passing out of an accustomed world and were hearing its language for the last time. One day when some boys had gathered around a priest under the shed near the chapel, he had heard the priest say:
> I believe that Lord Macaulay was a man who probably never committed a mortal sin in his life, that is to say, a deliberate mortal sin.
> Some of the boys then asked if Victor Hugo were not the greatest French writer. The priest had answered that Victor Hugo had never written half so well when he had turned against the church as he had written when he was a Catholic. . . .[12]

That narrowness of life is the extreme opposite of true Catholicity. The great enemies of catholicity are those forces which keep the church bound too closely to a particular cultural form or a specific national group. Michael Novak has defined "Catholic" to mean unfettered by a mentality which is sectarian, ethnic, exclusive, or closed.[13] To that short list I would only add that a truly Catholic church is as prompt to learn as it is to teach.

The sectarian temptation is to see the church as being a closed-off social structure containing a membership totally homogeneous who regard themselves as the saved or the righteous. The Catholic church, by contrast, is a church of saints and sinners, perfect and imperfect; its parable is that of the field with both wheat and tares. It is a church which can accommodate both a Daniel Berrigan and a William F. Buckley, Jr., while expecting each of them to grow and learn while they try to teach.

---

* I would consider its greatest practical achievement to be the development, after World War II, of the notion of a Christian Democracy under the leadership of de Gasperi, Schumann, and Adenauer.

A truly Catholic church is not ethnic even if it often expresses itself through ethnic realities. To identify the church with this or that ethnic group is not only to deny the largeness of vision which is Catholic but to accede to a form of racism. Some years ago I said to a priest friend that I thought that he would be a bishop some day. "Never," he replied, explaining that to be a bishop one needed a name which began with an "O," not one which ended with one. Bishops were named O'Reilly; they were not named Romano—at least not in this country. To the degree that was true catholicity was diminished. It diminished catholicity in the same way that a Vatican with names that end in "O" exclusively also diminishes catholicity.

The ethnic component of religion will never disappear (nor should we want it to) precisely because religious systems are such potent carriers of cultural identity. The strength of Polish Catholicism today is not rooted in the innate holiness or moral superiority of the Poles, but it has much to do with the role of the Polish church as a preserver and propagandist of Polish national identity. One of the functions of religion, as Durkheim pointed out decades ago, is to provide social cohesion for a group. The great danger comes when those social ideals become absolutized in the name of religion so that this or that culture becomes ipso facto a "Catholic" or a "Protestant" culture. If the sectarian temptation is the regnant temptation of the left, the prevailing temptation of the right comes from its misidentification of cultural forms with genuine religion. When someone becomes overly enamoured of the "cross and the flag" or some variant of that theme, the suspicious religious mind should automatically switch to "ready alert."

The ethnic impulse is not confined to this or that country. In a sense the Roman Catholic church has always had to fight against its own internal temptation to overemphasize the adjective *Roman* so as to make Catholicism identifiable with Western cultural forms. The older insistence on Latin as the predominant language of the church, both in liturgy and as an "official" language for theology and church communication, was one sign of this tendency. The export of the Latin language, European architecture, schools, etc., to the mission lands of Africa and Asia was one way in which Catholicism came to be considered just one more manifestation of Western colonial expansionism in the last century. The degree to which the church is able to accommodate cultures alien to Western values is a test of catholicity.

That such accommodations are difficult can be seen in the refusal of Pope John Paul II to participate in an Africanized liturgy when he visited Zaire in 1980. Pope John Paul evidently felt that a totally Africanized Mass (and all that it symbolized) was too radical a departure from the larger Catholic reality of the liturgy. In his address in Kinshasha on that occasion (where he celebrated the liturgy in French) the pope said that such changes as those envisioned in the liturgy must derive from "a wide exchange among yourselves, in union with the Universal church and the Holy See."[14]

What one sees in the Kinshasha incident is a microcosm of the problem of catholicity. Let us view it from the side of the pope and then from the side of the archbishop in Zaire. For the pope the issue is this: How does one remain faithful to the tradition of the church while allowing a legitimate expression of cultural diversity? For the archbishop: How can I integrate the words, symbols, rituals, and concepts of the West into a culture which is completely foreign to these notions? In both cases the crux is the avoidance of ethnocentricity in favor of catholicity. The problem, of course, becomes all the more magnified when certain cultural issues impinge on more central structures of the faith. In Zaire, for example, there is not only much sentiment for a married clergy but for a legitimation of African polygamy. It was an open secret that some priests and bishops were, de facto, already married, some with more than one wife. When Pope John Paul II spoke in Kinshasha, his talk was not only on liturgy but on the defense of the traditional view of marriage.

To choose catholicity over ethnocentricity or partisanship is a difficult choice to make even on an individual level. Our own sense of who we are, where we belong, and what we have to be proud of is so much a part of our ethnic and national backgrounds that it is difficult to hold that sense of ourselves in check. To be truly Catholic demands some degree of self-abnegation.

But such openness can occur. The greatest recent advance in the expansion of the spirit of catholicity in the church has been in the positive effects of ecumenism. For the past two decades the Catholic church has been nurtured and enriched by its willingness to step out of its defensive trenches and *listen* to the insights of other Christian traditions; indeed, I think it is fair to say that such listening has been a two-way street. As a result of that listening (that receptive silence of which we speak elsewhere) the Catholic church has been enriched by the Reformation's emphasis on the word and by the Eastern Orthodox concern for wisdom and the Spirit. Openness to these rich spiritual veins illustrates how the church can grow and learn. To accept insights from other traditions is to admit that others can instruct. That admission is at the heart of catholicity. Catholicity is not being everywhere but listening to everything.

The willingness to listen to the other Christian experiences has been paralleled by attention to the religious experiences of those who are outside the Christian tradition. Some of the most striking formulations of Catholic piety have come, in recent days, from those who are willing to learn from the world outside Christianity. We all know how powerful a witness we have received from the spirituality of Thomas Merton, Bede Griffiths, John Dunne, and those others who are listeners and learners.

One of the most interesting of these patient listeners was the French priest Jules Monchanin (1895–1957) who founded a contemplative center in India patterned after the traditional Indian ashram. Monchanin died on the eve of the council, but his life was a witness to the openness of catholicity. He wanted to live a life which was totally Indian and thoroughly Christian. He labored first as a village pastor in India and then as a contemplative hermit; in both roles he portrayed a profound love for India and an equally profound love for Christ. When Father Monchanin (and his first collaborator, the Benedictine monk Father Le Saux) started their contemplative experiment, they printed a small booklet entitled *A Benedictine Ashram* to set forth their ideas. It is a model of the kind of catholicity which is at the heart of the church:

Christ expects of each land and of each people an outburst of praise and love, which they alone can offer him. Very often the church is compared by the Fathers to the *polymita tunica* (the coat of many colors) of the patriarch Joseph, to the splendidly adorned mantle of the bride of Solomon *circumdata varietate.* A particular type of Christian spirituality has to evolve out of the particular genius of the people of each country. The qualitative universality of the Church, nowhere foreign, never outdated, but contemporary with every age and connatural with every civilization, is but the final harmonizing and synthesizing of all civilizations, assumed by Christ, the absolute man, into his theandric pleroma.[15]

That kind of catholicity is sharply distinguished from a simple-minded syncretism which takes in anything but lacks a fundamental position from which to discriminate the useful from the harmful. Catholicism begins with an irrefragible position (roughly being: "Jesus is Lord."), but is open to the new; it is not, however, true catholicity to simply vacuum up whatever ideas happen to be lying about. To be open to other traditions does not mean uncritical acceptance; it does mean willingness to listen—and that is very difficult in its own right. The capacity to listen *religiously* to other cultures is a great gift. Here is how William Johnston, after a quarter of a century in Japan, expresses it when speaking of Christian-Buddhist relationships:

Now I believe that a time will come, probably in the next century, when we or those who come after us will forge a common way of speaking and even some kind of common theology. At present I think it is only possible for a Christian to speak from a Christian viewpoint and for a Buddhist to speak from a Buddhist viewpoint while we work towards mutual understanding, cooperation, and love. . . . Let me write about Christianity as an insider and about Buddhism as a sympathetic outsider who has learned very much and wishes to learn more.[16]

Catholicity and Skepticism

To this point we have emphasized the rather paradoxical fact that true catholicity is conservative and open. We have insisted that Catholicism has the constant dialectical task of balancing its memory with what it learns in each new age. To achieve that balance requires the cultivation of a subtle sense of discrimination so that memory does not ossify and openness does not become promiscuous. The great threats to the catholicity of the church are uncritical rigidity and uncritical faddishness.

Let us try to make this a bit more concrete by posing this question: How do I become a better *Catholic* Christian (with *Catholic* being understood not in the denominational sense)— one who is rooted in the memory of Christ and open to the complex unfolding of the world? My short answer would be that I must cultivate that basic attitude which has been called Christian realism. The term *Christian realism* (or variants of it) is used by a number of contemporary theologians like Richard McBrien, John and Denise Carmody, and Michael Novak for somewhat different but not necessarily contradictory ends. By the term, however, we mean something like a balance or golden mean by which we find reconciliation amid a number of pressing religious polarities:

1. *The dialectic of sin and grace:* The Catholic tradition has never accepted either the notion of total human depravity or the idea of human perfection. To be Catholic means never being surprised by the fact of human sin but, at the same time, never being overwhelmed by it. Catholicism has always rejected the notion of the church as a perfectionist group of "saints"; it is more at home with the model of the field which has both grain and tares.

2. *The gnostic temptation:* There has been a persistent strain of religious thought with which catholicity has contended from the beginning. It is the notion that there is in religion a more perfect way—a *gnosis*—free from the muck of ordinary existence and the sweat of human history. The gnostic, by instinct, is a spiritual snob. To have the truth in spirit is to stand beyond the mob and, easily enough, to despise it for being a mob. Catholicism does have avenues for the pursuit of perfection and it provides recognition for those who pursue those paths. Saints are the religious virtuosi of Catholicism. The great lesson of the saints is that closeness to God comes by the transformation of the ordinary: It is the "little way" of Thérèse

of Lisieux; the simple joy of St. Francis; the charity of a Vincent de Paul; the earthy good sense of the mystic St. Teresa of Avila; the personal simplicity of a Thomas Aquinas. The gnostic is an elitist and a perfectionist; the Catholic is a democrat and a realist. The gnostic hates the world, wishes to destroy it as it is and start over; the Catholic understands the world, loves it, suffers no illusions about it; looks to the future.

3. *Reality and Idealism:* The Catholic is one who refuses the simple-minded empiricism of "what you see is what you get" as surely as she or he rejects an idealism unattached to the real textures of the world. The Catholic, in short, is suspicious of the naïve realism of the fundamentalist (whether religious or scientific) and the uncritical mind of science partisans of "going with the flow" or "getting it" or whatever the current cliché is. McBrien, utilizing categories from Bernard Lonergan, states the Catholic middle way with succinctness:

> Critical realism, or what Lonergan calls Christian realism, insists that experience alone is not enough. One can "take a look" but one cannot be sure that what one sees corresponds entirely to what is real. . . . Christian realism also rejects the notion that clear and distinct ideas (doctrines, dogmas, canonical directives) are equivalent to the real itself. . . . Just as Christian realism rejects biblicism and moralism in favor of a critical and systematic approach to reality, so Christian realism rejects dogmatism and legalism in favor of a critical approach to reality, an approach that goes beyond what seems to be there and that takes historicity into account in the use and interpretation of ideas and principles.[17]

4. *The World and Eternity:* Catholicism is a fleshly religion; it affirms the Incarnation and defines itself as a sacramental church, i.e., a church made present by visible and tactile realities. It feels no compunction in its appeal to the senses; it is iconic, tuneful, colorful, and sensual. It has not hesitated to superimpose itself on older forms of religious life when those forms were closely tied to the ancient earth religions of the world. For all its rootedness in the earth, however, Catholicism also insists that there is something more, something beyond, something that is not yet. The great balancing act of the true Catholic is to keep in mind that "not yet" without

losing a love for this world or, contrariwise, to love the world with fullness without losing sight of what is beyond it. It is that battle to reconcile matter and spirit which Walker Percy has called the struggle against angelism/bestialism. In his satirical novel *Love in the Ruins* (1971) he explored that tension between love of the world and the transcendent horizon of reality as thoroughly as any theologian of our time. The hero of that novel, the existentially shaky Doctor Thomas More, cries out a prayer from his hospital bed (he had bungled a suicide attempt), which is one of the most Catholic prayers I have ever read:

> Dear God, I can see it now, why can't I see it at other times, that it is you I love in the beauty of the world and in all the lovely girls and dear good friends, and it is pilgrims we are, wayfarers on a journey, and not pigs nor angels. . . .[18]

Points for Meditation

1. If you had to list ten things which were "typically" Catholic, what would they be? What would your list say about your concept of catholicity?

2. What do you think Protestantism most has to teach Catholicism? And vice versa?

3. To what degree do you equate uniformity with catholicity? To what degree do you think that various regions of the world (e.g., Africa) should be permitted to "go it alone" in terms of their liturgical or personal styles of life? How would you still keep a catholicity of intention in such churches?

4. Do you think being Catholic has made you an open person? If not, do you see that as a personal or ecclesiastical flaw?

5. What do you most love (or dislike) about being a Catholic?

Notes

1. Hans Küng, *The Church* (New York: Sheed and Ward, 1967), p. 297.

2. John Henry Newman, *Apologia Pro Vita Sua*, ed. David DeLaura (New York: Norton, 1968), p. 99.

3. Owen Chadwick, *The Victorian Church*, vol. 1 (New York: Oxford University Press, 1966), p. 180.

4. Karl Adam, *The Spirit of Catholicism* (Garden City: Doubleday Image Book, 1954), pp. 153–541.

5. *Dogmatic Constitution on the Church*, art. 8, in *The Documents of Vatican II*, ed. Walter Abbott (New York: Association Press, 1966), p. 23.

6. Hans Küng, *On Being a Christian* (Garden City: Doubleday, 1976), p. 503 and passim.

7. Richard McBrien, *Catholicism*, vol. 2 (Minneapolis: Winston, 1980), p. 1080.

8. This is a commonplace in the sociology of religion; see Werner Stark, *The Sociology of Religion*, vol. 3 (London: Routledge and Kegan Paul, 1967), and Michael Hill, *The Religious Order* (London: Heinemann, 1973).

9. John W. O'Malley, "Reform, Historical Consciousness, and Vatican II's Aggiornamento," *Theological Studies* 32 (1971) 573–601; "Developments, Reforms, and Two Great Reformations: Toward a Historical Assessment of Vatican II," *Theological Studies* 43 (1983) 373–406.

10. O'Malley, "Developments, Reforms", p. 406.

11. George Orwell, *The Road to Wigan Pier* (New York: Harvest Paperback, 1958), pp. 177–78.

12. James Joyce, *A Portrait of the Artist as a Young Man* (New York: Penguin, 1977), p. 156.

13. Michael Novak, *Confessions of a Catholic* (San Francisco: Harper and Row, 1983), pp. 101–8.

14. Quoted in George H. William's *The Mind of John Paul II* (New York: Seabury, 1981), p. 304. For a survey of African theologies, see Justin S. Ukpong, "The Emergence of African Theologies," *Theological Studies* 45 (1984) 501–36; for an overview of African Catholicism, see the issue "Learning From Africa," *Cross Currents* 27, no. 4 (Winter 1978–79).

15. J. G. Weber, ed. and trans., *In Quest of the Absolute: The Life and Works of Jules Monchanin* (Kalamazoo: Cistercian Publications, 1977), pp. 76–77.

16. William Johnston, *The Inner Eye of Love: Mysticism and Religion* (San Francisco: Harper and Row, 1978), p. 16.

17. McBrien, *Catholicism*, vol. 2, p. 1179. The work of Bernard Lonergan he refers to is "The Origins of Christian Realism," in *A Second Collection*, ed. F. J. Ryan and Bernard J. Tyrrell (Philadelphia: Westminster, 1975), pp. 239–61.

18. Walker Percy, *Love in the Ruins* (New York: Dell, 1972), p. 104.

Selected Readings

Boff, Leonardo. *Church: Charism and Power*. New York: Crossroad, 1985. Catholicism from the perspective of a theologian of liberation.

Cunningham, Lawrence. *The Catholic Heritage*. New York: Crossroad, 1983. A study of ideal types in the Catholic tradition.

De Lubac, Henri. *The Splendour of the Church*. New York: Sheed and Ward, 1956. A classic study characterized by deep learning. Invaluable.

Gilkey, Langdon. *Catholicism Confronts Modernity*. New York: Seabury, 1974. Catholicism from a Protestant perspective. Important.

Haughton, Rosemary. *The Catholic Thing*. Springfield: Templegate, 1979. A wonderfully readable attempt to get at the Catholic essence.

9

COMMUNITY

Toward the end of Ignazio Silone's classic novel *Bread and Wine* the hero Pietro Spina (masquerading as a priest) is at the home of a family whose son had been tortured to death by the fascist police. Pietro himself is in hiding from the police. The dead boy's father offers to the assembled visitors at the farm house the traditional peasant food of bread and wine which were the products of their own humble farm. It is "his" bread and wine the grieving father insists since he cultivated the grape vines and helped with the sowing of the grain. Pietro Spina sits at the table with the peasants and comments:

"The bread is made from many ears of grain . . . therefore it signifies unity. The wine is made from many grapes, and therefore it, too, signifies unity. A unity of similar things, equal and united. Therefore it means truth and brotherhood too: these are things which go well together. . . ."[1]

That particular scene, like many in the novel, echoes the language of sacred scripture. Silone, writing as an antifascist (and as an anticommunist), wanted the hero of his novel to be understood as a new kind of priest who would teach people to live with a passion for justice, a prophetic disdain for social and personal evil, and a burning love for neighbor. That new kind of priest was to preside over a new eucharist, i.e., a meal of peasant food—bread and wine—at which, in the very sharing of the meal, people would have a strong sense of belonging, of community, of solidarity.

Silone's novel *Bread and Wine* was written in the 1930s and reflects the novelist's own strong stand against the totalitarian state. What is interesting, however (and rarely ever pointed out), is that Silone anticipates by decades the major themes of current liberation theology. Silone's vision of Christianity was a radically new one based on a model which is strongly oriented to the future, evolving out of lay reflection and committed to the poor and dispossessed. The vision of the church reflected in Silone's novels is a church which is hidden, small, prophetically engaged, and, above all, communitarian. It is a church radically alienated and estranged from the power and prestige both of official church and of official society. It is at odds with what the liberation theologians call, with bitter irony, "Christendom."

The point that Silone emphasizes time and again—and it may serve as an entry point for this chapter—is that people do not create community by going out and starting one ("let's begin a congenial and sympathetic community"). Communities are born and nurtured by those who find a common sense of purpose which is recognized and celebrated. Communities are the natural product of deep convictions which overarch the individual impulses of this or that person. When conviction is felt and expressed, then community is born.

One common expression of that shared conviction is the ritual of the communal meal. Silone argues that the words "companion" and "brother" both have etymological links to the notion of shared eating: "companion" from the Latin *cum pane* ("with bread") and "brother" from the old Germanic root *brod* (bread).* We become "companions" when we share a meal; sharing bread makes us brethren. Eating together, in short, has profoundly deep social meanings.

That the central act of Christian worship should be centered on a meal should not surprise us. In line with its Jewish antecedent (the Passover meal) the Eucharist is a symbol of unity and reconciliation. At the Eucharist we recite a common creed, beg forgiveness for our sins, exchange the Kiss of Peace, recite the Lord's Prayer in unison—we perform, in short, a

---

* I have not been able to verify the latter etymology; it is not indicated in the *OED* as an etymological source for the word "brother."

whole series of symbolic gestures to indicate our unity at the Lord's table.

The idea that a meal expresses unity is deeply rooted in common experience. Most of us, in fact, have had such experiences in our own ordinary life which give empirical force to the proposition. In the round of family life festal meals like those at Christmas, Thanksgiving, Easter, etc., are occasions when families reunite, when efforts are made to be nice to the more odious relatives, and when, obviously, the occasion is freighted with more than the simple act of eating. Because of the special character of such meals, great pains are taken to avoid any disturbance or discomfort which would mar the festive mood of the meal. That is why disturbances at such meals seem so terrible and discordant as readers of Joyce's account of a spoiled Christmas meal in *The Portrait of the Artist as a Young Man* will readily recall.

The eucharistic meal is the preeminent sign of Christian unity and Christian community. It is for that reason that so much attention has been paid to the question of intercommunion among Christians. The question of an ecumenical communion is a very complex one, but at its heart there is this single issue: Should the sharing of the Eucharist signify a unity already achieved or could it be seen as an instrument for the seeking of unity? It is the former sentiment which has been most prominent in the Catholic tradition; indeed the Second Vatican Council taught that divine law itself forbade any common worship (*communicatio in sacris*) which would "damage the unity of the church or involve formal acceptance of falsehood or the danger of deviation in the faith, of scandal, or of indifferentism."[2]

Ecumenical discussion, cooperation, and common prayer have all done much to bring the various Christian bodies closer together over the decades since Vatican II. Consensus about theological issues has been reached with a number of ecclesial bodies so that the official possibility of sharing the Eucharist with some non-Roman Catholic churches is on the horizon. When such Eucharists are celebrated, it will be in the nature of a momentous event since in those celebrations the deepest power of the symbolism of the Eucharist as a meal will become manifest.

For the ordinary Catholic who goes to Mass each Sunday the Eucharist is also a sign of unity. That sought-after unity operates at a number of levels in ordinary life. At the beginning of the Sunday liturgy we confess our sins and ask for God's reconciliation so that, in the first instance, we be not estranged from God. Secondly, we try to be reconciled with those who are bonded to us either by blood or by relationship since we are admonished in the Gospel to "leave your offering there before the altar, go and be reconciled with your brother first, and then come back and present your offering" (Mt. 5:24). Finally, we are bound in unity not only with those who are present at church with us but with the entire body of believers who profess the same faith and share the same meal. The unity which derives from the celebration of the Eucharist is beautifully attested to in the *Didache*, one of the earliest noncanonical Christian texts we possess:

As this broken bread was scattered over the hills and then, when gathered, became one mass, so may thy church be gathered from the ends of the earth into thy kindgom. For thine is the glory and the power through Jesus Christ forevermore.[3]

It may seem banal to insist on the point, but parish life, summed up in the liturgy, should be the communitarian apex of the daily Catholic experience. It is in that corporate act of worship that we make concrete "one faith, one baptism, and one Lord."

It has been argued, however, that parish life is too impersonal, too large, too "mechanical" or rationalized to provide a sense of community either at the liturgical or at the social levels. For that reason there have been any number of attempts to create alternative, intentional, voluntary, communities as substitutes for the traditional parish as we know it. Even within parishes there have been experiments with small group worship services (neighborhood "living room" liturgies). Experiments of this kind (and the more radical moves to found alternative communities to parishes) have had a varied history of success in attempting to provide an alternative for those who find ordinary parish life a trial.

It would be utopian to think that the parish structure or some variety of it will disappear from church life in North

America in the near future to be replaced by smaller, more intimate communities. Given the current structure and understanding of the church, the parish probably should not disappear. What the typical parish does provide is a structural umbrella for smaller interest groups (e.g., Cursillo, St. Vincent de Paul societies, etc.) to meet and still provide some way of manifesting their larger sense of Catholic community at Sunday Mass. It is, I would submit, good for the *cursillista*, the Marriage Encounter couple, the charismatic, etc., to be together in the pews on Sunday. On that issue I am unabashedly nonelitist and egalitarian: Let the most "advanced" of us take our place in the parish on Sunday. It is there that we celebrate in time and space the catholicity of our religion. It is from that base that we move to take our place in other communities of interest.

The Search for Community

The family and the parish are the "base communities" for most of us who are Catholics in North America. It is there that we share our meals (communion) and it is there that we attempt to affirm ourselves as a community. However much family and parish have functioned as the anchors of community, they never did exhaust the desire for other networks of support. They certainly do not do so today when both institutions have come in for both attack and a weakening of their relevance.

When we look back into Catholic history, we see a plethora of attempts at creating community in order to satisfy the religious exigencies of people. What is monasticism, after all, but an attempt to live out a certain ideal of Christian community free of egoism and material striving and rooted in mutual cooperation, sharing, and charity—a community where everyone is "sister" or "brother" under the benevolent direction not of a boss or a master but a "father" or a "mother."

In one very real sense monasticism (and its many offshoots in religious living) has been an exercise in social fantasy, i.e., monasticism attempts to show the larger world how life could be lived if people would subsume the ego needs of the individual for the great good of the whole after the pattern of the Gospel.

One of the earliest books on monasticism explicitly compares the "peaceful kingdom" of the desert ascetics with the social horrors of the cities of the world:

> So their cells in the hills were like tents filled with divine choirs—people chanting, studying, fasting, praying, rejoicing in the hope of future boons, working for the distribution of alms, and maintaining both love and harmony among themselves. It was as if one looked on a land all its own—a land of devotion and righteousness. For neither perpetrator nor victim of injustice, nor complaint of tax collector was there. And there was a multitude of ascetics, but among them all there was one mind and it was set on virtue. . . .[4]

That demonstrative side of religious life often had a prophetic edge to it. The medieval mendicant brotherhoods like the Franciscans arose in the cities as alternative communities for those who would not accept the mercantile values of the newly powerful city elites. The Franciscans must be seen—at least in part—as a prophetic challenge to the greed and materialism of the age. It is not accidental that St. Francis of Assisi's father was a merchant and that central to the story of Francis is the breach between the saint and his father over the disposition of goods for the poor.

The Franciscan challenge to its age is only one example from many in the history of the church where communities were created to challenge the exigencies of the time. The great clerical societies founded at the time of the Counter-Reformation (the Jesuits, the Theatines, the Oratorians, etc.) were powerful countersigns for the demoralized, corrupt, and undereducated clergy of the time. The spectacular growth of active women's religious societies started after the pioneering foundation of the Sisters of Charity (founded by St. Vincent de Paul and Louise de Marillac in 1673 in Paris) was a sign of the gradual emancipation of women in the church as well as a recognition of a need for social services. It was the examples of groups like the Sisters of Charity, for example, which would lead women like Florence Nightingale in the nineteenth century to envision other ways for women to enter into social service.

It should also be noted that during the entire Middle Ages

(indeed, as early as the sixth century) there were confraternities, pious societies, and *ordines* in which lay people could express their desire for a more perfect life by a loose confederation with established religious life. Indeed, as recent scholarship indicates, the distinction between those who were technically in the religious life and those who wished to live in the lay state and follow a life of greater piety could not always be distinguished with ease. Whatever the canonical clarity of the distinction between "lay" and "clerical" status in the medieval period, it was, in part, theorizing: "Distinctions were constantly blurred and monastic and clerical prerogatives were quickly imitated by the laity."[5] One conspicuous example of this blurring was the rise of the so-called third orders by which lay people belonged to a branch of a religious order like the Franciscans or Carmelites.

Our present age is the heir of this long and complex tradition of religious orders, third orders, confraternities, lay organizations, and so on. It is very difficult to see what the direction of such communities will be, although the decline in membership of religious orders is a conspicuous fact of contemporary life. The number of women religious who have departed regular life in the last two decades is staggering; the number of male priests and religious, alarming. Some religious communities are beyond crisis; they are in their death throes. Unless there is a reversal of current trends (and there is no convincing sign of such a reversal), we can only say that a certain kind of religious community is on the wane with no clear indication of what will replace it.

While I say that I do not see any clear indication of what will replace (or reshape) religious community life in the future, it is equally true that one sees certain experiments which have taken place in modern times as telling us something about the culture in which we live. These experiments reflect not only the exigencies of contemporary culture but the impulses of the church itself.

One thing that strikes the careful student of modern Catholicism is the number of attempts made in our age to get close to the poorest and most alienated of the world while, at the same time, breaking down the artificial barriers of traditional religious life. The Little Brothers and the Little Sisters of Jesus founded on the ideals of Charles de Foucauld (1858–1916) have attempted to lead a contemplative life not in the fastness of a rural monastery but in the midst of the worst economic "deserts" of our contemporary world. They desire to live among the poor as the poor and establish a "presence." Thus, typically, a small group of brothers or sisters will take a slum apartment, work for a living if work is available, develop a regular life of prayer, and simply "be there." They are the new desert dwellers of the church except that they live in artificial deserts; they are to be found living on junks in Hong Kong harbor; among the nomads of Algeria; in shanty towns around the vast cities of Latin America; a few of them even live with women prisoners in pentitentiaries or in gypsy caravans. Their mission is a blend of the very traditional spirituality of the church and a radical understanding of the alienation of our world. The sympathetic journalist Peter Nichols writes of the Little Sisters:

> They accept that whatever happens to the Church happens because of the action of the Holy Spirit. They prefer to work among non-Christians but if they are with nominally Christian people they accept the normal structures, going to church like exemplary parishioners. The one distinction they make is to wear their habits. They want it to be clear that they are Christian sisters, even if they are evicted from their homes like the Black neighbors among whom they have been living in a South African city. . . . They are treated with awe by other missionaries. They are not even missionaries in any classical sense of the term because they do not preach as such. They show people what Christians should be.[6]

The Little Brothers and Little Sisters are vowed religious; some of the Little Brothers are ordained to the priesthood. They can be distinguished from those layfolks who either make a temporary or a lifelong commitment to serve the poor while living in community. The Catholic Workers, founded by Peter Maurin (1877–1949) and Dorothy Day (1897–1980) in the Depression days of the 1930s, are committed to living in community with the poor in what they call "houses of hospitality," providing shelter, food, clothes, warmth, and care for the poorest, most bewildered, and neglected of our cities. The Workers live in voluntary poverty to serve the poor whose poverty is neither voluntary nor redemptive. Numerically the number of Catholic Workers has been quite small, but their impact on the American church has been large indeed both by reason of their example and by their commitment to the principles of Christian love and witness. It is safe to say, I think, that Dorothy Day is one of the most loved and revered persons in American Catholicism.

One other contemporary experiment in community, of a totally different type, is the community known as *L'Arche* ("The Ark"). It is a movement which provides a familylike atmosphere of living for mentally handicapped people. Begun by the Canadian philosopher Jean Vanier (1928–   ) in 1964, there are now over fifty L'Arche communities in the world where volunteers live in family settings with those who suffer from mental illness or mental deficiencies. It is a committed Christian alternative to the faceless warehousing of the mentally handicapped.

Vanier has meditated and written upon community with much persistence. His L'Arche families are ecumenical in their makeup (one community in Northern Scotland has eight different Christian denominations represented) but, in the final analysis, are rooted in a common faith in Christ and a shared willingness to celebrate that faith. Vanier sees a profound connection between faith-ful celebration and community:

> A celebration, you know, is quite different from a leisure activity. We could talk for hours about the importance of celebration. No, celebration is not the same as leisure activity; it is much closer to thanksgiving. It isn't simply a diversion. And if we want to celebrate in this world of ours, we have to celebrate as a community, whether it be a family community or any other in which it's given us to live. Our family community or the community in which we live together is this earth, where we can grow like children, in tenderness and fidelity. That's where we can welcome one another and ourselves with all our frailty, and discover the mystery of God, present in the wound of our own being.[7]

Vanier and his fellow members of L'Arche have had over

two decades of experience with living in community. His reflections, both written and spoken; reflect both his idealism and his realistic assessment about the living out of community ideals.

Vanier knows about human weakness, the fragility of faith, the irritations of living together, the sheer tension which comes from human effort. He also recognizes that communities like L'Arche require a special calling and a special readiness to be self-giving; how many of us, in all honesty, could even conceive of living in an extended family with mentally handicapped persons? Still, Vanier is convinced that within the church there ought to be a wide variety of community possibilities both to reach those who are wounded and as vehicles for those who desire to deepen and expand their sense of being a Christian. The very plethora of communitarian efforts, whether permanent or not, testifies to the creative desires of those in the church who wish to incarnate their deepest desires into some kind of tangible and imitable reality. On this Vanier writes:

> Our world has more and more need of "intermediate communities"—places where people can stay and find a certain interior freedom before they make their decision. They either cannot stay in their family or don't want to; they are not satisfied with life alone in a hotel, hostel, or apartment. They need somewhere where they can find interior liberation through a network of relationships and friendships, where they can be truly themselves without trying or pretending to be anything other than what they are. It is in these intermediate communities that they will be able to shed what is weighing them down and preventing them from discovering their deep selves. It is only when they have been exposed to the poor and to other values that they will be free to choose and construct a project which is truly their own, not that of their parents or the people around them, nor something set up in reaction to it, but one which is born of a real choice of life, in response to an aspiration or a call.[8]

Vanier's comments are both shrewd and timely. They underscore the essential catholicity of all serious attempts at community building. Charles de Foucauld, Mother Teresa, Jean Vanier, Dorothy Day, Peter Maurin, and all the other persons who have attempted to bond people together to serve the needs of the Gospel have understood two things simultaneously; that there are real needs to be served in the world beyond our own and that these needs can be served when "two or three" are gathered in God's name. The many experiments in intentional community are evidences, in the last analysis, of the abiding reality of the Incarnation and incarnational spirituality. They are genuine efforts to make tactile and real the presence of Christ among the people of the world. The vocations of the various communities are complementary; they all add to the maturing of the Gospel in the world: They are all branches of that unique community which is the church, the mystical Body of Christ. He is the vine of which the communities are branches.

Basic Christian Communities

One of the most intriguing and fast-growing phenomena in contemporary Catholicism is the growth of what are called *basic Christian communities* or, simply, *base communities.** Such communities are found, for the most part, in the Third World areas of Latin America, Asia, and Africa. They are most conspicuous in Brazil which has about seventy thousand of them. While the term is a common one, the reality is a bit more complex. For our purposes we can distinguish those communities which are founded primarily for pastoral strategies and those—predominantly but not exclusively—where a definite political agenda is part and parcel of the community's purpose.

Pastoral base communities were proposed over a decade ago as useful alternatives to European style parishes by a number of African bishops in countries like Malawi, Kenya, Uganda, Tanzania, and Zambia. The bishops proposed small communities under lay leadership to both promote the long-term health of the local church and to serve as an instrument for further evangelization. By helping people to stay together, the communities hold weekly Bible services, encourage both adult and youth education, prepare couples for marriage, foster

---

* The English terms, as inelegant as they are, attempt to translate the Spanish phrase *comunidades eclesiales de base.*

interest in the sacramental life of the community, promote social self-reliance both for the village and in relationship to the church. The communities, under lay leadership, in short, do everything that a parish could do except exercise those ministries peculiar to the ordained priesthood.

Such communities, in short, are miniparishes under the lay control of catechists or other similar ministers. They exist to foster intimacy, relieve an overburdened clergy, and actively involve people in the life of the church community. They are of crucial importance for the maintenance of the life of the church and may well evolve into models for the future church when the older notions of ministry and organization will no longer be functional.

In Latin America the basic Christian communities have taken on a more explicitly political character as they have evolved. Indeed, for some theologians the base communities reflect both a new kind of theological understanding and a new manner of structuring the church (i.e., the church of the people) according to the theology of liberation. Base communities started from those small groupings of individuals who came together as intentional groups seeking to strengthen their life of prayer and their life of sharing the Gospel. From this purely spiritual start (the original idea of the base community has much in common with the older notion of the Catholic Action "cell") the communities developed through two other stages:

> communities which, in addition, devote themselves to certain social tasks, to charitable action, to mutual aid within the neighborhood, and begin to think about improving or building collective facilities like dispensaries or primary schools, etc. (communities of mutual aid); communities which go a step further along the road to political awareness and begin to demand social reforms (communities which change society).[10]

It is estimated, as we noted, that there are about seventy thousand of these communities in Brazil alone with many of them existing among the poorest neighborhoods. Some have been in existence for some time and reflect attempts to keep Christian communities together where there was a lack of clergy; they evolved from models of lay Christian groups like the Legion of Mary or the Better World Movement of Father Lombardi. In their present state they are seen as paradigms for a new kind of church. The Brazilian theologian Leonardo Boff sees them as the emerging vanguard of a new Christianity.[11] Father Boff sees this church, incarnated in the *comunidades,* as having a new character and possessed of new ecclesial notes (*notae*). His concept of this new church is radically different from older ecclesiologies. This people's church is made up of the poor, the despoiled, and the disenherited; it is a lay church in the sense that it is made up of the people (*laos*) by definition. This church experiences a fellowship of power (i.e., it can do things; it can liberate), it is wholly ministerial, and it is in diaspora, i.e., it is separated, scattered, and in tension with the power pretension of "Christendom." This new church liberates people and symbolizes and sacramentalizes that liberation both as an individual and as a social reality. It is a church which continues what Boff calls "the Great Tradition" which Boff considers to be the church of the Acts of the Apostles and the church of the martyrs, and the various prophetic movements in the church that have repeatedly arisen. It is in communion with the "Great Church" as a concrete manifestation of its continuing presence among the poor. Its unity is rooted in its identification and solidarity with the poor of the world while its primary mission is to liberate those people wherever they may be. That is also the dimension which justifies its catholicity since it links together everyone who opts for justice and love. Its apostolicity is an imitation of the Twelve who were a messianic community and a collegial body. Finally, this church creates a radically new kind of spirituality appropriate both to its mission and to the present age:

> But the grassroots ecclesial communities are creating the conditions for another kind of holiness, that of the militant. Rather than concentrating on the fight against one's passions, which remains a permanent struggle, one fights politically against the creation and use of exploitive mechanisms of accumulation; and one fights for the establishment of more well balanced, communitarian relationships. The new virtues find expression in class solidarity, participation in community decisions, mutual aid, criticism of abuses of power, endurance of slander and persecution for the sake of justice, unjust imprisonment, loss

of one's job, and aversion to private profit and accumulation that is devoid of social responsibility. . . . Many communities are preserving and cherishing the name of their confessors and martyrs. The recall them in their celebrations, and celebrate their victories.[12]

One need not read a great deal of liberation theology to see how radically new the theoreticians of the *comunidades* conceive them to be. They see these small groups, held together by a common passion and a common faith, as the vanguard of a popular church which will radically reform (if not sweep away) the older models of Christianity.

What is to be said of these communities?

First of all, they are a reality in the contemporary church and apart from the theorizing about their significance we need to say that their evolution comes from recognizable Catholic forms. It also seems indisputable that they reflect an intense desire for the poor to have some sense of support and some feeling that they could claim control over their lives and understand their plight as well as some need for a language to express those transcendent needs for liberation, freedom, and human love. Secondly, it seems equally clear that they provide a sense of community and fraternal support in a way that the older parishes never could. Indeed, in the case of the African bishops, the parish (in the European sense of a territorial parish) was rejected as an alien and unworkable concept for the reality of Africa. The emphasis on manageable community was sociologically and anthropologically closer to the intense kinship bonds of African culture. The same, *mutatis mutandis*, is true in Latin America especially in view of the fact that the ratio of clergy to layfolks is so wide and so many communities could not experience the normal life of a parish.

Whatever the circumstances that triggered the rise of the communities and whatever their utility with respect to certain situations, one must still ask whether their *theoretical* justification and their direction are something to be viewed with equanimity. The Vatican evidently doesn't think so. According to press dispatches (e.g., NC News Service—3/25/84) the prefect of the Congregation for the Doctrine of the Faith, Joseph Cardinal Ratzinger, sees much of liberation theology as an absorption of the Gospel into the categories of historical materialism and Marxist ideology. He recognizes that there is great appeal to the formulations of liberation theology because of its total commitment to the poor, but sees its theology as basically inimical to the Gospel. The great problem for the church, the cardinal concluded, was how to oppose liberation theology in its more Marxist manifestations without seeming to abandon the poor in their need.

From reading apologists like Boff one does get the sense of special pleading. The notion of the elect (i.e., the poor), the utopian wistfulness, the strong identification with a prophetic minority, the simple dismissal of other viewpoints as irrelevant or mystifications, the total politicization of theological language, the ideological reading of the Gospel—all these make one suspicious that the apologists for the *comunidades* are falling prey to a kind of sectarianism and enthusiasm against which the church has always struggled.

There is, of course, theory and practice. It may well be premature (or even gratuitous) to judge the movement of the *comunidades* based on the writings of theorists. My own inclination, writing as a North American with no experience of these movements first-hand, is to apply the principle enunciated by Rabbi Gamaliel in the Acts of the Apostles: It will fail as a movement if it is the work of human agency; it will be unstoppable if it is the work of God.

Whatever may be the long-term of the *comunidades* (to say nothing of their future shape), it is clear that they are only one recent manifestation of something which is a constant in the Catholic tradition, i.e., the search for meaningful and manageable community. That search for community reflects the deep conviction of the Gospel that the Good News is not preached exclusively to individuals but to those who are in communion with each other and with the Lord. It is in that community that Jesus was "known to them in the breaking of the bread" (Lk. 24:35) which led them to conclude that it was a worthy thing to persist in belief, devote themselves to the teachings of Christ, and "fellowship, to the breaking of bread, and prayer" (Acts 2:42).

That intimate bond which ties together small (and, in the

case of parishes, not so small) bodies of believers into community is part of that larger reality which we call the universal church (what Boff calls "the Great Church"). That is why it has been common for centuries to call each worshipping community an *ecclesiola*—"a little church." These small worshipping communities are microcosms of the reality of the great church. Andrew Greeley puts the matter nicely:

> The Eucharist was the public celebration of and the response to Jesus. But the Eucharist was a local event enacted where humans lived and worked. It was a grass roots experience. Humankind responded to God in the same way it lived, not as isolated atoms or a massive collectivity but rather as a collection of small local communities, united in a common faith and a common goal. Global in its aims and vision, local in its daily life, federal in its organizational structure, the assembly offered the model by which human unity would eventually be restructured; that is, universal world vision, local autonomy, and organic structure linking the various local communities in a variegated but integrated unity.[13]

Petrine Community

It would be impossible (or totally perverse) to write a book on Catholicism and not discuss the papacy: *Ubi Petrus, ibi ecclesia* ("Where there is Peter, there is the church"), as the old formulation would have it. In the last analysis what makes the church Catholic (as opposed, say, to Orthodox or Reformed) is that it organizes its *ecclesia*—its community—around the figure of the bishop of Rome who is, Catholics affirm, the successor of the Apostle Peter.

To write of the papacy, then, is a necessity. It is also a heavy burden and, given the complexity of the subject, a risk. The papal office is a lightning rod for all manner of controversy, most of them acrimonious, some of them long standing, and not a few of them current. Within the contemporary church there has been a raging debate over the papal charism of infallibility ever since Hans Küng's *Infallible? An Inquiry* (1972) was published. That debate is intimately linked with the larger discussion of the relationship between papal power and the integrity of the local church. Outside the communion of Roman Catholicism other churches debate and discuss the role of the papacy in the larger context of Christian unity. The strong personality of Pope John Paul II (as well as his biography as a Christian from the Eastern part of Europe) has created interest in the papacy on the part of many who normally take little interest in ecclesiastical affairs.

In the Christian world the papacy is inescapable both as fact and as symbol. To simply visit the Vatican the way a tourist might with a quick tour of St. Peter's Basilica and a very selective glance at some of the treasures of the Vatican museum along with a short visit to the Sistine Chapel (all done before the bus takes the tourist back to the hotel for lunch) forces the question: What, in God's name, does this all have to do with the man who said that while the foxes have barrows and birds nests he had nowhere to lay his head? To stumble upon a full-scale, no holds barred, polyphonic, papal ceremony in the basilica of St. Peter does not encourage thoughts of early Christians breaking bread in upper rooms on the back streets of Mediterranean cities.

It is not the large-scale opulence of the Vatican that raises these kinds of questions as much as the complexity of the history of the Vatican which stands behind such opulence. Even the short American Express tour lets us know that the Vatican functions as a sort of warehouse for Western culture. One can find everything from antique statuary to contemporary art. One walks through St. Peter's and sees a medieval bronze here, a Michelangelo there, the entrance to an early cemetery blocked by a Canova sculpture done in the last century, the fragment of a Giotto fresco facing a bronze door cast by the contemporary sculptor Manzú. These historical artifacts reflect the long line of popes who have lived in the Vatican. That historical line has been a source of unending fascination for the historian. That history has had its glorious moments, its transcendently holy ones, and periods which are so ignominious that one hesitates to remember them. The papal line includes among its number those who died for the faith, those who would have killed to attain the office, those who saw the papcy as a rich sinecure, and those who used it as an opportunity to transform the church and the world.

The papacy is so much a part of Catholicism that Catholics, often pejoratively, were simply called "papists." Such allegiance to the papacy was considered, in the period of the Reformation, a sure sign of corruption and false religion. "Who can count the staff of the pope and the cardinals, even when the pope rides out for pleasure? He is accompanied by three or four thousand on mules, as much as an emperor or a king. Did Christ or Saint Peter go on foot, in order that their vicar might have the more pomp and pride to display?"[14] asked Martin Luther in one of his more restrained outbursts against the Renaissance papacy.

A good deal of the polemical virulence toward the papacy (except among some marginal sectarians) has abated over the years. Ecumenical discussions since the conclusion of the Second Vatican Council have not only helped to clarify the essentials of the papacy for non-Roman Catholics, but also put into perspective the role of the papacy for Catholics. One positive result of these discussions has been a deepening understanding about the place of the papacy in the community of the church.

The literature on the papacy and its role in the church published since Vatican II has been enormous. Some of the most suggestive of these writings have been the reflections of George Tavard who has served as a *peritus* for many official ecumenical discussions between Roman Catholics and other Christian bodies. Tavard argues that when one tries to see the papacy (or, as he would prefer to say, the "Petrine function") as a whole, one must account for a rather complex set of data: the role of Peter in the New Testament and the continuation of Peter's function in the subsequent history of the church; the complexities of the historical developments of the Petrine function; and the theological interpretations attached to the Petrine office and function over the centuries.[15]

Recent scriptural scholarship has helped us get a better understanding of the role of St. Peter in the New Testament church.[16] We also understand that the papacy took on any number of responsible roles in the long course of history. We can see the development of papal offices as the papacy became regarded as the authentic locus of orthodox teaching; when it became a court of last resort for ecclesiastical conflicts; when the pope became understood as being the "vicar of Christ;" when the pope became the supreme governor of the church. In all of these developments there were historical pressures for the papacy to assume roles. This long line of historical development can also be seen, as Tavard insists, as a theological development necessitated by the complexity of life in the universal church and, as such, manifests one constant in this development: The entire history of the papacy, regarded theologically, can be seen as a providential development oriented toward the universality and the unity of the church.

Tavard envisions the papacy as an office (or "function") which would help the church as a whole to express its universality and unity. In that desire his vision is not totally dissimilar to that of Hans Küng who affirms the Petrine office, but, at the same time, wants it to be understood not as an absolute monarchy but as a servant office existing for the good of the entire church. Understood in those broad terms, Küng's vision is an unimpeachable one which strikes me as acceptable to both "conversatives" and "liberals"; nor would this servant office be without relevance for those Christians who are not now in communion with the Roman church. Küng writes:

> Perhaps the Eastern Orthodox or Protestant Christian will be able to sympathize a little with the Catholic in his conviction that something would be lacking in his church and perhaps in Christendom as a whole if this petrine ministry were suddenly to disappear: something that is not inessential to the church. How much it would mean to Christendom if this ministry were freshly understood dispassionately and unsentimentally in the light of Holy Scripture as what it ought to be: service to the church as a whole.[17]

In God's good time we will see some Christian consensus about the Petrine office which will permit it to be a locus of unity for all of Christendom. In the interim, we must ask about the papacy today with respect to its relationship to the local community of faith. Let us leave aside the tensions between papacy and local churches on this or that particular issue (e.g., the almost total lay and largely clerical repudiation of the papal teaching on artificial contraception); such tensions are endemic in the church. The main point is this: For the Catholic, the papacy is the visible guarantee that the church is not merely a sectarian or ethnic or national reality but a *Catholic* one. The pope cannot side with this or that particular ideology or national interest; the pope acts for the good of the universal church and the values of the Gospel.

The papal ministry, then, can be thought of as a servant ministry, i.e., one which attends to and entirely symbolizes the needs of the whole church. That is the deepest meaning of the old papal title *servus servorum Dei*—the servant of the servants of God. It is the privilege and power of the papacy to articulate those truths which are of common concern to the Catholics of Africa, Latin America, Oceania, or North America. The papal presence, in itself and through its utterance, expresses the common faith of the *Catholic*, which is to say, the universal church.

To see the papal office as a servant office is to view it from the angle of the papacy with respect to the church. From the angle of the local church with respect to the papacy there comes the concomitant obligation to hear the voice of Peter with the utmost respect. The papal voice cannot be regarded as just one more voice among others. It must be heard with a faithful willingness to see that voice as expressing the unity of the church. In moral matters the court of last resort for action is the well-formed conscience, but that conscience cannot be formed without reference to papal teaching. In matters of doctrine there can be no sharp disjunction between the faith of the local church and the faith of Peter without, at the same time, wounding the unity of the church. The delicate balance between listening in faith to the voice of Peter while remaining faithful to the Spirit of Christ as experienced in the local church is one of the neuralgic issues of contemporary Catholicism.

The tension between the papal office and the local church has been a prominent issue in recent decades. It is far outside the scope of this chapter to even touch on those issues. However, in a chapter on community, it would be useful to point out that the good of the church is not served by the intransigencies of either the left or the right. The speed with

which the extreme right issues anathemas and excommuni-
cations is as shameful as the cavalier indifference of the left
to the voice of Peter. That such things should happen is not a
surprise to those who read church history, but historical
precedent does not always temper the chagrin one feels at
experiencing such excesses. For those who truly seek, community strategies must be developed to keep such divisions
from running away with the church. Such strategies include
not only dialogue but the cultivation of those virtues which
most build community while assuaging bitterness: humility,
charity, patience, and that serene maturity which allows for
divergence of opinion.

That the pope should exercise his ministry in the ancient
city of Rome in the Vatican seems neither inappropriate nor
scandalous. The presence of the papal office in that city reminds
us, first of all, that Catholicism is a tradition and that the
tradition has been represented in a special place for two
millennia. The historical character of the papacy is both a
burden and an opportunity. Whoever assumes the chair of Peter
assumes both the glory and the shames of his predecessors just
as he assumes his role as defender of the faith, voice of the
concerns of the Catholic church, and arbiter among the churches.

One of the carryovers from past history is the tendency to
see the papacy as the apex of a great pyramid whose base line
is the local church. This monarchical view of the papacy,
inherited from medieval and post-Reformation factors, will not
do for the contemporary church. It does not seem true either
to the needs of the church or to the actual role the papacy
plays in the church. It also exists as an insurmountable
ecumenical stumbling block. Moreover, this structured model
is in tension with those new understandings of the church
which we have received from the Second Vatican Council.

The fascination with the church as a rigid hierarchy has
given way to an understanding of the church as a people on
the way, the church as pilgrimage, the Body of Christ, as a
Christian community, and so on. With these metaphors there
is little room for an absolute monarch; new images must be
found which will do justice both to the integrity of the local
community and to the central role of the Petrine office as the

guarantor of unity and universality in the church. This is a task of great magnitude as John Wright has pointed out in an important essay:

> Catholics in communion with the bishop of Rome, being the largest single Christian body, bear an enormous resposibility at this period in the church's history. The Apostolic see of Rome is a symbol of the unity, universality, and historical continuity of the Christian church. As recent ecumenical conversations have made clear, there is a place in the future united Christian church for the papacy. But the gift of the papacy must be given without arrogance or self-righteousness, with a desire to serve and not to dominate, and with a recognition that it is the function of the papal church not to suppress the episcopal, presbyteral, and congregational elements in the organization of the visible church, but to strengthen, support, and unify them. As Christians through prayer and discussion discover their inner unity in Catholic faith, in recognizing all baptized believers as members of the one body of Christ, they will endeavor to give appropriate external manifestation and support to that unity in the visible form of a renewed church.[18]

My Community

Religiously speaking, I may belong to a number of communities varying in their intensities and closeness. There is the family circle with its own memories, celebrations, and shared memories both religious and social. My family, in turn, extends, together with other families, into a worshipping community which may provide, under its aegis, any number of smaller groups that may gain my allegiance for a particular spiritual and/or social purpose. Our worshipping community, again, has links with the local church under the bishop even if that link is less intense and immediate. The local church, finally, finds itself in communion with the bishop of Rome who stands as the representative and head of the entire Catholic community.

In this complex web of relationships there should be (and ideally will be) a series of mutual interactions by which the various communities are linked together. I emphasize the word *mutual* since without that mutuality there can be no true community. Authority which is univocal or monodirectional creates, not community, but corporations. True community cannot occur when everything comes from the head and the members are only passive vessels for the receptions of order and direction. Community has at its heart the sense of sharing and the sense of interchange.

That concrete mutual interchange means, basically, that the bishop of Rome must listen to the local church with the same respect and attention that the local church shows when listening to him. To be authentically catholic is to be nourished by, and to nourish, all the different communities which make up the great church with some spirit of organic wholeness. In the concrete that means that my family, my study group, my parish, my diocese, and *my* (I emphasize *my*) papacy influence me precisely to the degree that I desire to be a Catholic Christian. In turn, my experience as a Catholic nourishes the community which desires to be worthy of the name Catholic.

It is that sense of connectedness that gives deep meaning to the concept of Catholic community. In this regard it is instructive to see how Karl Rahner answered the rather basic questions: Why, given so many options in Christianity, be a Catholic? Rahner answers that one can be confident in being a member of the Catholic community if one is satisfied that the Catholic church meets three criteria with respect to Christian revelation: continuity, fidelity, and authority.[19]

By continuity Rahner simply means that one can look at the history of the church and ask if its history appears to reflect something vital and connected to New Testament origins. In other words, is there some organic connection with the reality of the present-day church and the church of the apostles. Do they connect?

By fidelity Rahner means something similar, but in this case the "something" is oriented to basic faith. Can one have confidence that the Catholic church is faithful to, and allows for the profession of, that basic New Testament revelation which says that Jesus is Lord? That affirmation is closely allied with Rahner's third criterion of authority. Can the church make that profession of faith in Christ with sufficient vigor? Has it protected the ways that faith comes to us? Does it have the power to affirm that Jesus is Lord?

In thinking about those issues, Rahner implicitly pays tribute to the church both as a community of actuality (can I do this or that today?) and as a community of memory (is this connected to the witness of the New Testament?). In affirming our sense of this community, we are not only enriched as Christians by the community of the church, but we then also bring our gifts to the church and enrich it.

It is for that reason that the church sees an intimate connection between community and catholicity. In line with the Pauline metaphor of the Body of Christ the church sees the contribution of individual and corporate members of the church as those elements which build up the church. That common effort to bring the church to a great realization of Christ by such communion of effort is attested in the description of the church outlined at the Second Vatican Council: "In virtue of this catholicity each individual part of the church contributes through its special gifts to the good of the other parts and of the whole church. Thus through the common sharing of gifts and through the common effort to attain fulness in unity, the whole and each of the parts receive increase."[20]

That, of course, is a noble sentiment but hard to put into practical action. Yet the sentiment needs to be repeated often if for no other reason than to remind the members of the many communities in the church that they have a responsibility both to the parts and to the whole. Only by constant reflection on that truth does the Catholic escape a certain sectarian myopia which allows concern only for this parish or that cell or the other organization. Community, paradoxically enough, demands both an ever closer cohesion of members and a certain concomitant forgetfulness of cohesion as it expands out to embrace others not yet a part of the community. In that regard I have always loved the sentiment of the great evangelical reformer John Wesley who, while laboring for very particular groups, still conceived of his parish as the world.

The universal church is the great community. That great community, we must remember, exists in time and space. It is composed of men and women who are lovable before God but also sinful. The great community has all the frailties of human constructions; it can only hope to escape the exigencies of imperfection and blighted dreams in the *eschaton*. Its manifestation as the Catholic church will never be more perfect or credible than its parishes or communities. The great church is only the generalization of the church in miniature—the *ecclesiola*. If we can see the church in that fashion, we can avoid perfectionist temptations and despair at the limitations of the church enterprise. We can move ahead in faith and trust. The church seen in that fashion gives special power and urgency to the words of Rahner:

> . . . We are obliged to see the church in its concreteness, in its finiteness, with the burdens of its history, and with all its negligences and perhaps even false developments, and in this way to accept this concrete church without reservations, as the realm of our Christian existence: with humility, with courage and sobriety, with a real love for this church and a willingness to work for her, and even with a readiness to share her burdens in ourselves and in our lives, and not to add the weakness of our own witness to the burdens of the church.[21]

Points for Meditation

1. In what ways and under what circumstances have you experienced your Christian faith as an experience in community or of community?

2. Do you consider your own family as a community? How does it relate to, and become a part of, the community of believers?

3. What do you see as the great impediments to Christian community in your parish or in your locale? In the "great church"? With other Christian bodies?

4. If you were to imagine an ideal Christian community, what shape would it take? Would its orientation be toward prayer or social action or a combination of both?

5. Is it possible, within the structures of the church, to create a sense of community with those who are at the margin? I have in mind here the less "fashionable" minorities: the aged, the addicted, the mentally handicapped, the urban homeless, the criminals, and so on.

6. How—if at all—does the papacy impact on your Christian life in terms of community? What do you think of the "servant model" of the papacy? What practical reforms would have to be undertaken to make actual such a concept of the papacy?

Notes

1. Ignazio Silone, *Bread and Wine* (New York: Signet Classic, 1963), p. 270.
2. *Decree on Eastern Catholic Churches*, art. 26, in *Documents of Vatican II*, ed. Walter Abbott (New York: Association, 1966), p. 383.

3. *The Didache*, trans. J. A. Kleist, in Ancient Christian Writers, vol. 4 (Washington: Ancient Christian Writers, 1948), 9.4.

4. *Athanasius: The Life of Anthony*, trans. Robert Gregg (Ramsey, N.J.: Paulist, 1980), p. 64.

5. Duane J. Osheim, "Conversion, *Conversi*, and the Christian Life in Late Medieval Tuscany," *Speculum* 58 (1983) 368. This article has an abundant bibliography on lay communities in the medieval period.

6. Peter Nichols, *The Pope's Divisions: The Roman Catholic Church Today* (New York: Penguin Books, 1982), p. 328.

7. Jean Vanier, "A Wound Deep in Our Hearts," *Cross Currents* 33, no. 2 (Summer 1983) 157.

8. Jean Vanier, *Community and Growth* (Toronto: Griffin House, 1979), p. 157.

9. Ibid., p. 43.

10. Gottfried Deelen, "The Church on Its Way to the People: Basic Christian Communities in Brazil," *Cross Currents* 30, no. 4 (Winter 1980/81) 389. For a fuller description of these communities, see Harvey Cox, *Religion in the Secular City* (New York: Simon and Schuster, 1984).

11. Leonardo Boff, "Theological Characteristics of a Grassroots Church," in *The Challenge of Basic Christian Communities*, ed. Sergio Torres and John Eagleson (Maryknoll, N.Y.: Orbis, 1981), pp. 124–44.

12. Ibid., p. 142. See also Leonardo Boff, "The Need for Political Saints," *Cross Currents* 30, no. 4 (Winter 1980/81) 369–76.

13. Andrew Greeley, *The Great Mysteries: An Essential Catechism* (New York: Seabury, 1976), p. 92.

14. From "An Appeal to the Ruling Class," in *Martin Luther: Selections from His Writings*, ed. John Dillenberger (New York: Anchor Books, 1961), p. 424.

15. George H. Tavard, "What Is the Petrine Function?" in *Papal Primacy and the Universal Church*, ed. Paul C. Empie et al. (Minneapolis: Augsburg, 1974), pp. 208–12; also George H. Tavard, "The Papacy and Christian Symbolism," *Journal of Ecumenical Studies* 13 (Summer 1976): 345–58.

16. See Raymond Brown and John Reumann, *Peter in the New Testament* (Ramsey, N.J.: Paulist, 1973).

17. Hans Küng, *On Being a Christian* (Garden City: Doubleday, 1974), p. 500.

18. John H. Wright, "The Structure and Meaning of Catholic Faith," *Theological Studies* 39 (1978): 711.

19. Karl Rahner, *Foundations of Christian Faith* (New York: Seabury, 1978), pp. 342ff. On this section of Rahner's study, see Michael Fahey, "On Being Christian— Together," in *A World of Grace*, ed. Leo O'Donovan (New York: Seabury, 1980), pp. 120–37.

20. *Dogmatic Constitution on the Church*, art. 12 in *Documents of Vatican II*, p. 31.

21. *Foundations*, p. 390.

Selected Readings

Cox, Harvey. *Religion in the Secular City*. New York: Simon and Schuster, 1984. Good reflections on contemporary concern with community.

Dulles, Avery. *Models of the Church*. Garden City: Doubleday, 1974. Different ways of understanding the church as community. Basic.

Granfield, Patrick. *The Papacy in Transition*. Garden City: Doubleday, 1980. A thorough discussion of the papacy today. Important.

Hellwig, Monika. *Understanding Catholicism*. Ramsey: Paulist, 1981. A general introduction with a strong emphasis on community.

Miller, J. Michael. *What Are They Saying about Papal Primacy?* Ramsey: Paulist, 1982. Excellent coverage of current ecumenical discussions.

10

EXPECTATIONS

All religious traditions have at least this in common: the articulated perception of a gap between what is and what should be; between reality as actuality and reality as an ideal. Both Buddhism and Hinduism, for example, perceive a tension between this world of material suffering and desire and the genuine world of the realized self. Islam contrasts an idealized world of believers submissive to the will of Allah (Islam means submission) and an actual world in which this is not the case. Pious Jews yearn for the day of full Torah observance for it is then when this imperfect reality will be supplanted by the Messianic era.

Christianity also posits a tension between what is (the old dispensation; the old Adam; the state of original sin; the "world") and what is to be (the filling up of all things in Christ; the New Jerusalem; the triumph of grace; the new heavens and the new earth). There is a strong element of eschatology in all of Christianity; a pointing to the final things. The gospels are rife with images (many of them clustered in the parables of the Kingdom) which point out the unfolding of events as they point to a "not yet": the wheat and the tares; the separation of sheep and goats; the growth of the mustard seed; the conditions of the wedding feast, and so on. Furthermore, the New Testament makes any number of demands, some of them stark in their absolute formulation, by which the putative follower of Christ might bridge the gap between the present imperfect and the future perfect: Give up everything; turn the other

242

cheek; take up a cross; abandon father and mother for the sake of the Kingdom; possess no goods; refuse marriage; and so on.

It is a historical truism to say that the Catholic tradition gives no evidence that the "what should be" has ever existed as more than a hope and an aspiration toward which the church is directed. The church exists in a state of imperfection; it is always *in via*. Consciousness of that imperfection constantly leads the church back to its sources: *Ecclesia semper reformanda* is the shorthand description of that dynamic. The church must always be reformed.

The history of the church's tradition demonstrates quite clearly that at crucial periods in the church's life when the gap between the "what is" and "what should be" becomes visibly acute, there arises a desire for reform; for a desire to go back to the sources; to seek out models of an earlier, less tainted age, of Christian witness. This is a desire which explains most of the reforming impulses of religious orders such as the medieval Cluniacs, the Cistercians, the mendicants, and, in the post-Tridentine era, the Jesuits and the Capuchins. These reform impulses are never completely successful, as history again shows, since they also demand their own reforms. Thus, the Cistercians were seen as a reform of the Cluniacs. The sweeping successes of the friars gave way in time to fractiousness and faint ridiculousness (see Erasmus's *Praise of Folly*) just as the post-Tridentine orders became domesticated by the forces of the Enlightenment.

If here I have insisted on the reforming impulses of the religious orders, it was for a reason. They represent a strong perfectionist strain within the church. Reformed Christianity has also had its perfectionist impulses but largely unable to channel them into religious orders (which were "sects within the church," as one scholar has called them) they tended to separate. Separatists in the Reformed tradition quite consciously saw themselves as a gathering of the saints or a conventical of the elect who both resisted the world and served as a sign of what true faith ought to be.

When one compares, for example, the severest of the separatist groups of the Reformation (e.g., the Old Order Amish) and the traditional monastic orders, the similarities are patent.

Both insist on strict separation from the world, a distinctive rhythm of life, and an integration of daily culture and life. In both cases these groups act out, albeit without explicit intention at times, a projected vision of what the ideal Christian community ought to be and how that life should be lived. They both attempt to be, to use an old monastic term, "schools of perfection."

Obviously not all impulses to bridge the "what is" and the "what should be" are as formal as the founding of religious orders or the establishment of conventicles of the saints. The perfectionist impulse can operate at far more modest levels; it is part and parcel of the reformist dynamic of recovery and renewal. One sees such impulses at work in everything from the movements to promote parish renewal, a better world, or a new restatement of theological truths. Every attempt to do such things is an implicit statement that things as they are do not constitute the norm or the desideratum. Such impulses, almost by definition, point to an as yet unrealized future.

The perfectionist/reformist tendency has always been present in the church, but the sweeping changes after the Second Vatican Council may be considered as radical in the sense that a genuine "horizon shift" has taken place in the church. Everything from the reforms of the liturgy to the announced determination to speak to the world with a new openness was done along with the rallying cry of repristination and reformulation of old truths in new language. While this last council was a reforming council, it was not responding to a well-articulated crisis as was, say, the Council of Trent in the sixteenth century. Vatican II's impulses derived from a half-articulated sense that the church vis-à-vis the world needed to make itself over in order to get a hearing in a culture which was fast becoming pluralistic.

The dynamic of reform and perfectionism (reform can be seen as a cautious and disciplined expression of the perfectionist spirit) are central to the Catholic tradition. To be satisfied with "the way things are" is a kind of ossification, while the desire to thrust forward an antinomian utopianism is at variance with the sense of Catholicism as a tradition and memory. If there is anywhere where one can invoke the ideal of the *via media,* it is when one is called upon to choose between ecclesial stasis and formless anarchy. That *via media* begins with the conviction that the present moment is historical and contingent. One lives in this moment but with the conviction that it does not sum up or fully contain all that there is of Gospel truth; there is always something more. Such a conviction is called, commonly, hope.

Hope and the Church

The preeminent sin against hope is despair; the "giving up" of reaching a goal which, as St. Thomas says, is "difficult but possible" (*arduum possibile*).[1] Despair can be dramatically existential as when, for example, the very strength of going on with life is doubted or when, to be more theological, the possibility of salvation or the availability of God's grace is denied. Desperation can also manifest itself in less crucial aspects of religious life. We can speak of "despair of the church" in the sense that people can—and, in fact, often do—feel that being in the church is simply not worth it. Such people simply cannot look ahead and see that there is anything of value which convinces them to remain "in the church."

Despair of the church takes on many hues and shades. We all know people who have left the church after some bitter personal experience that has permanently alienated them. Those experiences may be triggered by the proverbial religious who hit them in grammar school or an unfeeling cleric who failed them in a moment of great need. More commonly one sees many people who simply drift away from the church with the same lack of reflection or purpose that accompanies growing away from certain one-time friends or social habits. Anyone who has spent much time in university environs knows scores of students who simply quit actively practicing their faith because there is nobody—most usually a parent—to rouse them on a Sunday morning or to reinforce other manifestations of church behavior. Many of these students later return to the practice of their faith as one more part of their increasing maturity and seriousness. They become churchgoers about the same time that they begin to get three-piece suits, briefcases, and their first employment. Others drift off into rather permanent but hostile nonobservance with the self-description of being a Catholic "but not a very good one."

It is one of the conceits of the committed Catholic that such departures, either hostile or unreflective, carry with them a certain degree of regret, anxiety, and a half-articulated desire to "return to the fold." That is the case with some people to be sure, but for many it is not. Life in the church for many people was a sociological fact and not a faith decision. Their departure from the church is rather like outgrowing the Boy Scouts or a college fraternity. Life moves on. In place of anxiety such persons feel, at most, a certain sense of nostalgia for a time when the church was a comfort linked to family ties or old familiar social rituals. The church is part of the furniture of the past like half-remembered small town life during adolescence.

There are others, of course, who feel a deep tie to the church, but find active membership in it an *arduum impossibile*. One frequently finds friends of my generation who will confess in a moment of confidentiality that they are "out of the church" or, more poignantly, "kicked out of the church" because of a canonically irregular marriage or a style of life which they will not or cannot rectify. One senses in their confidences a kind of desperation which they see as only partially of their making. They see their lives as caught in a kind of Hobson's choice between their actual lives and the seemingly irreducible demands of the church. Between those two competing realities there appears to be an unbridgeable gap.

The examples we have cited above are pressing pastoral problems which the contemporary church attempts to answer through various strategies. But there are many people who are still "in" the church while feeling a certain sense of unease about the whole enterprise and their part—however modest—in it. Let us leave aside those who have a quarrel with this or that aspect of church polity as well as those who are in the church because that is where they are and could not conceive of being elsewhere. The more interesting issue, which has been addressed over and over again by Karl Rahner,[2] is this: Why does one, upon reflection, stay in the Catholic church? How does it contribute to a fundamental Christian life? The pious answer, of couse, paraphrases the Gospel: Where else could one go? The church possesses the words of eternal life. Fortunate the person who can say that with tranquility and without hesitation.

The question of "why the church?" can be framed adequately only after the issue of fundamental Christian faith is settled. When one affirms a basic act of faith in the order of transcendence as it is exemplified and revealed in the person of Jesus the Christ, then—and only then—can one frame the question of the church. At the level of faith the two questions are closely entwined. One says, in essence, that one believes in Christ and then proceeds to ask if that faith is nurtured and confirmed in the church or not.

When the two issues of faith in Christ and ecclesial faith are seen in tandem, then one can faithfully ask if the church* has the resources, powers, and metaphors to give sustenance and shape to one's more basic existential Christian faith. Karl Rahner puts the issue nicely:

> Quite enough terrible and base things have happened in the history of the church. There is so much that is terrible and base that the only hopeful answer is this: where else would we go if we left the church? Would we then be more faithful to the liberating spirit of Jesus if, egotistical sinners that we are, we distanced ourselves as the "pure" from this poor church of sinners? We can do our part to remove its meanness only if we help to bear the burden of this wretchedness (for which all of us bear some guilt), if we help to bear the responsibility of constantly changing it from the outside.[3]

Two observations seem to be in order here. First, we need admit that the terrible and base things which happen to people may drive them out of the church and the church may well be at fault. Roman Catholics find it difficult to admit that the church may be at fault for church defections, but it is an unassailable fact which should be clearly recognized. Secondly, Rahner makes a helpful, if implicit, distinction which is worth

---

* It should be clear that the term *church* is used here to mean the believing community as it concretely manifests itself in that observable reality called the Roman Catholic church.

keeping in mind: The church has obligations to us, but we also have obligations to the church.

Those who make an option for the church even when that personal choice seems painful or wearisome need cultivate that kind of hope which permits them to live in the current moments of unhappiness or dissatisfaction while looking to the future in that spirit of hope. The cultivation of that ecclesial hope accepts the notion that the community of believers, both with its memory and its actuality, will provide the sustenance to grow in Christian perfection. One expects that in the preaching of the Gospel, in the constant celebration of the Eucharist, in its attempts to re-form itself after the fashion of the apostolic faith, one still senses God's presence in Christ made actual and palpable. That sense makes the effort of being Catholic worthy and useful.

To live in such hope in the church demands a certain gritty realism about the church. To be hope-filled, to be expectant, does not mean to be unrealistic or utopian. Hope must be grounded in the *possibile*, but it is a *possibile* that is *arduum*. Those who forget the historical and contingent nature of the church as an institution are shocked by its earthliness and limits only because they confuse a church which is at the end of history with the church which now lives immersed in history. Here is a mild paradox: One lives in the church with expectant hope but without hoping for too much.

For the hope-filled Catholic the church is seen as no more perfect or perfectible than those who make it up or give it substance. It is an imperfect vessel. We are permitted to be radically shocked by the church only if we never find anything shocking about ordinary human behavior. To simply look around a Sunday morning congregation should drive home the point. In that gathering there are persons of genuine piety and others who are, at best, habitual but undistinguished congregants. Some of the community is capable of heroic virtue while others are weak or given to fits of maliciousness. The point is—and this can never be said enough—that this is the church in the concrete.

My local parish congregation does not model the church completely. Monks and nuns at prayer, *comunidades de base* in Brazil, papal liturgies (yes, even papal liturgies), home Masses, and eucharistic congresses with a cast of thousands—all of these manifest the church in concrete reality and form part of its total reality. What all those gatherings have in common (at least, ideally) is their corporate expression of faith in Christ and their common human frailty. Like Chaucer's pilgrims they are a cross-section of humanity who share a common destination which is to say, a common hope in the future not yet realized.

About those gatherings one rightly asks whether one receives nourishment from them but also, as Rahner notes, whether the community is somehow diminished by our absence. We receive grace to be faithful in community. That grace, in turn, brings obligations. We owe something to the church itself.

That point is sometimes lost on the self-appointed "guardians of orthodoxy." I was once told while discussing my reservations about *Humanae Vitae* that I should either accept the church or "get out." I declined to do that both because being a Catholic is who I am and because the church may be diminished in some miniscule manner by my retreat. The church is not an institutional reality which one enters and leaves like membership in a country club. It is a gathered community which takes on an institutional form. Hans Küng who has been as contentious as most (and disliked by the guardians of orthodoxy more) makes the case for staying in the church as eloquently as most. Writing over a decade ago, he said:

> . . . despite everything, in this community of faith critically but jointly we can affirm a great history on which we live with so many others. Because, as members of this community, we ourselves are the church and we should not confuse it with its machinery and its administrators, still less leave the latter to shape the community. Because, however serious the objections, we have found here a spiritual home in which we can face the great questions. . . . We should no more turn our backs on it than on democracy in politics, which in its own way is misused and abused no less than the church.[4]

Hope as Direction

The 1967 translation of Jurgen Moltmann's *Theology of Hope* triggered an intense interest in hope as a theological category and oriented theologians to a more serious and sophisticated consideration of the future.[5] The emerging theology of hope, in turn, shaped, and was shaped by, the interest of theologians in political theology in general and the liberationist themes of political theology in particular. The theological advances made in the various areas of liberation theology are many, complex, and not full matured. What we can glean from this theological ferment, however, is the fundamental insight that hope can be seen as confidence in, and direction toward, the future. The future, in this context, can be denominated as that limitless horizon which the New Testament calls the coming Kindgom and the definitive coming and triumph of Christ.

That fundamental datum of the future is at the very heart of the New Testament vision of reality. The urgent call of Jesus to repent in anticipation of the Kingdom, the Pauline urgency about the imminent return of the Lord, the apocalyptic vision of the new heavens and the new earth all oriented the early Christian communities to look to the "not yet." In time the urgent expectancy of the not-yet Kingdom becomes domesticated, but the Christian community never really lost its sense of futurity. While the church could become complacent at times in its acceptance of the status quo, there was always an undercurrent, prophetic in its urgency, which reminded the church that we live between the times and the "not yet" is still to come.

The future is of a polyvalent reality. For many, in religious terms, it is the crisis moment of death: In my future there is death at the end of *my* life. Will I be found wanting as that life is judged? A good deal of energy has been expended in Catholic circles promoting that notion of the future as individual judgment. Its most macabre and vivid manifestations appear in those large mechanical clocks which one can see in the public squares of some European cities on which, when the hour is struck, there is an animated parade of apostles followed by the angel of death with scythe and hourglass to remind the populace that we are dust and to dust we will return.

However Gothic the Catholic imagination could be in promoting the *memento mori* theme, there was another side of the coin: the expectation of final happiness to be found in Christ after death. Death, in the future, becomes for those who hope, not the final testing of human effort, but the *transitus gloriae* (as the Fathers called it), the passage to glory. The more modern formulation of that expectation is that in the resurrection of Christ we are sustained in the hope that our individual lives will not dissolve into nothingness and insignificance but that we will live in some transformed manner. That transformed living is guaranteed by one's faith in the resurrected Christ. Our ultimate trust, then, is placed in *our* individual future beyond the thresholds of ordinary time and space. It is confidence in our right to claim resurrection after the manner and through the pledge of the resurrection of Christ.[6]

We should note, however, that the future need not be conceived of only as that absolute moment of our death. The future also includes the hope that in this passage through life— this pilgrimage *in via*—we are capable of those transformations (those "resurrections" if you will) which are rightly called "conversion." Conversion is not a once and single affair. We look forward in our lives to those graced moments in which we can be led to larger, more generous, and fuller understandings of our role as Catholic Christians. If the example of the great saints teaches us anything, it is that radical transformations can and do happen in our time-bound futures. After all, both Teresa of Avila (as well as the contemporary Teresa of Calcutta) and Francis of Assisi were already converted to the religious life long before they had deeper conversions to the style of life which was to mark their real mission in life. Our future is to be conceived, then, not only in terms of the end of our future in death but in those incremental steps by which we seek to act out more fully what it means to be a person of faith after the manner of Christ.

What we have spoken of above is, of course, a very individualistic reading of futurity. The church, it needs to be said, sees our destiny not only at the level of the individual but also at the level of the corporate. The church envisions a future not only for this or that individual but for those individuals as members of the human race, graced by Christ the New Adam, and the church as the *sacramentum* of Christ's presence on earth. That corporate notion, rooted in biblical eschatology, was systematized in Augustine's *City of God* and, through that work, enters the cultural life of the West in variegated forms.

The corporate future of humanity, eschatology, and apocalyptic vision are part and parcel of the imagined future from the Christian perspective. In that perspective we need to note that there is much room for the corrective of basic Christian realism. Somewhere between those who would canonize a static view of the church relative to time (e.g., "Europe is the Faith") and those who pine for apocalyptic renewal by the tumbling of the structures (a notion at least as old as Joachim of Fiore and as new as certain liberationist tendencies) there is ample space for a position toward the future which is critically prophetic in its skepticism toward the "now," generous to the lessons of the past, and hope-ful about the future.

A genuinely Catholic sense of futurity can be constructed only by a blend of critical judgment and the power to imagine. Critical reflection provides that basic dissatisfaction with the imperfections of the present that moves one toward change while, at the same time, damping down any temptation toward complacency with the "now." That spirit of reflection and judgment derives from the full integration of spiritual awareness and the exercise of charity in the world. It is rooted in an awareness that the redemptive power of the Gospel is not fully present now in this particular place. It is that critical spirit which allows us to live in our time and in our place while feeling a certain homelessness as well as an impulse toward an expansive universality which is deeply Catholic. Its spirit is captured in some words Thomas Merton wrote for a Latin American edition of his writings:

> For me Catholicism is not confined to one culture, one nation, one age, one race. . . . I cannot believe that Catholicism is tied to the destinies of any group which confusedly expresses the economic illusions of a social class. My Catholicism is not the religion of the bourgeoisie nor will it ever be. My Catholicism is all the world and all ages.[7]

That sense of critical reflection which judges the "now" and "not yet" must be accompanied by imagination, i.e., the power to construct alternatives to the present. That power to imagine looks to the future but is nourished by the memory of the past. Recent scholars have strongly emphasized the importance of imagination in theology,[8] but I would simply point out here that imagination can be used in the circumscribed sense as the ability to hope *in the concrete* for a more loving future and a more just ambience for the world.

One of the primary functions of the preaching church is to set out, as unambiguously as possible, images of hope: Christ as healer of hurts, as provider of needs, as prophetic judge of the present, as the nourisher of the poor, as the instigator of the reign of justice, and so on. The grasp of these images as "doable" or "fleshable" and, most importantly, as "possible" (i.e., "Yes, this can happen!") defines the precise character of Christian hope both individually and socially. That hope may range from a simple individual act of conversion or a complex scheme of changing this or that aspect of mundane reality. In the final analysis, the dynamic is the same: a sense of the provisory nature of the "now" and the power to imagine a "something else."

In this discussion I am very hesitant to invoke the term, much in currency today, of utopian thinking or imagining. There is some scholarly disagreement as to whether Sir Thomas More meant his utopia (the word literally means "no place") as a real blueprint for a livable society. One thing is very clear. If he did think of utopia as a real place to live in (he may well have, given his strong monastic bent), damn few of us would want to be numbered among its citizens. Utopian thinkers are, almost by definition, negators of history. They envision societies freed from the impurities of human experiment, human failures, and the historical impurities which derive from such failure. Utopian fantasies are generally harmless and, at times, therapeutic as critiques of historical reality. They begin to be dangerous only when a utopian thinker has the power to implement what he or she imagines. It is one thing for a utopian thinker to gather together an intentional community (as did the monks and nuns of old), but it is quite another thing to have the power to establish "perfect" societies. Every time I am the least beguiled by the vision of a utopian community of justice somewhere in the world, I am called back to reality by memories of the more energetic utopian thinkers of our age. Pol Pot is one of the more recent and grimly determined of the lot: His desire for an agrarian society of Cambodia, a mad brew of historical nostalgia and rigidly idiosyncratic Marxism, yielded one of the more gruesome pages of history in this century.

The Catholic imagination—even while imagining the "not yet" of the future—must root itself in the realities of history and accept those limits which derive from the very nature of our contingent and historical condition. One of the great and bitter lessons of history is that the combination of imagination and power engenders that great temptation to begin *de novo;* to initiate that demonic exercise of nostalgia for a totally ahistorical and blissful utopia in which our primordial parents once lived. It is a temptation, when indulged, that triggers the storm of rooting out, destroying, and laying waste of the old in order to start afresh. The one thing that all of our modern literary disutopias have in common (*Brave New World* and *Nineteen Eighty-Four* are conspicuous examples in literature) is a hatred for, and an obliteration of, the past. Christian realism, by contrast, demands a finer balance between what is imperfect yet perfectible (i.e., our world) and the absolute "not yet" which will come in God's own good time.

An unsympathetic reader of the above might see my plea for "realism" as a plea for a "middle of the road" attitude which would have gainsayed all the revolutions, historical and social, which have enriched our human journey in the past. It is not. History demands its revolutions as it has had in the past. Revolution can be a harbinger of peace for, as the late Paul VI has said, peace comes from the doing of justice. Solidarity's revolutionary impulses was as rooted in justice as was the overthrow of Somoza in Nicaragua. It is what comes after a revolution which is at stake. It is then that the temptation to abstraction and destruction seems so strong.

Christian realism demands that the church, the community of believers extended in time and space, hate injustice in both its individual and its social manifestations as much as it loves justice as an ideal and as a reality to be enfleshed. The actual dynamics of overcoming injustice and the implementing of justice may be a matter of dispute; the ends of justice and love are not. Is that not precisely the issue which separates good people who debate real political and social strategies both at the domestic level (how does one best erase poverty or discrimination?) and at the international one (how best implement justice in the countries of the Third and Fourth worlds?).

Strategies, then, can be a matter of dispute; the ends of justice may not. When, recently, conservative critics rejoiced at the Vatican's monitum on the subject of certain themes in liberation theology, they conveniently overlooked the ringing affirmation made in that document about the immorality of a neutral attitude about present injustice. Certain strategies might impede the coming of the "not yet," but, as the document states: "More than ever, it is important that numerous Christians, whose faith is clear and who are committed to live the Christian life in its fulness, become involved in the struggle for justice, freedom, and human dignity because of their love for their disinherited, oppressed, and persecuted brothers and sisters. More than ever, the church intends to condemn abuses, injustices, and attacks against freedom, wherever they occur and whoever commits them. She intends to struggle, by her own means, for the defense and advancement of the rights of mankind, especially the poor."[9]

The doing of justice is, at once, simple and complex in the sense that the demand for justice is straightforward in the social sphere while its practical implementation can be painfully difficult. At the very least we must be clear about the irreducible demands that the church proposes for all of us who are called to be doers of justice. We need, at the offset, ringingly affirm something that every Roman pontiff from Leo XIII to the present pope has taught as being at the core of social justice: The good of the individual is prior to the good of the state. In other words: All social institutions can be judged by the criterion as to how they cultivate or harm the full humanity of the individual. Both conciliar and papal teaching over the past century has rigorously insisted that every human being has a strict right in justice to certain basic goods needed for human life: bodily integrity, freedom of growth in physical, intellectual, and spiritual ways; basic sustenance and shelter; freedom to be part of a family; and so forth.

The above list of human rights may seem so obvious to us (who possess them as a matter of course) that their recital may appear otiose. But let us make a concrete application of the demands deriving from that list. Suppose our local pastor were to take the pulpit to point out that our city has large numbers of homeless bewildered people who sleep in parks and eat from dumpsters. Their lives are indecently poor. Suppose that same pastor says that those people have a right in justice (not simply the hope for charity) to housing, etc., even if it means our giving up of our excess. Suppose, in short, that the pastor says that there is room at the table and we need provide it. Would we honor that demand? Would we grumble about "politics in the pulpit" when it was plain that he was invoking, not political discussion, but the demands of justice? How would we feel if we were able to imagine his talk transferred from the local situation to the global one? How would we begin to "imagine" the ways to provide room at the table?

In proposing such scenarios, the church, in the first instance, demands that we think about the status quo—about *our* status quo—in radically different ways; that we think about another way of being or doing. That is future thinking at its most elementary level. Christian realism holds that justice does not reign, but should reign; that one must move from what is not to that which should be. At the same time, Christian realism demands that we hold in some kind of creative tension the ultimate religious meaning of life which is, to use Teilhard de Chardin's lovely phrase, the Christification of both the social order and individuals who make it up through the here and now affirmation of justice and love for every individual person.

The dialectic of present and future becomes clearer when we consider the nature of the church's fundamental mission. What, to use the scholastic term, is the final end or *telos* of the church? This question has received a good deal of attention in recent theological discussion. Francis Schüssler Fiorenza writes that the traditional understanding of the church's mission was understood in terms of the supernatural end of man. The stronger the emphasis on the distinction between nature and supernature, the clearer the emphasis on the purely transcendental goal of evangelization and redemption: "The objective of the church is to evangelize, not to civilize. If it civilizes, it is for the sake of evangelization," said Pius XI. "The Church," the Second Vatican Council affirmed, has "no proper mission in the political, social, or economic order. The purpose He [i.e., Christ] set before her is a religious one."[10]

Of course, the vexatious issue is to define what that religious role or purpose is. Should the church do the works of mercy merely as religious acts when there are other agencies that also can do them? Is it required to perform them, as it did in earlier times, when there are no alternative agencies? Should the church energize Christians to work for the social reality of Gospel values as part of its mission to make incarnate the work of Christ in the marketplace? That was surely the strategy of the European notion of Catholic Action.

Recently, some theologians have begun to speak of missions rather than mission of the church. The reason is simple: It seems impossible to disentangle the service of the church to all strata of society from its goals of evangelization. Arguing for this complex understanding of the church's *telos* and, in the same breath, trying to overcome a split between human and divine ends, Roger Haight writes:

> . . . The church is not primarily in service to itself. This statement represents the most radical shift for one's understanding of the church today. It marks a certain about-face in relation to many ecclesiologies of the past. And yet it seems inescapable. . . . The church from the beginning was in service to the *missio Dei* and presumably the object of that is universal human history and the world. The church is primarily in service to the world; it is sent to those outside itself. There is no need to interpret this exclusively; one need not deny that the church is a community of worship and mutual support and nourishment in the faith. But this aspect of the church's life should always nourish and lead to the expectation of the church's primary mission.[11]

To hold in tandem the twin goals of humanization and divinization[12] as poles of the church's mission helps to prevent the church as well as the individual in that church from becoming preoccupied "merely" with the state of one's soul or becoming "merely" a social service agency with a thin patina of theological language. To hold that tension creatively also aids in the development of that critical sense about the relationship of social activism and spirituality. More pertinently today, it illumines the relationship between politics and faith—an issue which vexes many in various parts of the world not excluding our own.

In a world as pluralistic as ours only the most naïve hope to shape the political order along "Christian" or "Catholic" lines. That is not to suggest that one must bracket faith in order to live and exercise in the sociopolitical order. In a society such as ours, for example, the state has assumed many of the tasks which were once the provenance of the church. Today, it is the state which acts as the primary provider of social services to the poor, elderly, those in need of massive medical assistance, etc. If, however, the agencies of the state or their strategies do not effectively act with justice or in a way that promotes basic human needs, then it would seem clear that the church has both the right and the duty to press for the doing of justice and for that regard for the human which is the basis for all human life. If the church ceded to the state the responsibilities for social welfare (inevitable, given the complexities of our society), it has not—and cannot—accede to any silence with respect to the demands of justice. It is precisely because the individual as well as the community of faith has responsibility for the other that it is impossible to disentangle the life of faith from the life of the commonweal, which is to say, the life of politics.

But what has all this to do with futurity? With what we have called *expectation?* Only this: We are not yet at the end of that process which the Christian tradition describes variously as a way, a pilgrimage, a journey. We are, as a matter of fact, *in via.* At any stage of the journey we move forward, but we are not in possession of that fullness of Christ or that fullness of catholicity (I would see the two as interchangeable) to which we are called and toward which we are drawn. As a strict consequence of that fact, the committed Christian cannot afford the luxury of looking back to a putative "Golden Age" (i.e., The thirteenth, the greatest of centuries) nor be seduced by the charms of the zeitgeist. The state of being Christian should be rooted in a dissatisfaction with the present (and not mere querelousness) and an abiding hope for the future (and not mere wistfulness for something better). That tug of the future which is, in fact, God's future, demands that we bring it about and not merely loiter about waiting for it to happen. In that "bringing about" it is the vocation of each individual to bring to fruition his or her perception of Christ as part of the unfolding of the Christian presence in the world.

The Church Again

We end this chapter (and this book) with a question asked at its beginning: Why the church? If, as a serious person (even a serious believer) concerned about the texture of my life, the life of the world around me, and about the ultimate questions that well up from such concerns, I am still "in the church" or, at least, at its edges I can still ask what I am doing there and why.

It is hardly a new question. Many people come to the church out of deep needs or because of intuitions which are so compelling that they cannot even begin to articulate them. When John Henry Newman became a Roman Catholic in 1845, he left a religious and cultural milieu which was part of his very bones in order to join a church which was largely perceived as alien, decadent, and antithetical to the national cultural consensus. It was a church, as Ronald Knox was to remark about such converts, that was unsure what to do with him when he arrived. For those who watched Newman convert in England in 1845 it was as big a shock as we would experience if Karl Rahner had announced that he was becoming a Mormon.

Not all associations with the church are that dramatic nor are such conversions so unusually wrenching. Many of us are Catholics because that is what we are. We were born to the faith or we assumed its identity as naturally as putting on an old familiar sweater. The one thing that might make us a bit different today is that we do not suffer our disenchantments as quietly (or as heriocally) as did Catholics in the past. We are not as generously or as elegantly forgiving as was, for one example, Henri de Lubac in his magisterial *The Splendour of the Church*. De Lubac quietly obeserves that common human failure tends to be magnified when that failure occurs in the church. Given de Lubac's own unhappy and unjust experiences with the authoritarian nature of the church, one sees the saintly poignancy of his observation that in the church we tend to accept the power to hurt and wound when such exercises "would be a violation at the hands of any other power. For this is precisely the situation into which Catholic obedience, in its most common form, takes us."[13]

Despite some persistent attempts at demanding that kind of obedience today, most contemporary Catholics who don't vote with their feet (alas, many do) and remain in the church resist such ham-handed methods. It seems clear that the days of "pray, pay, and obey" are over. In fairness, one must say that generally speaking such servility is not often demanded. Nor is it seen as much of an issue for many Catholics who do not much see the church as a rigid reality to which one must conform. Today there are avenues of redress and ways of seeking consensus. There is also the possibility of simply joining the "loyal opposition."

That spirit of loyal dissent is a new reality for most Catholics. Some deplore it as a rending of the seamless garment of the church and as a source of scandal. I do not see it that way. While there have been excesses, it is not clear to me that spirited discussion is harmful; it can be, to use Peter Maurin's happy term, a means of clarification. Leaving aside purely doctrinal disputes (e.g., the extent to which trends in liberation theology may or may not reflect Marxist deviations), most current church disputes center either on ethical issues (the nature of economic justice, peace issues, family planning, etc.) or on pastoral strategies which may touch on doctrinal understandings: women in the ministry, marriage annulments, liturgical adaptations, etc. In those areas does any person seriously wish to argue that the church is better off without serious debate on these issues? Would the North American bishops in their pastorals on nuclear warfare have been better advised to have spoken *ex cathedris* rather than seek a consensus hammered out by using what Newman has called "the clash of mind with mind"? Is the church's position on contraception more compelling today because *Humanae Vitae* was issued as a preemptive strike against further discussion and against the consensus of the majority of the birth control commission? The unhappy history of dissent from, and general resistance to, the church's position on contraception would seem to suggest not.

Still, for most of us, dissent plays a very small role in our lives as Catholics. We may be chagrined and/or outraged by the petty (and not so petty) injustices and stupidities in the church while marvelling at the inertia resisting the forces of change. At our more reflective moments, we may even be generous enough to think that such inertia may be a brake on the more enthusiastic flirtations aimed at the zeitgeist. Those of us who watch these struggles from the sidelines are often tempted to pronounce a pox on both houses. For every loony proposal of the radical left there seems to be an equally loony reaction from the decidedly unfashionable right. What one hopes for is that we can salvage a mediating language that permits honest discussion to take place. The absence of such language will unhappily result in dissent giving way to competing factions and special interest partisanship. Democracy, a system to which the church is now making its first nod, is notoriously susceptible to factionalism and its inevitable by-product of rancor and power play.

What to do? To have even human faith in the church's future—to be expectant—demands a sense of the church's traditional nature and its conservative function. Such a sense teaches one very clear message: The church survives its own worse instincts and what is more important, produces those figures who can show us intellectually and spiritually how to live in times fraught with tension and unhappiness. If anything should innoculate from the twin evils of rightist despair (the church is in a shambles) or leftist presumption (let the entire structure crumble; begin anew), it is a sense of tradition and continuity. To succumb to either temptation is to live solely in the present without the willingness to look backward or forward. Such a stance betrays a lack of faith in the church both as a community of memory and as a community which hopes for the not yet. It is, in short, a denial of the historical texture of the church and flight from the gritty realities of human life and failure.

A sense of the church as community of memory is the key to understanding the church as that community which looks to the future. For hope in this instance is simply an expectation that in the church there are those who will help us reach forward to the *arduum possibile* of living as Christians "between the times." Those who remain in the church, either out of duty or with love, continue to affirm that the church has something to say about those deep existential questions which are posed by all authentic religion. Such fidelity affirms that the peculiar memories of the church, its struggle to hand on the Gospel, to be in the world as a witness, has given it a perspective on life which is very much pertinent to our attempts at puzzling out meaning.

One remains in the church, finally, because one still finds in that community a source of edification. The word *edify* has a certain inescapably smug ring about it ("She is such an edifying person"; "That was such an edifying sermon"; etc.) which belies its richness. Derived from the Latin verb *aedificare* (to build or construct), one who edifies in the church helps to construct that reality which is Christ in the world within the confines of the church. In the community of faith, in short, one is "built up" by those who, singly or in consort, help us to see the rich possibilities of the Gospel. Conversely, by our exercises in fidelity, we add to that building of the church. We should remember, in this regard, that in the famous promise to Peter (in Mt. 16) Jesus did not say that he *had built*, but *would* build his church. The church is not a finished building (*aedificium*) but one in the process of construction.

That process of edification, of building, occurs at a grand level when someone contributes so conspicuously that their contribution becomes a model for our activity and our labor. When that effort has been truly great, we all know of it and we honor such builders with the name of saint. But that same process occurs at a far more intimate level, one observable by just looking around us. For professional reasons I spend a fair amount of time reading about saints and heroines in the Catholic tradition, but, in fact, the most common sources of edification for me are much closer to home: the ordinary parish priests who unfailingly listen, visit, celebrate, console, and serve their communities; the families of modest incomes who raise their own children and expend their time and energies on those less fortunate than themselves; those who care for elderly parents or handicapped dependents without self-pity and with great devotion; the religious women who work with families of prisoners, with the down and outers, with the poor who have missed the safety net, with the children; the missioners, lay and religious, who labor (like a classmate of mine who has spent two decades in the mountain villages of Peru) in obscurity and poverty; the unfamous contemplatives who stay in prayer and whose stability consoles so many who find themselves at their places; those people (they are in every parish in the world) who are so manifestly good and holy in their ordinary lives that one feels, alternately, shamed and edified to be near them; those who have been given terrible crosses to bear and who bear them.

Are these people not the people of God? And is not the people of God, finally, the church? When the headlines tell of this scandal or that disagreement or this condemnation or that failure—when, in short, we are sick and tired of the posturings of the George Kellys, the Hans Küngs, the Cardinal Ratzingers, the Ernesto Cardenals, and the Archbishops LeFevres of the world—is it not to those hidden builders that we should turn and ask if the church is worth it? I think so.

Over the years I have read, and been most edified by, those books which have gotten close to the experience of the common voice and allowed it to speak of the human condition in the finely grained texture of ordinary lived life. I have in such works as Robert Coles's fine studies of children written under the rubric "Children in Crisis"; the oral histories of Studs Terkel in books like Division Street and Working; the luminous portraits of English village life in Robert Blythe's now classic work Akenfield. It has long been my conviction that there is a great book to be written after the model of those authors by someone who would go out and listen to the experiences, not of the professional or "star quality" Catholics, but of those thousands of ordinary Catholics, clerical and lay, who have taken their faith seriously enough to make it the shaping influence on their lives. They, after all, are the true builders of the church.

It is not a flight of fancy to say that those informal networks of builders are the visible reality of the truth of the Gospel as well as a concrete expression of the dynamic life of the Body of Christ. Those networks touch other ones and a mapping of them in their totality is that palpable reality which is the deepest meaning of the church: a *magnum sacramentum*. To the degree that we are aware of, participate in, and give extension to, those networks, we become increasingly conscious of our catholicity, not as a given, but as a growing reality not yet here but one to be expected. It is through the work of "edifying others" that we do the works of love in faith.

Why Catholic? Because, first, it is in that process of edification understood as building up that one finds hope and direction toward the future.

Why Catholic? Because in the many *ecclesiolae* one sees opportunities and the possibilities for the living out of the Gospel. Despite the failures, the scandals, the disappointments, and the sin, there are still those who edify. As long as that happens (and we have the promise that it will continue to happen), we can look for the Lord in confidence. The gates of hell have not prevailed.

Points for Meditation

1. From the angle of your own life, how do you see the direction of the church's future? How would you like to see it?

2. If you were asked to make an *apologia* for being a Catholic, how would you approach your task?

3. To what degree do you think the church would be diminished by your absence?

4. Are you "expectant" in the individual and social sense? How do you relate to the future understood as open possibility?

5. What makes you most helpful (and vice versa) about the church?

6. Can you name persons from the circles of your own life who "edify" the church? What would you see as their most conspicuous merits? Could they serve as paradigms for your own behavior?

Notes

1. I have borrowed that phrase from the *Summa Theologiae*, I II^{ae}, q. 40, art. 7.
2. See, for example, the essays in *Concern for the Church: Theological Investigations*, vol. 20 (New York: Crossroad, 1982).
3. Karl Rahner, *The Practice of the Faith: A Handbook of Contemporary Spirituality* (New York: Crossroad, 1983), p. 15.
4. Hans Küng, *On Being a Christian* (Garden City: Doubleday, 1974), p. 532.
5. See the survey of William Frost, "A Decade of Hope Theology in North America," *Theological Studies* 39 (1978): 139–53.
6. For a more radical approach, see Hans Küng, *Eternal Life?* (Garden City: Doubleday, 1983), and a trenchant review by Thomas Sheehan: "Revolution in the Church," *New York Review of Books*, June 14, 1984, p. 39.
7. Quoted in Michael Mott, *The Seven Mountains of Thomas Merton* (Boston: Houghton Mifflin, 1984), p. 315.
8. For a very brief survey of the topic, see Kathleen Fischer, *The Inner Rainbow: The Imagination in Christian Life* (Ramsey, N.J.: Paulist, 1983).
9. From the introduction to "Instruction on Certain Aspects of the 'Theology of Liberation,' " NC News Service, August 31, 1984.
10. Francis Schüssler Fiorenza, *Foundational Theology: Jesus and the Church* (New York: Crossroad, 1984), p. 200.
11. Roger D. Haight, "Mission: Symbol for Church Today," *Theological Studies* 37 (1976) 634–35. For a different view, see Robert T. Sears, "Trinitarian Love as Ground for Church," in ibid, pp. 652–79.
12. See Michael Fahey, "The Mission of the Church: To Humanize or Divinize?" in *Proceedings of the CTSA*, vol. 31 (1976), pp. 56–69 and the excellent discussion in Fiorenza's *Foundational Theology*, pp. 196–6.
13. Henri de Lubac, *The Splendour of the Church* (New York: Sheed and Ward, 1956), p. 59.

Selected Readings

Dulles, Avery. *The Resilient Church*. Garden City: Doubleday, 1977. A meditation on the resources of the church in a time of change.

Coleman, John. *An American Strategic Theology*. Ramsey, N.J.: Paulist, 1982. A very useful study of political theology in an American context.

Durkin, Mary, & Greeley, Andrew. *How to Save the Catholic Church*. New York: Viking, 1984. A proposal for the contemporary church.

Percy, Walker. *Lost in the Cosmos*. New York: Farrar, Straus, and Giroux, 1983. Witty but profound essays on the future of religion and the future of the church.

Perkins, Pheme. *The Resurrection*. Garden City: Doubleday, 1985. A scriptural study and meditation for the contemporary Catholic.

Index

Abba concept, 97, 100, 106, 121, 133
Adam, Karl, 192
altars, 16–19
Anglicanism, 191, 192
apolegetics, 192, 193, 205, 230
ascent, spiritual, 147–48
asceticism, 74, 134–37, 141, 181
Augustine of Hippo, Saint, 115, 141–42,
  160, 189, 191–92
autobiography, 140–41
  of Augustine, 141–42
  confession and, 144–47
  history and, 149–51, 153
  Merton and, 143–44
  spiritual journeys as, 147–49
  story of Jesus and, 140, 142, 144, 157–
  61

baptism, 48, 49, 51, 52, 132
basic Christian communities (base com-
  munities), 226–31
basilicas, 10–12, 15, 16, 22, 232
biography, 140, 142
bishops, 32, 83–84, 115, 141, 208, 209,
  226, 260
Boff, Leonardo, 228–31
Bonaventure, Saint, 64, 71, 123, 147
Bonhoeffer, Dietrich, 69, 106
Bread and Wine (Silone), 216–17
Buber, Martin, 73, 96–98
Buddhism, 211
Bühlmann, Walbert, 182
Burrell, David, 111

Catholicism, 32, 33, 182, 230
  in Africa, 209

in America, 27, 28, 58–59, 84, 206,
  219–20, 224
Anglicanism and, 91, 192
apologetics and, 192–93, 205
asceticism and, 134–37, 181
Catholic Worker movement and, 223–
  24
celibacy and, 201, 202
church structures and, 9–10
class tensions within, 173–76, 201
conscience, faith and, 144
contemporary change and, 153–54
contemporary injustice and, 53–58, 82–
  85, 204
Cursillo and, 109, 198
definition of, 189–91
despair and, 245–46
dissent and, 260–61
Edict of Milan and, 12
ecology and, 128, 129
ecumenical church and, 180
ecumenism and, 210–12, 218
edification and, 262, 264
in England, 88, 205
eshatology and, 250–52
ethnicity and, 208–9
feminism and, 155–57, 167–73
gnosticism and, 212–13
history and, 139, 141
hope within, 245, 248, 249
imperial toleration of, 12, 189–90
knowledge of God and, 124–25, 149
life-cycle rituals of, 48–52
liturgy of, 39, 44–46, 131
middle classes of, 204
middle way of, 212–13, 244–45

266

Catholicism (*Cont.*):
  neglected factions within, 175–80, 204
  Newman and, 191–92, 207
  obedience and, 260
  oriental religions and, 210, 211
  as orthodoxy, 189–91
  papacy and, 231–37
  paradigmatic people and, 165–67
  parish structure and, 219–20
  perfection and, 212–13, 243, 244
  poverty and, 177, 203–4
  prayers and, 78, 88–89
  Protestants and, 190–94, 197
  quietism and, 76
  sacramentality and, 115–16, 126, 128–30, 132, 194–95
  science and, 125–26
  shrines of, 22–28
  silence and, 64–66, 69, 204
  syncretism and, 211
  time concepts of, 38, 39, 103–4
  tradition and, 195–96, 198, 200–1, 205
  transcendence and, 213–14
  unity of, 218–19, 235
celibacy, 202
change, religious, 21, 33, 44, 153–55, 176
Chesterton, G. K., 70, 71, 124, 130, 205
children, 118
christology, 54, 151–52, 167, 177, 185
churches, 168–69, 232
  altars of, 16–19
  in America, 17, 18, 28
  architectural styles of, 11, 13–17
  Gothic, 11, 14
  Latin American, 27, 31–32
  paganism and, 22–23
  poverty and, 31–32
  romanesque, 13–14
  sacred nature of, 9–11, 17, 22
  spatial significance of, 9–10, 79
  worship outside of, 9, 20–22
communities, religious
  of Africa, 226–27
  Boff's concept of, 228–31
  Catholicism and, 195, 237–40
  of Latin America, 227–29
  links between, 237–40
  liturgy and, 60
  papacy and, 231–36
  Silone's definition of, 216
confession, 144–45, 160
conservatism, 170–71, 178, 199–200, 211
contemplation, 91, 99–102, 110, 137, 210
Cooke, Bernard, 133, 134
Cox, Harvey, 173

crucifixes, 152
Cursillo, 109, 198

Dante, 15, 147–48
Day, Dorothy, 45, 165, 223
death, 40, 48, 57–58, 65, 158, 159, 250–51
de Lubac, Henri, 33, 260
Divine Comedy, The (Dante), 147–48
Duby, Georges, 15

ecumenism, 210–12, 218
Eliade, Mircea, 28, 36–38, 117
Eliot, T. S., 38, 80, 88
eschatology, 240, 242, 250–51, 256, 258–59
Eucharist, 18, 32, 36–38, 78, 127, 131
  ecumenism and, 218
  Greeley's observation on, 231
  Jewish antecedent of, 217
  in Silone's novel, 216
  unity and, 218–19
events, contemporary, 52–53, 58–59
  christology and, 54–55
  church involvement in, 53, 55–57
  death penalty, Jesus ethic and, 57–58
  moral reaction to, 52–54
events, sacred, 19, 20, 36–39, 47–48, 61–62
  feast days as, 40–42, 146
  human growth and, 47–48
  liturgical, 39–43, 52
  sacraments and, 48–52, 132–33
evolution, 125

faith, 116–17, 134, 139–40, 144, 159
  Christian, 247
  contemporary experiences of, 154–55
  conscience and, 144
  edification and, 262–64
  fidelity and, 238, 262
  papal office and, 235, 236
  persecution and, 82
  and politics, 258
    radical challenges to, 176–79
  in the resurrection, 251
  science and, 125–26
  silence and, 82
  spatial concepts and, 30
  Teilhard de Chardin and, 125
feminism, 150, 156, 172, 178–80
Fiorenza, Elisabeth Schüssler, 156, 169
Francis of Assisi, Saint, 71, 109, 117, 119, 221

God, 9, 11, 14, 15, 17, 20, 29
  Augustine and, 141
  children of, 72, 185, 186
  as Creator and Giver, 126–28, 133
  existence of, 123
  Franciscan concept of, 71
  grace of, 114
  Jesus and, 55, 70
  knowledge of, 66–68, 124
  love of, 124, 128, 137, 214
  mystery of, 67, 96–97
  prayer and, 60, 67, 78, 92, 96–100, 137
  presence of, 31, 78, 100, 105, 137
  shrines and, 30
  silence and, 64–66, 69–75, 81
  spiritual growth and, 147–49
  time and, 61
  word of, 75, 76, 80
  the world and, 136
grace, 127–28, 130, 132, 160
  of Christ, 117, 185
  despair as negation of, 245
  forms of, 76, 114
  of God, 114, 118
  paradigmatic roles and, 164–67
Greeley, Andrew, 21, 43, 166, 231
Gregory I, Pope Saint (Gregory the Great),
  23–24

hagiography, 151
Haight, Roger, 257
healing, 20, 25–27, 253
heresy, 126, 178, 189, 192
history
  Catholicism and, 139, 141, 155, 161,
    195–96, 236
  change and, 153–55
  christification and, 156–57
  crucifixes and, 152–53
  egocentrism and, 160
  feminism and, 150, 156–57
  hagiography and, 151
  historians and, 149, 150
  Jesus and, 157–61
  mariology and, 168–69
  martyrs and, 153
  tradition and, 152, 154–55
homosexuality, 178, 200

Immaculate Conception, 168, 169
incarnation, 40, 101, 105, 136, 156, 167,
  185
individuality, 196
injustice, contemporary, 53–58, 81–85,
  204, 254–55

Jesus Christ, 5, 12, 17–19, 21, 29–31, 33,
  36, 39, 40, 48, 54–55, 60, 66, 70, 106,
  114, 116–22, 124–27, 130, 131, 133–
  34, 140, 144, 151–52, 156–61, 168,
  176–77, 182, 183, 185, 186, 191, 193–
  97, 230, 239, 247
John of the Cross, Saint, 76, 104, 147,
  166
Johnston, William, 76, 211
Joyce, James, 110, 207, 218
Judaism, 53, 82–83, 217

knowledge, 95
  of God, 66–68, 124, 148
  of self, 98–99, 148
  through silence, 66–67, 69–70
  vocational roles in the church and, 164
Krautheimer, Richard, 12
Küng, Hans, 193–94, 231, 249

Leukens, Veronica, 171
liberation theology, 55, 109, 179, 204,
  229–30
liturgy, 11, 13–14, 17–21, 36, 39–43, 47
  of African church, 209
  art and, 44–45
  change within, 21, 33, 44, 171
  confession and, 144–47
  Eucharist and, 36–37, 78, 127
  feast days and, 40–42, 146
  gratitude and, 127
  language of, 33, 44, 46, 171
  Latin usage in, 33, 44
  meaningfulness in, 44, 46
  monasticism and, 131
  prayer and, 104, 107, 108
  reform of, 131
  sacrament and, 127, 130–32
  silence and, 75, 78–80
  time and, 36–38, 60
Lonergan, Bernard, 213
love, 50, 76, 95, 100, 120, 193
  of enemies, 120–21
  of God, 124, 128
  of humanity, 120–21, 129–30, 136, 180–
    82
  missionaries and, 183–90
  of nature and the world, 123–29, 134,
    136, 214
  selfnessness and, 121–22

McBrien, Richard, 213
Mackey, James, 158
Malits, Elena, 143
martyrdom, 32, 82, 153

Mary, Blessed Virgin, 10, 23, 25–27, 40, 167–73
matrimony, 49–51, 108, 202
Merton, Thomas, 18, 60, 65, 73, 91, 92, 99, 102, 143–44, 148, 165, 252
Miles, Margaret, 135
missionaries, 23–24, 182–85, 257
modernism, 131, 170–72, 206
monasticism, 64, 74, 88, 80, 131, 165–66
  challenges of, 220–21
  as an idyllic community, 221
  religious orders and, 197, 221–23
  separatism of, 243–44
Monchanin, Jules, 210
mysticism, 18, 67, 69–71, 95–98, 103
  christology and, 151
  sacramental vision and, 116
  spiritual ascent and, 147–48
  of Teilhard, 125–26

nationalism, 26–27, 170, 208
Newman, John Henry, 191–92, 207, 259, 261
Nichols, Peter, 223

O'Malley, John W., 200–1
Orwell, George, 205

paganism, 9–12, 22–25, 168–69
Pannikar, Raimundo, 165–66
papacy, 23–24, 170, 171, 180, 185
  African liturgy and, 209
  Bayside revelations and, 171
  Catholicism and, 231–37
  history and, 236
  and Jews, 82–83
  of John XXIII, 55, 165, 174
  Marian piety and, 170
  social justice and, 255
Paul, Saint, 22, 32, 36, 66, 125, 126, 156, 163, 168, 185
penance, 40, 49, 118, 144–47, 160
Pennington, Basil, 99, 101, 120
Percy, Walker, 39, 59, 214
perfection, 212–13, 243, 244
Peter, Saint, 231, 233
poverty, 56, 119–20, 130, 160, 177, 203–5
prayer, 68, 72, 73, 75–78, 88–89
  Arnold's view of, 90
  Berger's comments on, 93
  centering technique of, 99–101, 104
  changing practices of, 108–11
  communal forms of, 101–3, 105–7, 198
  Communion of Saints and, 105–6
  contemplation and, 91, 99–102, 110, 137

God and, 60, 67, 78, 92, 96–100
horizon and, 94, 98
human framework of, 91–94, 98
informal types of, 108
Jesus prayer and, 199
liturgy and, 104, 107, 108
Lord's Prayer and, 100, 107
monastic, 88, 90, 92
of Percy's Thomas More, 214
places for, 89–90
Rahner's views on, 92, 94–96
rosary and, 198–99
as self-knowledge, 98
as signals of transcendence, 93
time for, 89–90, 110

quietism, 101
quietude, 64–66, 85, 178
  armaments and, 54, 83–84
  God and, 64–66, 69–75, 81, 144
  holocaust of Jews and, 53, 82–83
  knowledge through, 66–67, 69–70
  liturgy and, 75, 78–80
  martyrdom and, 82
  monastic, 74
  morality of, 81–85
  music, sound and, 68–70
  prayer and, 68, 72, 73, 75–78, 99–100
  varieties of, 72–75

Rahner, Karl, 21, 45, 67, 70, 92, 94–96, 143, 165, 186, 238–40, 246, 247, 249
reform, 131, 176–79, 243, 244
religious orders, 197, 221–26
resurrection, 37, 41, 48, 146, 158–59, 250–51
Romero, Bishop Oscar, 32, 153, 165

sacraments, 17–18, 48–49, 51–52, 114–15
  asceticism and, 135–37
  baptism among, 48, 49, 51, 52, 132
  children and, 118
  "Christ Meaning" and, 133–34
  in daily life, 130–33
  evolutionary views of Teilhard and, 125–26
  human growth and, 48–52
  humanity and, 117–22
  Jesus and, 117–22
  lepers and, 119
  liturgy and, 127, 130–32
  love and, 120–22, 128, 129
  matrimony among, 49–51, 108
  penance among, 40, 49, 118, 144–45
  reality and transcendence of, 115–17, 123, 125, 129, 130, 136

sacramental vision and, 116–17
saintliness and, 118, 122–23
self-sacrifice as sign of, 121–22
Teresa of Calcutta and, 119–21, 130
timeliness of, 49, 132
worldliness of, 123–29
Saint Peter's Basilica, 10, 12, 15, 16, 232
saints, 141, 151, 164–67, 174, 221
science, 125–26, 206
secularization, 20–21, 28, 64, 170
Shea, John, 142
shrines, 9, 22–28
silence. *See* quietism; quietude
Silone, Ignazio, 216–17
soul, 65, 147–48
Stendhal, Krister, 107
story. *See* autobiography; biography; history

Tavard, George, 151, 233, 234
Teilhard de Chardin, Pierre, 60, 125–26, 165, 256
temples, 9–11, 23–24, 28, 29
Teresa of Avila, Saint, 102, 104, 150, 213, 251
Teresa of Calcutta, 60, 119–21, 130, 251
Thomas of Aquinas, Saint, 57, 97, 121, 123, 154, 206, 245
time. *See* events, contemporary *and* events, sacred
Tracy, David, 46, 148, 167
tradition, 21, 131, 133, 152, 154
Catholicism and, 195–96, 198, 200–1, 236

liturgical, 45
marriage and, 202, 209
transcendence, 22, 26, 30, 93, 115

unselfishness, 121–22, 182
utopian concepts, 253, 254

van Beeck, Franz Josef, 158–59
Vanier, Jean, 224–25
Vatican I (First Vatican Council), 66, 124
Vatican II (Second Vatican Council), 17–19, 21, 30, 53, 55, 103, 105, 108–10, 129–31, 143, 150, 155, 168, 181, 198–200, 218, 239, 244, 257
visionaries, modern, 25–26, 171
vocation, 163–66, 173–75, 177, 178, 181–84
Christ and, 176–77
feminism and, 172, 178–79
reform of, 176–79
of Virgin Mary, 167–73, 179–80
of women to the priesthood, 178, 180
von Balthasar, Hans Ur, 184

Walthen, Ambrose, 74
Wilder, Amos Niven, 46
Williams, George Hunston, 170
women, 150, 156–57, 221–22
feminism and, 150, 156, 172
Mary among, 10, 23, 25–27, 40, 167–73, 179–81
as priests, 178–80
Wright, John, 237

Yahweh, 28–29, 81